POSTCARD HISTORY SERIES

Brookville

On the front cover: This postcard of three lady artists painting was made from a photograph taken by Ben Winans in 1906. The location is probably alongside the East Fork and in front of the Hermitage. In recent years, many Indiana plein air painters have come to the Hermitage in October to set up their easels along the East Fork. The Brookville Town Park north of the Hermitage offers many great views of the river, and many of the modern painters take advantage of the same views as artists J. Ottis Adams and Theodore C. Steele did a century before. (Courtesy Craig T. Chappelow.)

On the back cover: The photograph for this card was taken in 1908 when the Main Street buildings were decorated for the Brookville centennial. The prominent three-story building on the right was the Herman Trichler clothing store, which was located at Seventh and Main Streets. The lodge of the Independent Order of Odd Fellows, a fraternal organization, was located on the upper floors. The Odd Fellows lodge is no longer active, and the Trichler store location is the Tebbe Package Liquor Store. The Crystal Theatre was next door. In later years, it was a Western Auto store; today it is a video rental business. (Courtesy Tom Rowe.)

POSTCARD HISTORY SERIES

Brookville

Craig T. Chappelow and Donald L. Dunaway

ARCADIA
PUBLISHING

ISBN 978-0-7385-5158-6

Published by Arcadia Publishing
Charleston SC, Chicago IL, Portsmouth NH, San Francisco CA

Printed in the United States of America

Library of Congress Catalog Card Number: 2007931944

For all general information contact Arcadia Publishing at:
Telephone 843-853-2070
Fax 843-853-0044
E-mail sales@arcadiapublishing.com
For customer service and orders:
Toll-Free 1-888-313-2665

Visit us on the Internet at www.arcadiapublishing.com

Dedicated to Brookville on its 200th birthday

Contents

ACKNOWLEDGMENTS

When we set out to create this book, we had three goals in mind. The first was to celebrate Brookville's bicentennial by creating a unique historical record. The second was to do so in a way that would be interesting to readers. The third was to involve the people of the Brookville community to help us accomplish it.

All of the images in this book are made from actual postcards, and most of them were provided to us by deltiologists (the fancy name for postcard collectors) in and around Brookville, who brought them to us in envelopes, photo albums, old shoeboxes, and, in some cases, a single card carried by hand. We are very grateful that so many people let us scan and use their postcards for this book; it could not have been accomplished without their help. Here is a list of the individuals and organizations that helped us tell Brookville's story in postcards: Brookville Public Library (BPL), Brookville United Methodist Church (BUMC), Franklin County Historical Society (FCHS), Beverly Banks, Paul Baudendistel, Pam Beneker, George and Jean Cowan, Frank Deutsch, Dennis Fritz, Jim and Peggy Glascock, Victor Hauberg, Ron S. Houchin, Joe Jonas, Joan Koch, John Lamont, Janice Landreth, Tara D. Lea, Kathryn Quinton, Tom Rowe, Julie Schlesselman, Martha Shea, Don and Elaine Smith, and Stephen M. Weber. We have credited the specific collector at the end of each caption using their last name or abbreviation. If no credit is listed, the cards came from the collections of the authors or from collectors who requested to remain anonymous.

We also express our appreciation to the Indiana Historical Society, which now owns and houses the Ben Winans collection of glass and acetate negatives. A sampling of Winans's best photographs are contained in the society publication *The Photography of Ben Winans of Brookville, Indiana, 1902–1926*. Some of the postcard images in this book are also in the Winans book.

Introduction

Postcards were first available for purchase in Brookville around 1873, and they were a far cry from the postcards used today. At that time, the only postcards permitted to be mailed were those produced and sold by the federal government, and the only place you could buy one was at the post office. They came with the stamps already printed on them, were blank on both sides, and the sender had to write the recipient's name and address on one side and their message on the other. In 1898, an act of Congress allowed private printers to produce and sell postcards. To make them more interesting, printers created these "postals," as they were called, with a small image on the message side, thus starting a massive collection craze that would last for years.

By the beginning of the 20th century, postcard collecting in Brookville, as in other parts of the world, was nearly a mania. Between 1895 and 1920, a staggering 300 billion postcards were produced and sold worldwide. If you visited almost any home in Brookville at that time, you would probably spend at least a few minutes enjoying your host's collection of postcards. They might be neatly organized in an album or just piled on a table in the parlor. For the residents of Brookville, postcard collecting was an ideal hobby for hard-working people who had little time and less money to devote to creating a collection of anything more elaborate. Postcards were incredibly cheap (one penny to buy, another penny to mail), took up little space, and were widely available in many shops in town.

In order to understand this phenomenon, we must suspend our modern perspective of the postcard as something we send a friend or relative when we go on vacation. (Imagine the Statue of Liberty gleaming against a cloudless blue sky or the Golden Gate Bridge partially shrouded in fog.) This modern-day postcard is always taken by professionals and mass-produced in splendid color—a record of where we have been. By comparison, an early postcard collection in Brookville might have a few examples of some out-of-town locations, but many of the cards were local scenes—a record of where we are. Many of the postcards were never mailed, indicating that collectors would buy the cards to keep. Brookville citizens would peruse the postcard racks at shops like Gus Baither's variety store or Citizens' Drug Store eager to purchase the latest postcard made of a local scene or rural view.

Another reason for the popularity of postcards in Brookville was functional. Almost no private homes in the area had telephones until after World War I. The telegraph, in use from 1860 to 1915, was expensive and used mainly for business. Letter writing was for the elite, not the ordinary citizen, and for women more than men. The postcard served as primary means of communication for the common people. It was a cheap way to communicate and, compared to today's postal service, incredibly quick. It was expected for a postcard, mailed from Brookville in the morning, to arrive at the recipient's home in Cincinnati the same afternoon. The creation of rural free delivery in 1901 ensured daily delivery to families in the country, and it was possible that in-town residents sometimes received deliveries two or three times on the same day. As proof of this efficiency, there are numerous cards in our collections that carried brief messages telling the recipient to pick them up the next morning at the train station or asking them if they plan to visit the day after tomorrow. In their role as precursor to the telephone in Brookville and for their popularity as a collectible, postcards thrived.

Most of the postcards in this book are from 1905 to 1930, and are one of two types: picture postcards or "real-photo" postcards. Picture postcards made up the vast majority of postcards created during this time period. They were mass-produced by mechanical printing using letterpress halftones and created by professional printing houses. They typically featured a town's most prominent sites—in Brookville's case it was usually the Franklin County Courthouse or a scene along the Whitewater River—and marketed to tourists or collectors. The majority of these cards were produced in Germany because its printing methods were far superior to anything in the United States. One prominent producer of Brookville postcards was the Kraemer Art Company, founded in 1902 on Fountain Square in Cincinnati. All the color postcards produced by Kraemer were printed at its facility in Berlin. Other common publishers of Brookville cards were the Art Manufacturing Company of Amelia, Ohio, and Auburn Post Card Manufacturing Company of Auburn, Indiana.

The other form of postcards, called real-photo, are more intriguing and rarer. These cards were produced for one individual buyer at a time. The buyer would provide an original photograph made from film negatives or glass plates to a local shopkeeper, drugstore employee, or professional photographer. Using photographic equipment in their shop, they would reproduce the photograph onto heavy, sensitized photo stock and cut it to postcard size. These real-photo postcards were produced in very small batches of a dozen or less and sometimes just a single postcard. They were produced for ordinary people and feature more everyday scenes and subjects important to that individual, like a family portrait or exterior shot of one's house. The image quality varied greatly from amateurish snapshot to studio perfection.

Many of the postcards in this book were made from photographs taken by Benjamin Franklin Winans of Brookville. Winans was a printer all his life, from the age of 15 until he died just short of 90 in 1949. He called his print shop Winans' Printery. He took up the art of photography in 1902, and this became a sideline in his business. Fortunately, Winans wrote captions and dates on the envelopes for the negatives. Most of his photographic works are from 1902 to 1916 with a few dating to 1926. His collection of glass negatives and acetate negatives have been the subject of interest for Donald L. Dunaway, coauthor of this book, for more than 40 years. He held the collection for more than 20 years and donated it to the Indiana Historical Society in 2005 to insure long-term preservation of the 2,740 glass plate negatives—many of which are 100 years old.

But hiring a professional photographer was not the only option for Brookville residents. Credit George Eastman for creating the popularity of photography for the average citizen. He demystified the photographic process by simplifying the camera and making it affordable. In 1888, he introduced a Kodak box camera that used a paper-based film that would replace the heavy and fragile glass plates of the day. The camera was so popular that in 1900 Eastman introduced a sturdy cardboard camera he called the Brownie and charged the princely sum of $1. Suddenly photography was available to the masses. It is understandable that someone might pose for a family photograph, take it to the drugstore, have it made into a postcard, and send a copy to a dozen family members. Lucky for us, the citizens of Brookville got in on this trend, and in doing so, they created a unique historical record for the rest of us.

One

Businesses

Brookville in the early 1900s was largely a self-sufficient town. Most of the businesses were on Main Street at the south end of town. There were banks, hotels, grocery stores, a bakery, a dairy, clothing stores, stores that sold yard goods for making clothing, shoe stores, and jewelers. Brookville boasted pharmacies, physicians, dentists, lawyers, furniture stores, and hardware stores that sold a wide range of products from paint to windup record players and household appliances that used kerosene. Naturally there were agriculture-related businesses, like farm implement dealers, a grain mill, and livery stables. There were newspapers, a print shop, photographers, an electric generating plant, a telephone company, movie theaters, dance halls, and many saloons. When automobiles began to replace the horse, the livery stables were torn down or converted to automobile dealerships. The first filling station opened in 1922 and sold gasoline, tires, and other automobile needs. There were also manufacturing businesses, including a paper mill and furniture factory, which sold their products outside Brookville. There were cigar factories, a short-lived candy factory that was destroyed by fire, and a brick factory, which was destroyed by a great flood. Shipping to and from the town was provided by a railroad with connections to larger cities. After World War II, all of this began to change as people were able to travel in their automobiles to bigger and more distant cities. Present-day Brookville does not have nearly as many businesses as it did before the previous mid-century.

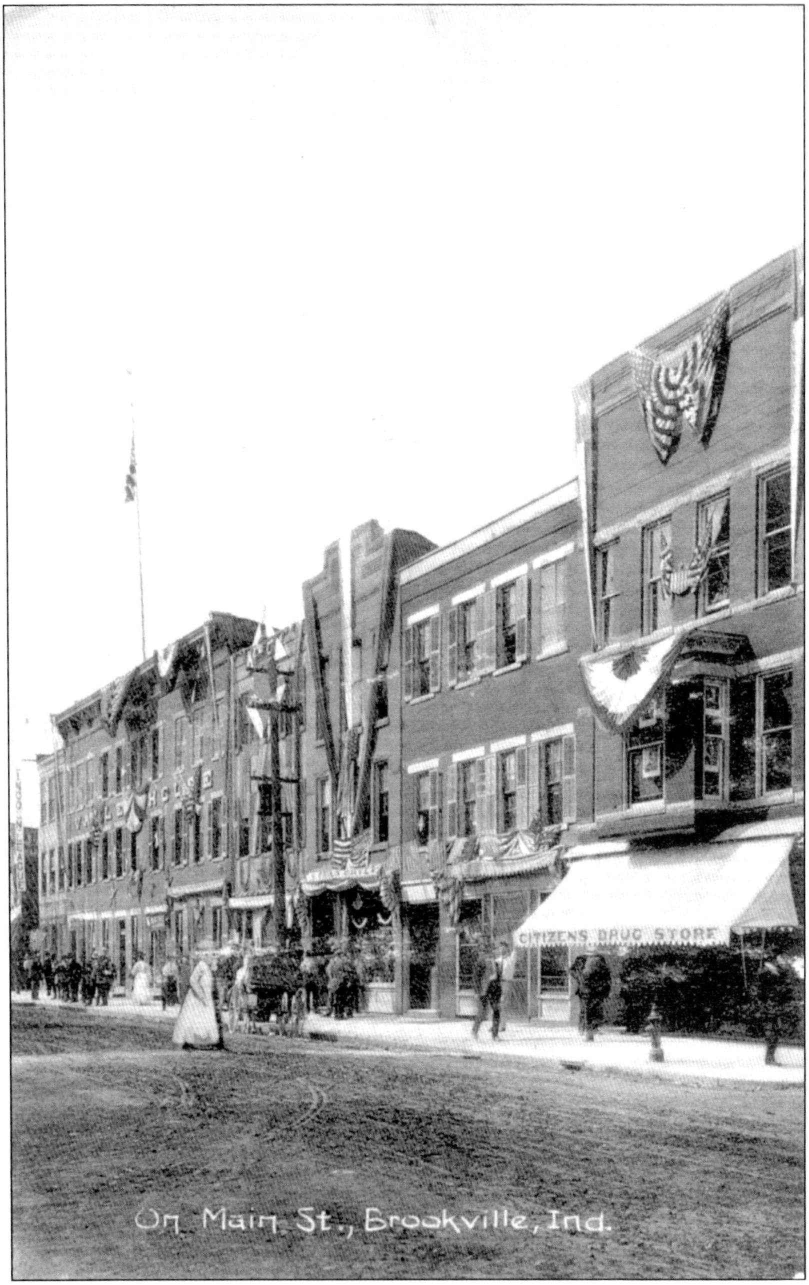

The heart of Brookville has always been at Fifth and Main Streets. This view shows the Citizens' Drug Store at the far right and the Valley House Hotel at the left. Small shops are located between the two. There is still a drugstore at this location, George's Pharmacy, but the Valley House has been closed for many years and has fallen into ruin. This postcard was made in 1908, and the buildings are decorated for Brookville's centennial celebration of that year. This photograph also shows that sometimes illustrators would enhance postcards to make the scene look more interesting. The woman in the white dress crossing the street was definitely drawn in after the fact. In the early 1900s, street fairs were held in this area facing the county courthouse. Imagine a Ferris wheel and other amusement rides and sideshows set up in Main Street.

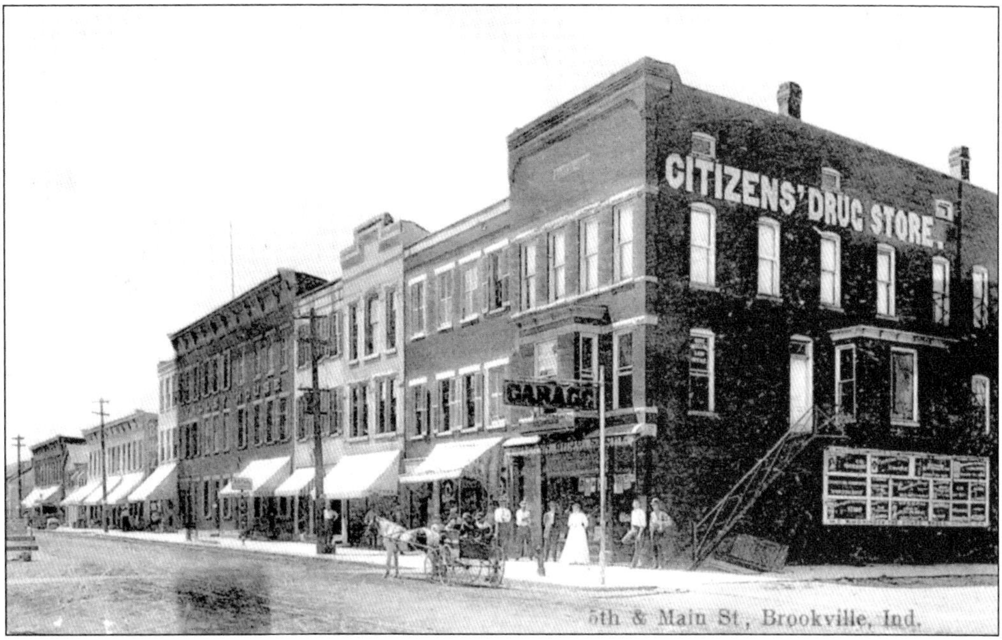

The Citizens' Drug Store was remodeled by Dr. Calvin Carter in 1907–1908. The lady in the white dress is probably Maggie Carter, his wife. She became a licensed pharmacist in 1904 and served the Brookville public at this location for more than 65 years. Calvin died in 1908 at the age of 51. Maggie married Frank Wright in 1914 and is better remembered as Maggie Wright. The postcard below is looking the other direction at Fifth and Main Streets. The prominent building on the left was the National Brookville Bank. Directly across the street is the building that preceded the Franklin County National Bank. It may have been a restaurant or a saloon. The carriages on the right are parked in front of a livery stable next door. (Above, courtesy Houchin; below, courtesy Smith.)

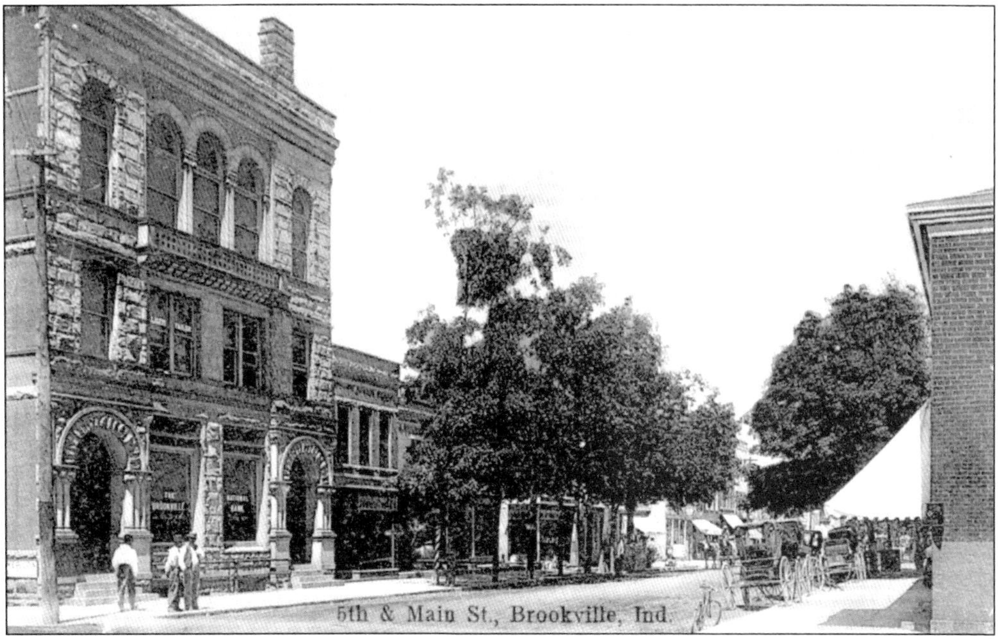

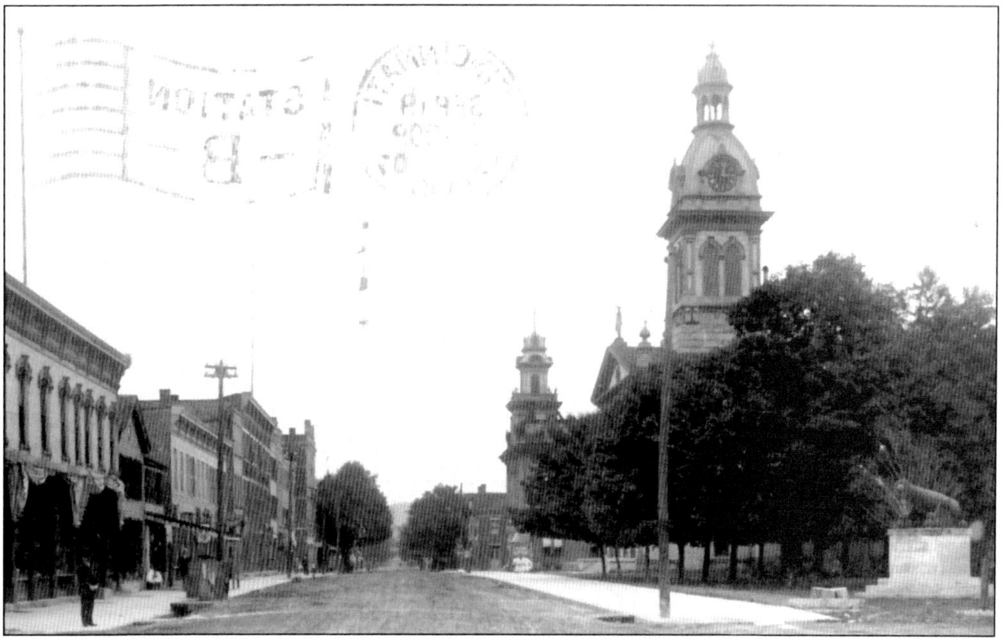

Abraham Bossert owned the two-story brick building on the far left. It housed three businesses on the street level, including a saloon, a grocery, and a dry goods store. Furman Hathaway's cigar factory was on the upper floor. Note the Civil War cannon in the Franklin County Courthouse yard. This image was made by Ben Winans in 1906. The view of Brookville's "Main Street Business Section" below was taken in the 1930s from the same place at Fourth and Main Streets and shows part of a sign identifying the Corner Café. Other signs hanging over the sidewalk identify "Lunch, Beer," Swayzee's Drug Store, Valley House Hotel, and Citizens' Drug Store. The towers of the Franklin County Courthouse and the Brookville Town Building are shown at the right. (Below, courtesy Fritz.)

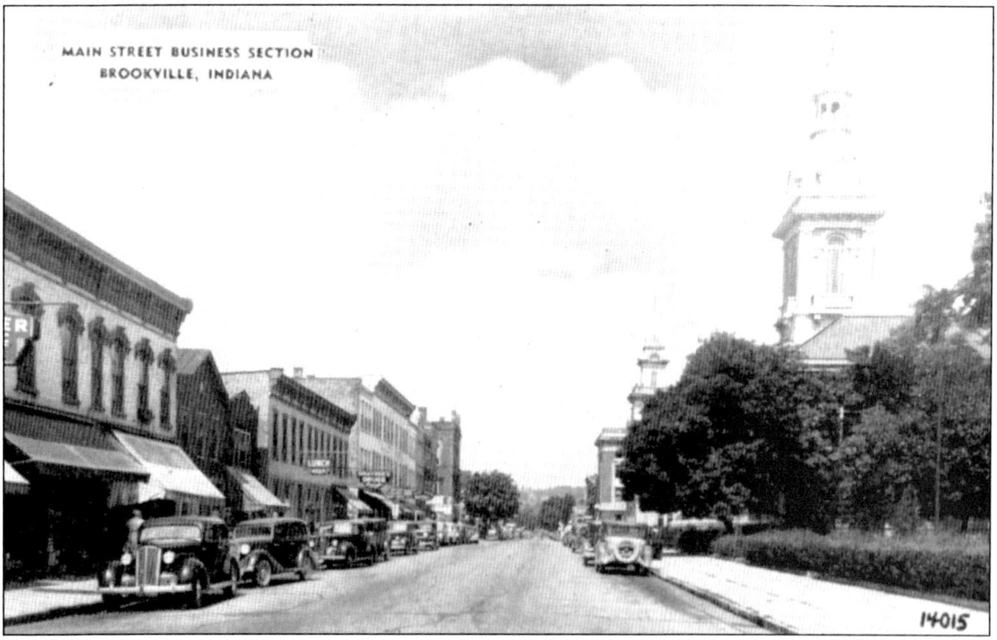

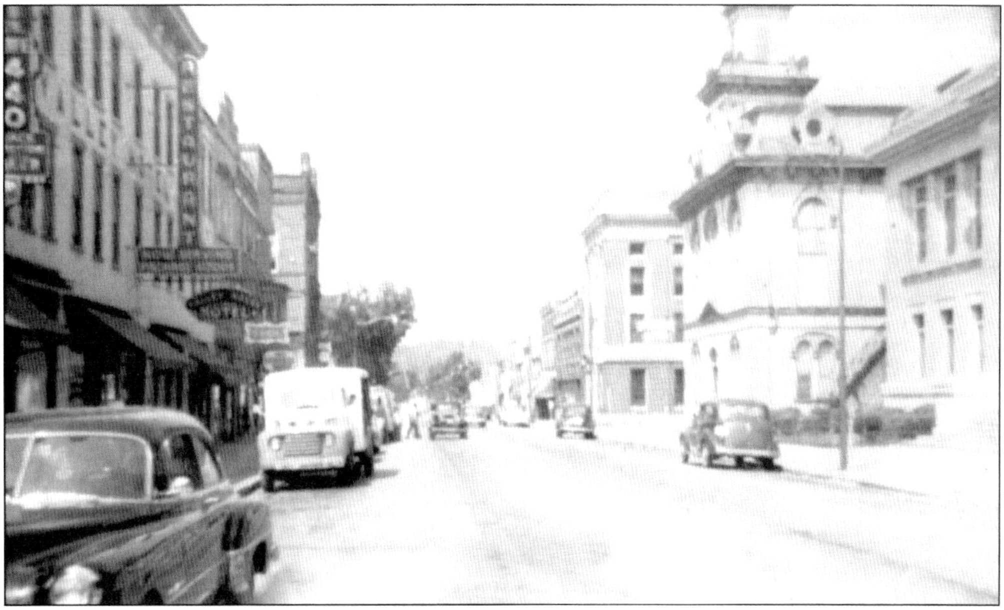

This view is looking north, and it captures the north half of the 400 block between Fourth and Fifth Streets. The 440 Café, which was also a Greyhound bus stop, is on the far left, the Valley House Restaurant and Hotel are next door. The automobiles date this card as late 1940s or early 1950s. (Courtesy Fritz.)

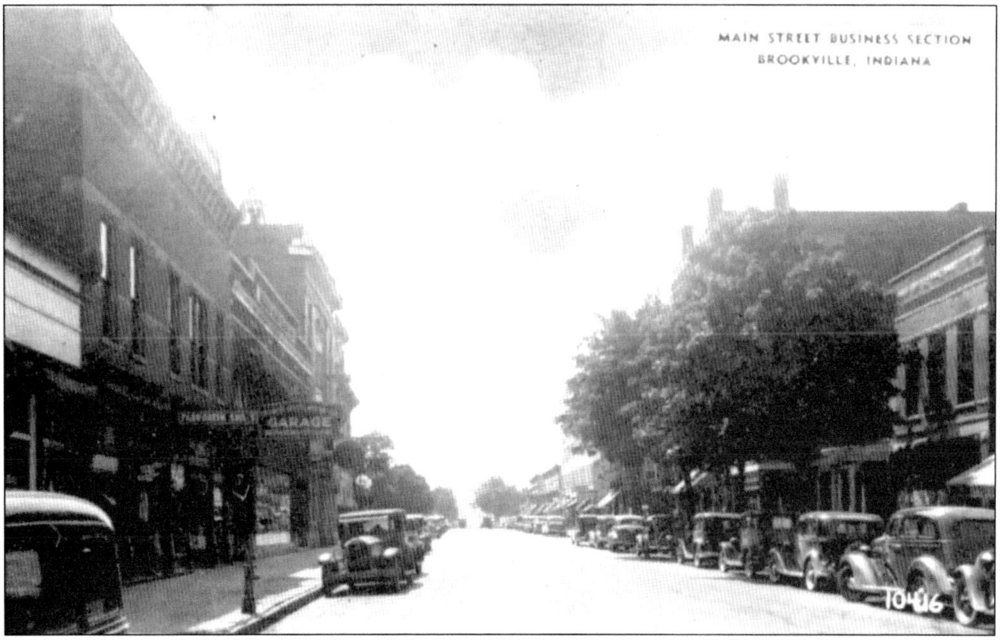

This view of Main Street was taken in the middle of the block between Fifth and Sixth Streets. The businesses on the left included Poppers, a men's clothing store, and under the garage sign was the Reidman automobile agency. The building on the right was Gus Baither's variety store—a prime source for Brookville residents to buy postcards. (Courtesy Fritz.)

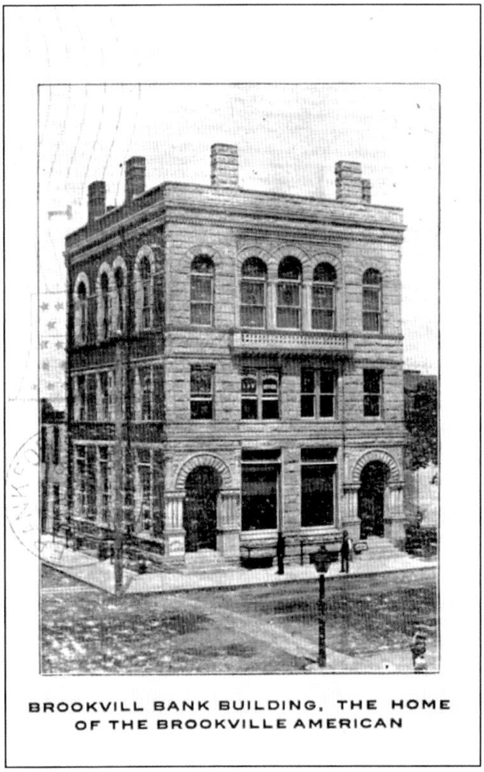

The National Brookville Bank was built in 1890–1891 at the northwest corner of Fifth and Main Streets. Its architecture is Victorian Romanesque, which is unique to Brookville. The bank, also known as the Shirk and Goodwin Bank, closed in 1939. Its assets were sold and deposits transferred to the Franklin County National Bank. A law firm was on the second floor, and the *Brookville American* newspaper was housed in the basement. This newspaper traces its beginning to 1832 and is still in business today. The Franklin County Farmers' Mutual Insurance Company now occupies the building. John C. Shirk, who served as president of the National Brookville Bank, was one of the organizers of the Farmers' insurance company. The bottom card shows the addition of a covering over the entrance and a fire escape on the side.

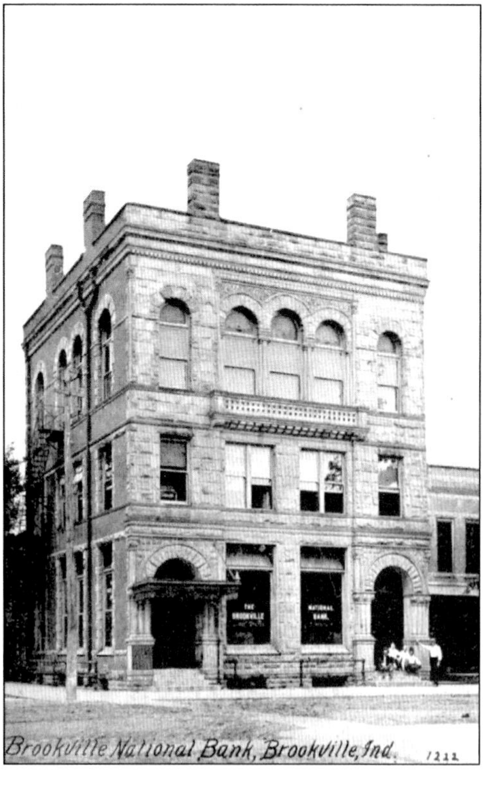

The Franklin County National Bank was organized in 1900 and moved into this new three-story building at the northeast corner of Fifth and Main Streets in 1913. The Knights of Pythias lodge had its meeting place on the third floor. Brookville dentist Dr. Charles Glaser had his office on the second floor, as did other professionals, until the bank needed the space and remodeled the entire interior of the building.

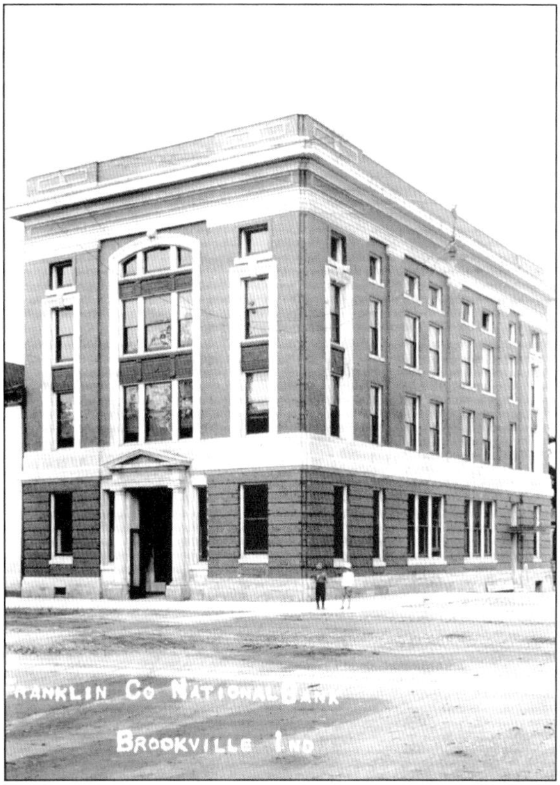

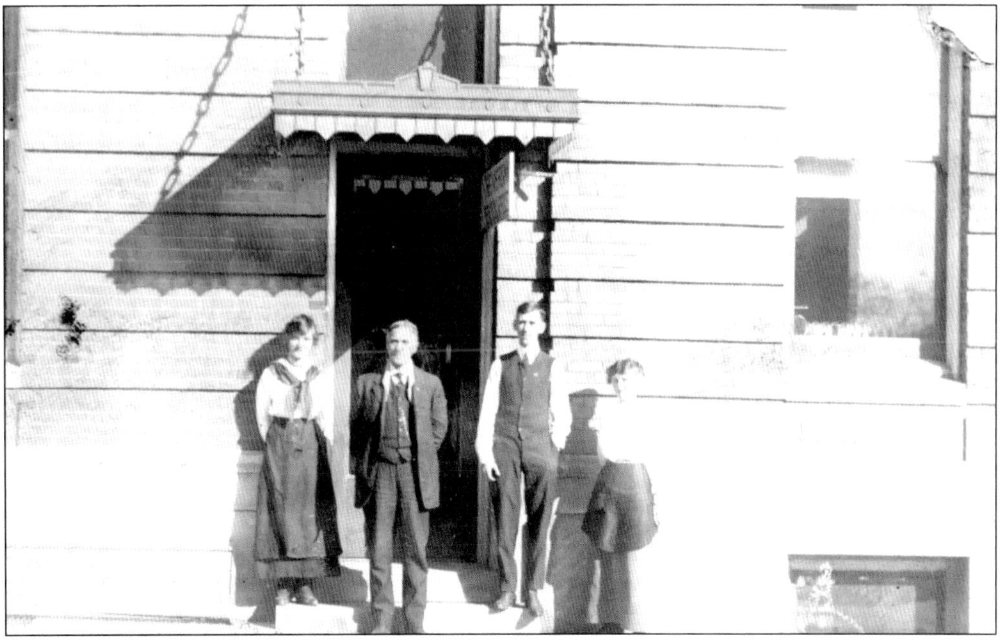

The staff of the *Brookville American* poses in front of their new office. They moved from the National Brookville Bank basement to the rear of the new Franklin County National Bank building and remained there until 1943 when they became part of Whitewater Publications and moved to the same building as the *Brookville Democrat.* (Courtesy FCHS.)

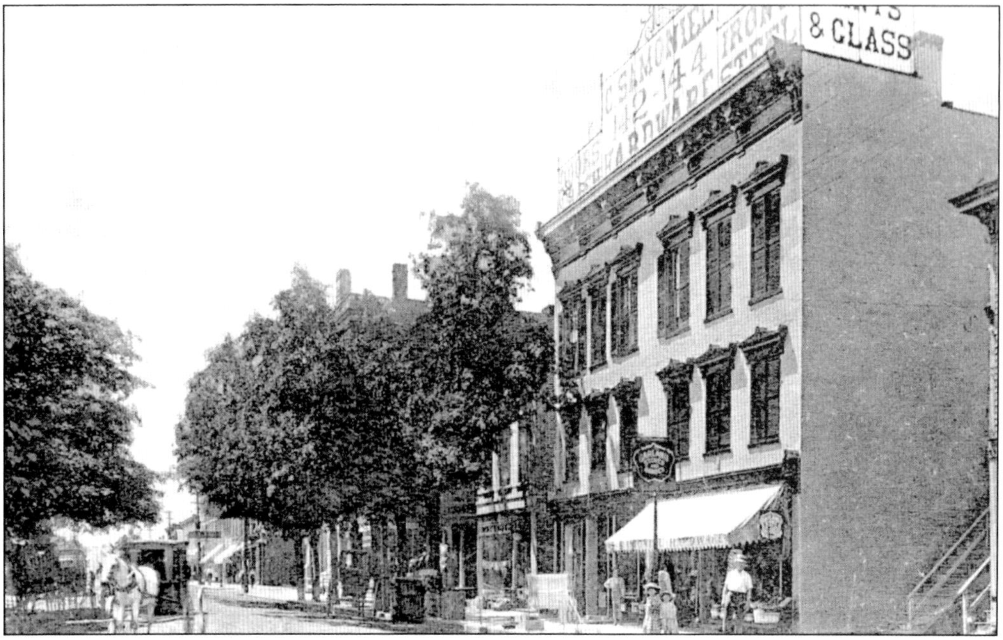

The most prominent feature of the Charles Samoniel hardware store was the large ornate sign displaying his name and describing his merchandise. Samoniel started his business in 1865. This building was built around 1880 and contained a wide variety of merchandise. Fries and Geis Hardware used the building in later years and closed in the early 1970s. (Courtesy Schlesselman.)

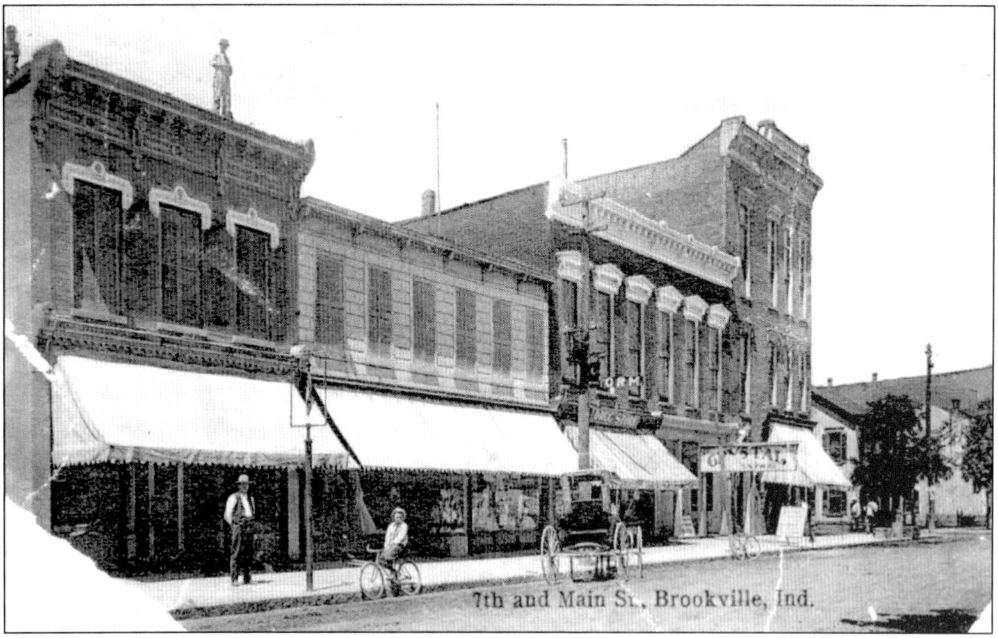

This postcard shows the north half of the 600 block from the southeast. The building on the left was a jewelry store owned by three generations of the Hornung family, then Huffine's jewelry and watch repair. The first and second buildings currently house the Rosenberger Main Meat Market. The Crystal Theatre and Trichler building are at the far end of the block. (Courtesy Shea.)

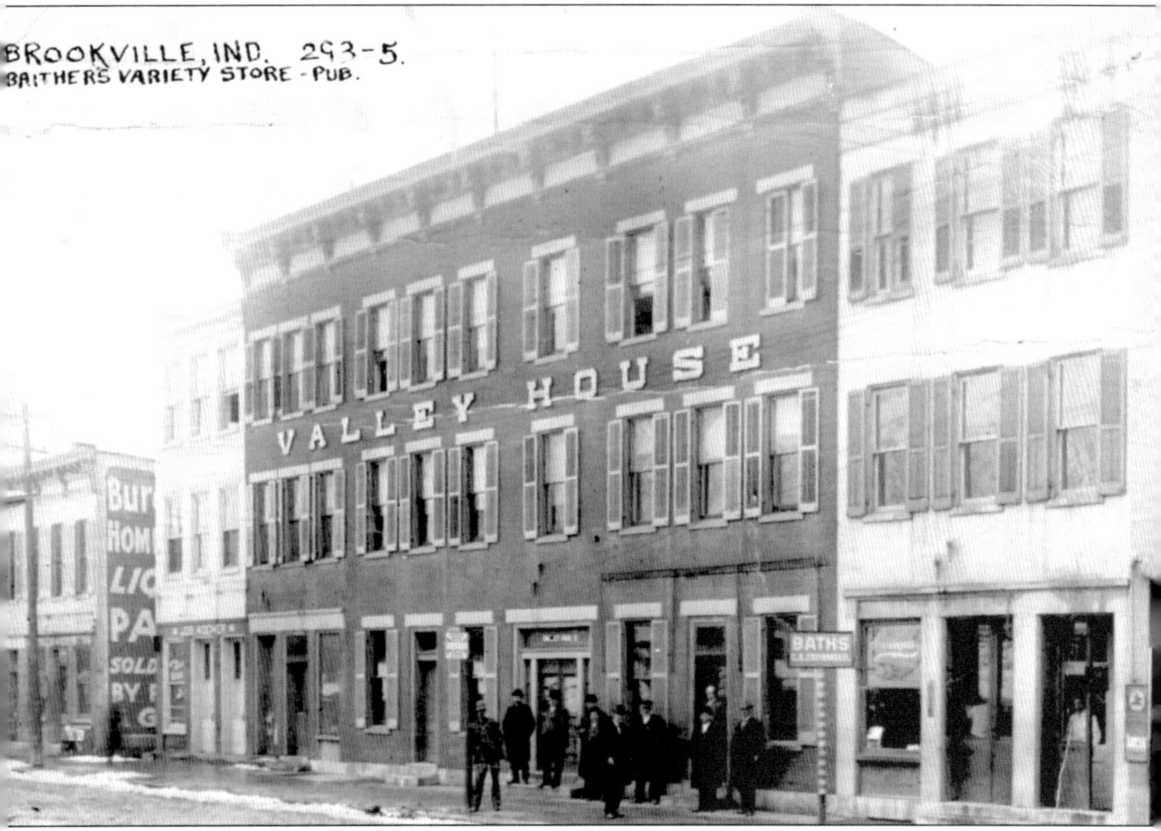

The Valley House was built in 1852 after the 1820 Brookville Hotel and other buildings on the block burned. Peter Schaf became proprietor of the Valley House in 1870, and under his management, the hotel gained a reputation for its hospitality. Casper Schuck's son-in-law Michael Senefeld continued the business until he died in 1913. In 1915, Senefeld's widow sold the business to Casper and Nora Schuck, who had owned the Brunswick Hotel. The Valley House's business declined during the Depression years, but the tavern and restaurant continued to operate. Edward and Nora Bath took over the business in 1938 and owned it until 1970. In 1977, George and Jamie Ballou restored the restaurant and barroom to an 1850s atmosphere. The food and atmosphere were well-received, but the business ultimately failed. In the 1980s, efforts by preservationists to purchase the old hotel and restore it were unsuccessful. Unfortunately this important Brookville landmark continues to deteriorate in the center of town. (Courtesy FCHS.)

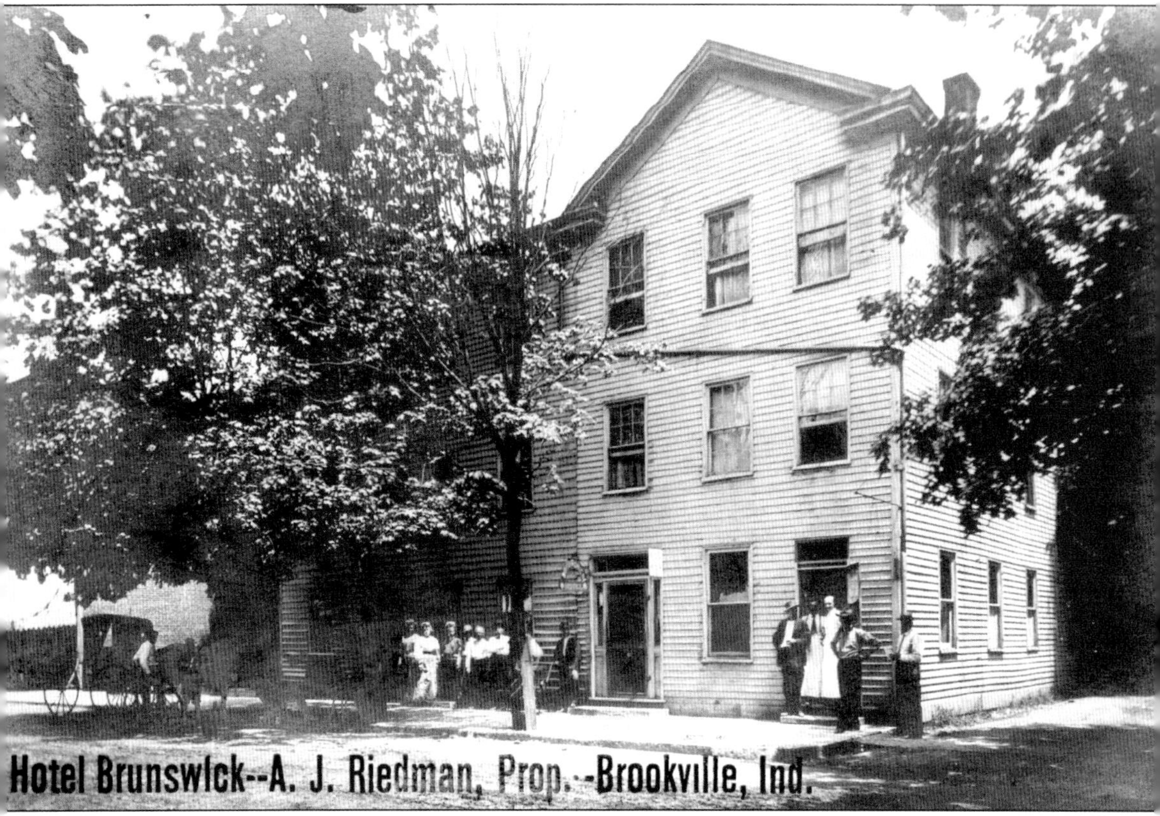

The Brunswick Hotel was located at present-day 647 Main Street. A contemporary account by Clifford Roberts told about life in Brookville in the 1914–1917 time period. He said, "In the front was the saloon, one of twelve in town. The saloon ran far back in the building to a large dining room where long tables were set for family style dining. Big steaming dishes of food would be passed around each table, home style. At the rear attached to the building was a livery stable. Out of town 'drummers' [salesmen] were the best customers for both the livery stable and the hotel." He said the owner of the hotel and saloon keeper was Casper Schuck. "His was the gathering place of the retired, beer drinking card players." Roberts remembered a vaudeville piano player and singer who entertained in the hotel's reception room when he was here in the off-season. The hotel was torn down in 1919, and Dr. Edward Glaser built a house on the site where he also had his office. (Courtesy Koch.)

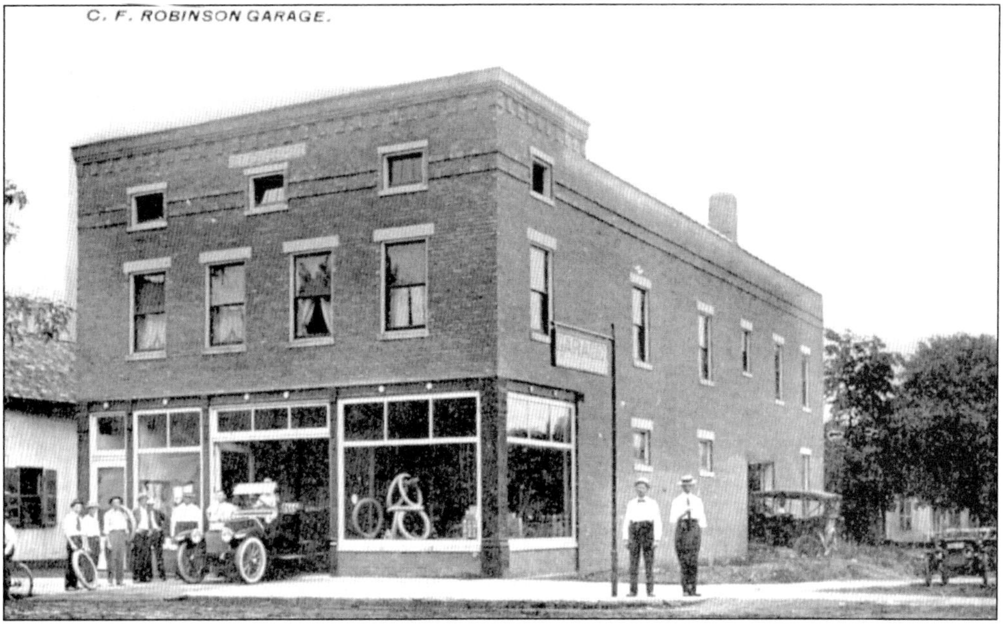

Charles Robinson built his business at the northeast corner of Seventh and Main Streets in 1913. In a December 1924 newspaper advertisement, he advertised a "Studebaker Standard Six Sedan" for $1,595. In later years, he and his son Percy sold Whippet automobiles, and later Percy sold John Deere tractors. Since then, the building has been a drugstore, a Southern Dollar Store, and a print shop, and it is now a beauty parlor. (Courtesy Schlesselman.)

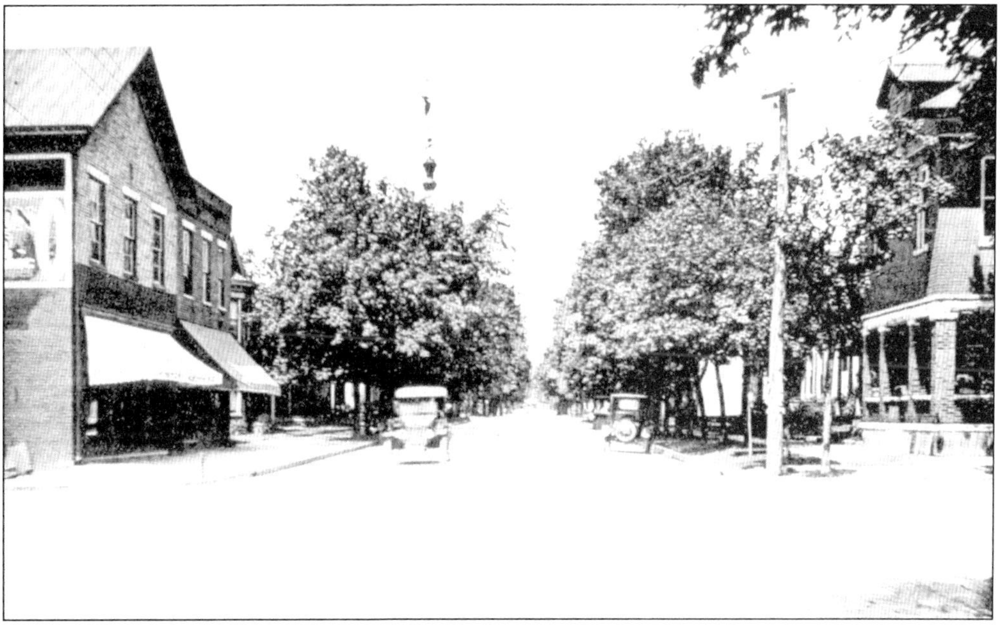

The Frank Masters building on the left sold threshing machinery and other farm implements. The building across the street was the James Buckley residence. He was one of the owners of the Brookville Furniture factory and maintained a furniture showroom in the house. In recent years, it was the Case House, a restaurant named after Dr. Clinton Case, who occupied the building at one time.

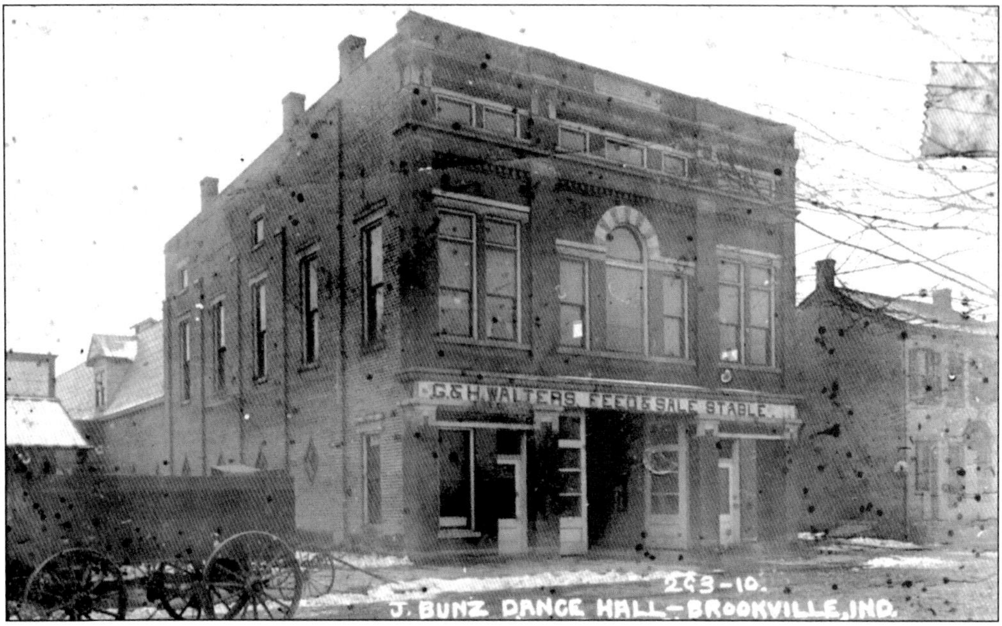

John Bunz built this brick building in 1909. The sign on the front of the building indicates it is a stable, but the description on the postcard refers to the second-floor dance hall—an interesting combination. The building has been used for a variety of purposes, including the Jay Garment clothing factory, a Ford agency, and a television repair shop. Today it belongs to the Knights of Columbus. (Courtesy Houchin.)

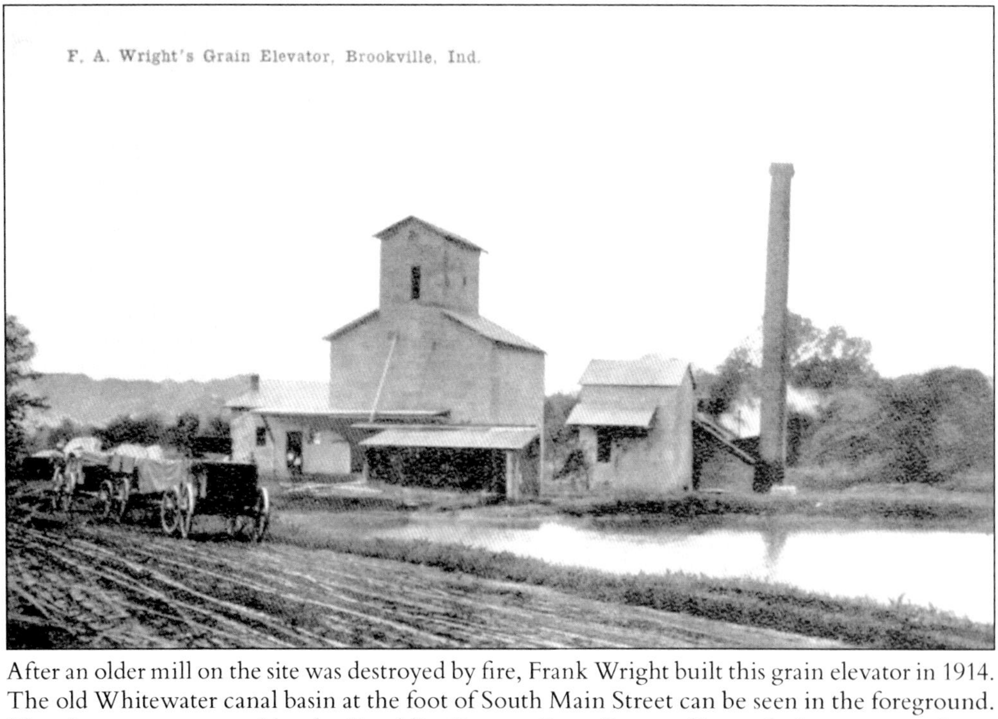

After an older mill on the site was destroyed by fire, Frank Wright built this grain elevator in 1914. The old Whitewater canal basin at the foot of South Main Street can be seen in the foreground. The elevator was owned by the Franklin County Farm Bureau Co-op in later years and was torn down in December 2006 after sitting idle for many years. (Courtesy Rowe.)

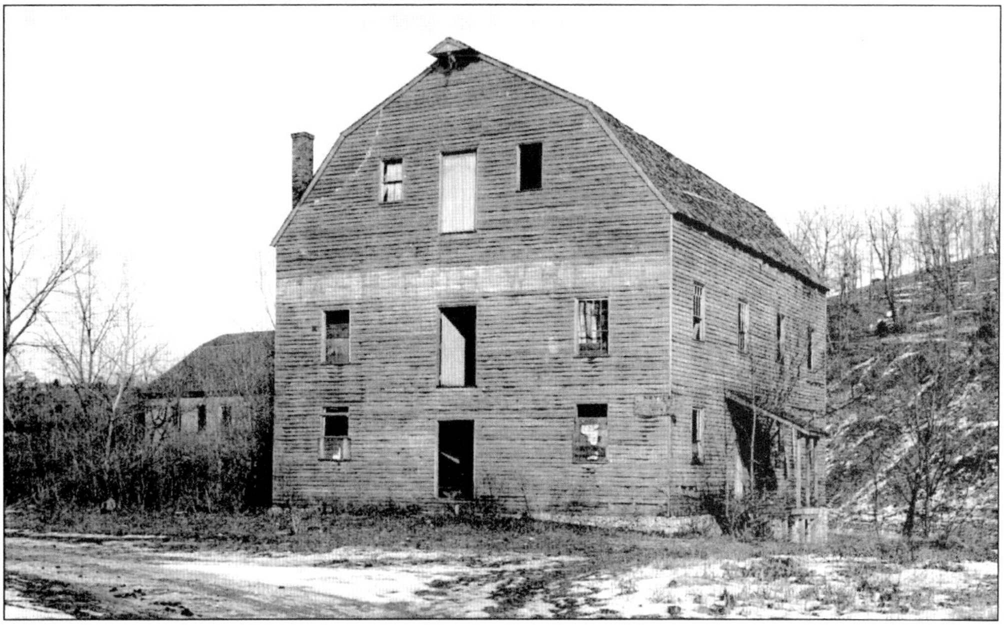

The Speer Flouring Mill stood near the Hermitage on the Whitewater's East Fork. This mill and the paper mill to the left rear were among the earliest enterprises in Brookville. The flour mill was torn down in 1905 and rebuilt as a farm barn east of town. The paper mill was razed in 1909 and the bricks reused in constructing the John Bunz building on Main Street.

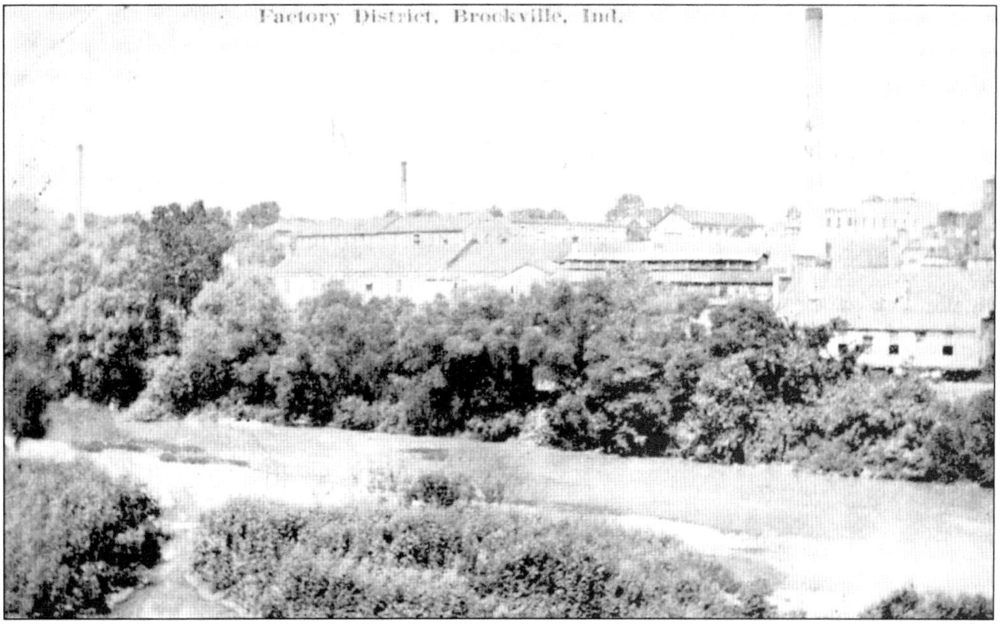

The Brookville Furniture factory and the Thompson and Norris paper mill faced each other across the remains of the Whitewater Canal and the Big Four Railroad. The railroad was built on the canal towpath shortly after the Civil War. Both factories used the railroad to ship their products. The West Fork of the Whitewater River flowed behind the paper mill. (Courtesy Rowe.)

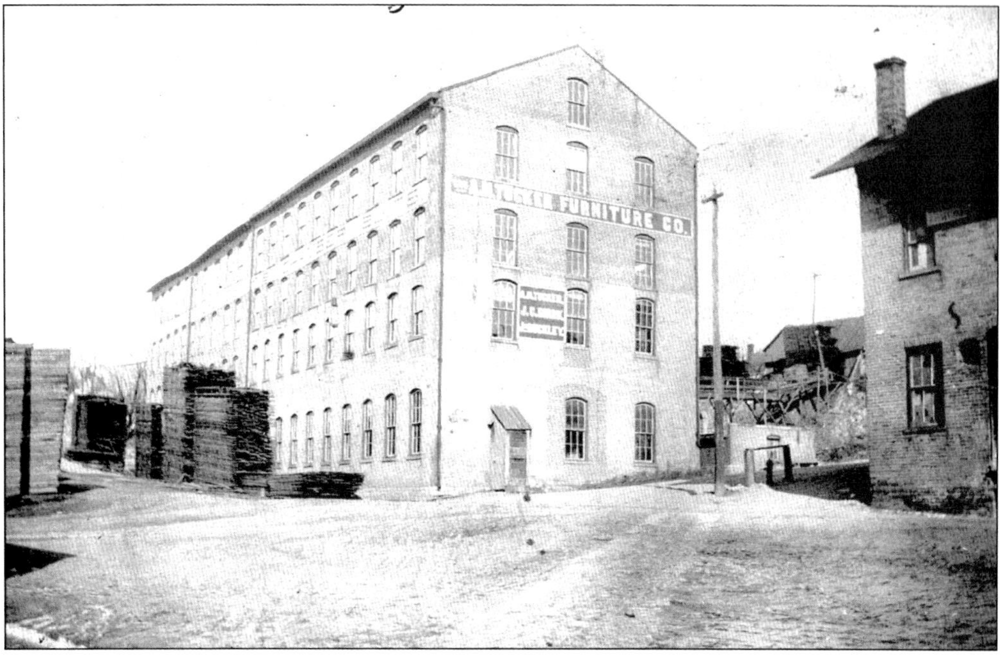

In 1897, A. M. Tucker and others formed the A. M. Tucker Furniture Company in this four-story brick building located at the foot of West Eighth Street, facing Cliff Street. In 1900, the officers were A. M. Tucker, president; John C. Shirk, vice president; and James Buckley, secretary. In 1907, Tucker sold his interest to Shirk and the business became the Brookville Furniture Company. In 1910, a four-story addition was built on the rear of the older building. This Brookville factory made high-grade walnut and mahogany furniture—primarily bedchamber suites—that were sold throughout the United States. The furniture factory closed sometime after the death of Shirk in 1924. The names on the old building could still be seen until the building was destroyed by fire in 1999. (Below, courtesy Houchin.)

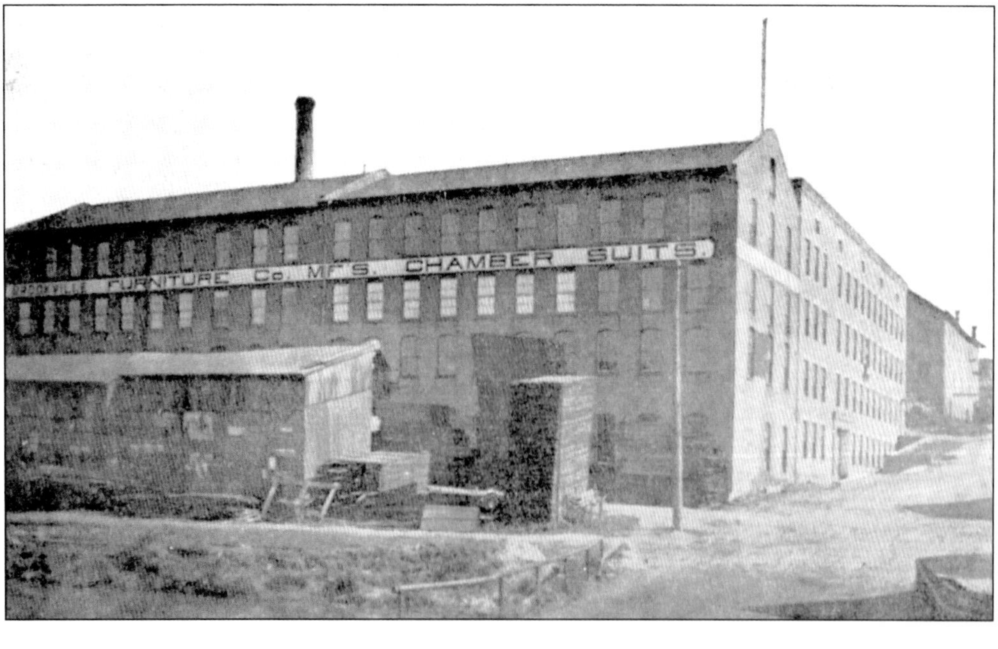

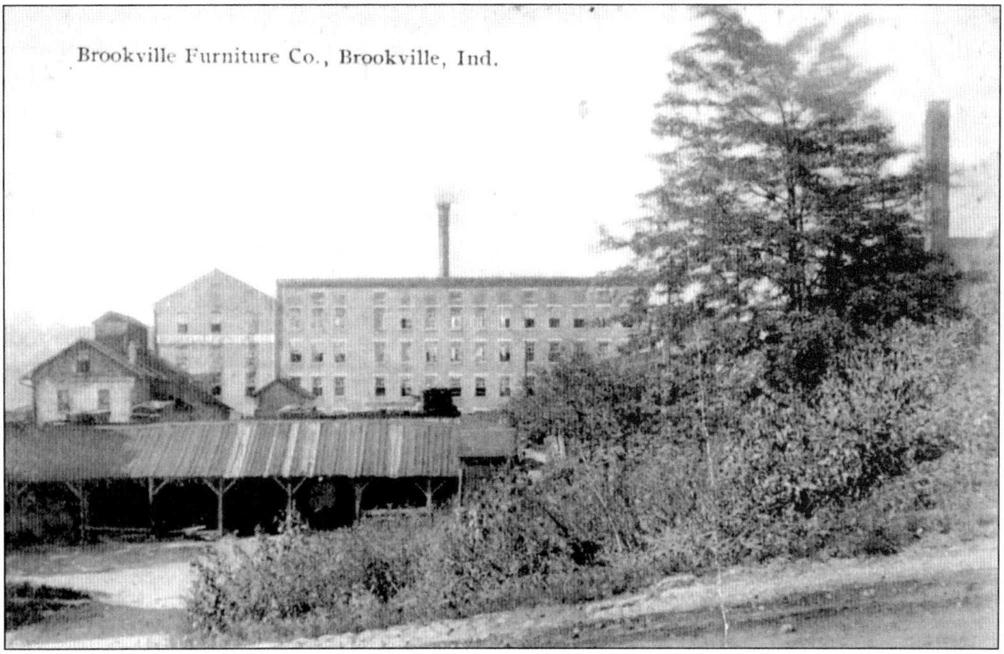

The Franklin Casket Company bought the old furniture factory buildings in 1937 and produced cloth-covered caskets. At one time, this factory employed 150 men but eventually closed in 1994. The building burned in 1999, and the site is now a vacant lot on West Eighth Street. (Courtesy FCHS.)

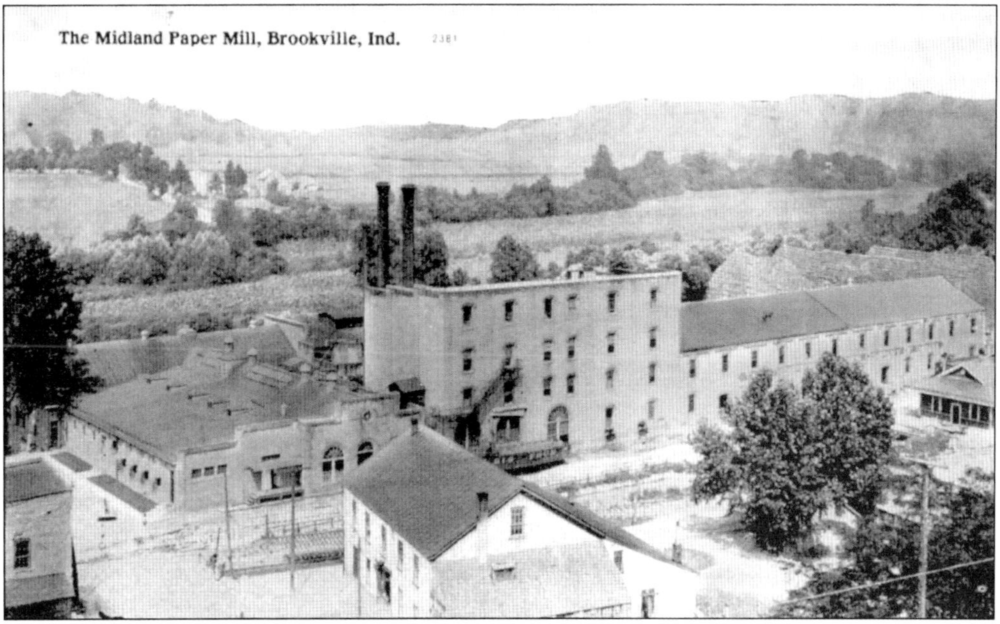

The Thompson and Norris Company purchased the remains of an earlier paper mill on this site in 1898. This plant made strawboard, used in corrugated paper and boxes used by shippers of glass, millinery and parcel post packages, and eggs according to one account. The building in the foreground was the Big 4 Saloon, and the Brookville train depot can be seen at the right. (Courtesy Lamont.)

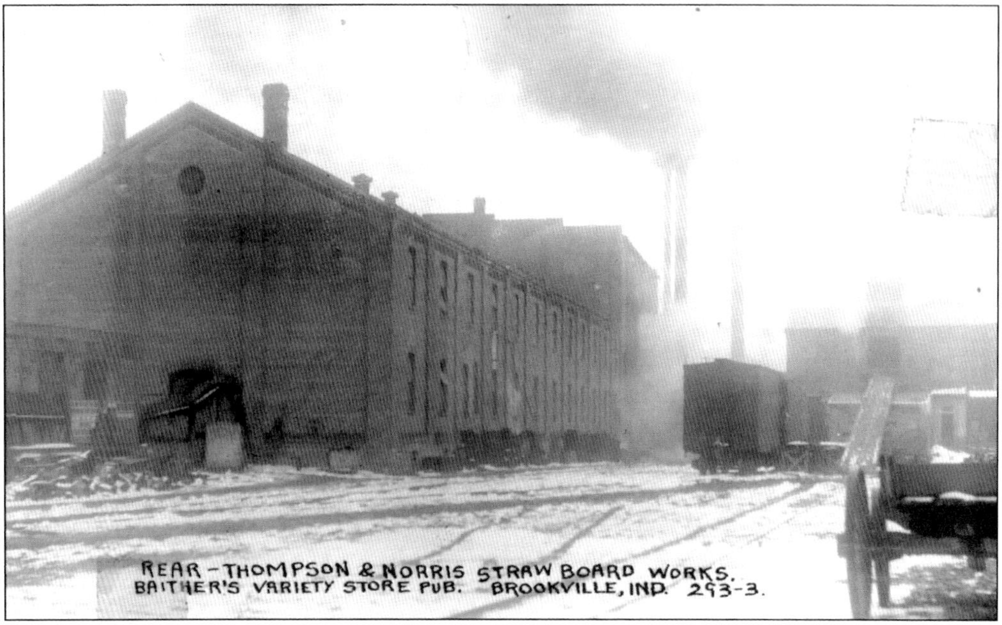

These cards show a similar angle of the Thompson and Norris paper mill. This building replaced an earlier structure that burned in 1911. In the plant's operation, straw was brought in and dumped into large vats for cooking and the strawboard product shipped via railcar. The dark plume from the smokestack was a fact of life until recently, when a roofing plant was put into operation on this location. When these cards were made, the railroad was vital in allowing this business and the furniture factory to ship their products to distant cities. The raw materials—straw for the paper mill and hardwood for the furniture factory—were grown locally and could be hauled in by horse and wagon. (Above, courtesy Houchin; below, courtesy Smith.)

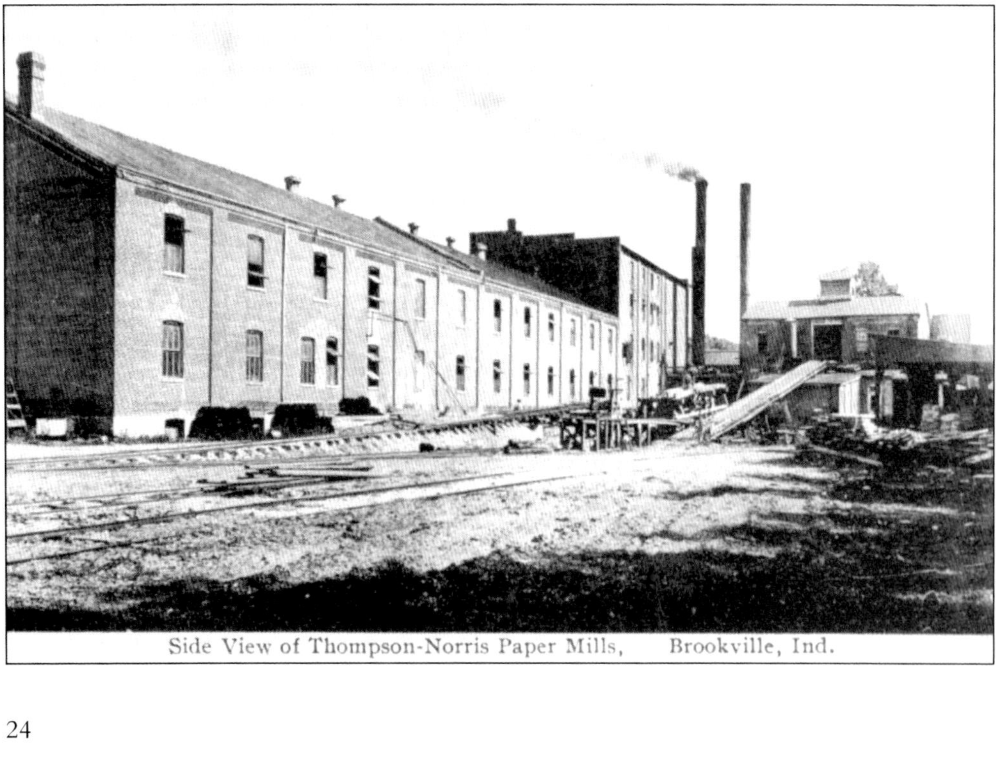

Side View of Thompson-Norris Paper Mills, Brookville, Ind.

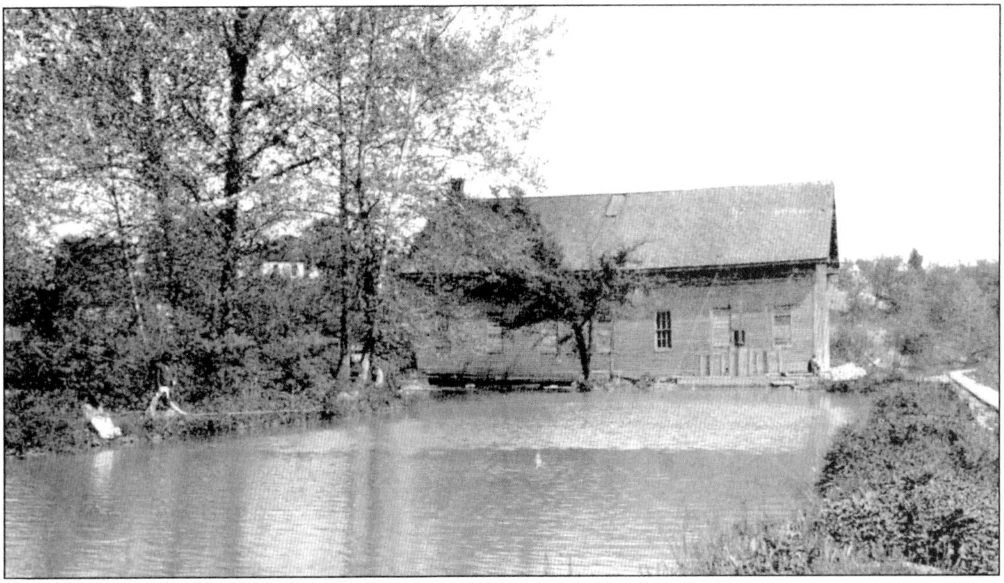

The Stewart Paper Company built this pulp mill near a canal lock on the northwest side of town in 1869. The main plant was the site later occupied by the Thompson and Norris Company. The pulp mill was damaged by fire and flood and finally destroyed by the 1913 flood. This was another Brookville swimming hole and place to fish until the canal was drained.

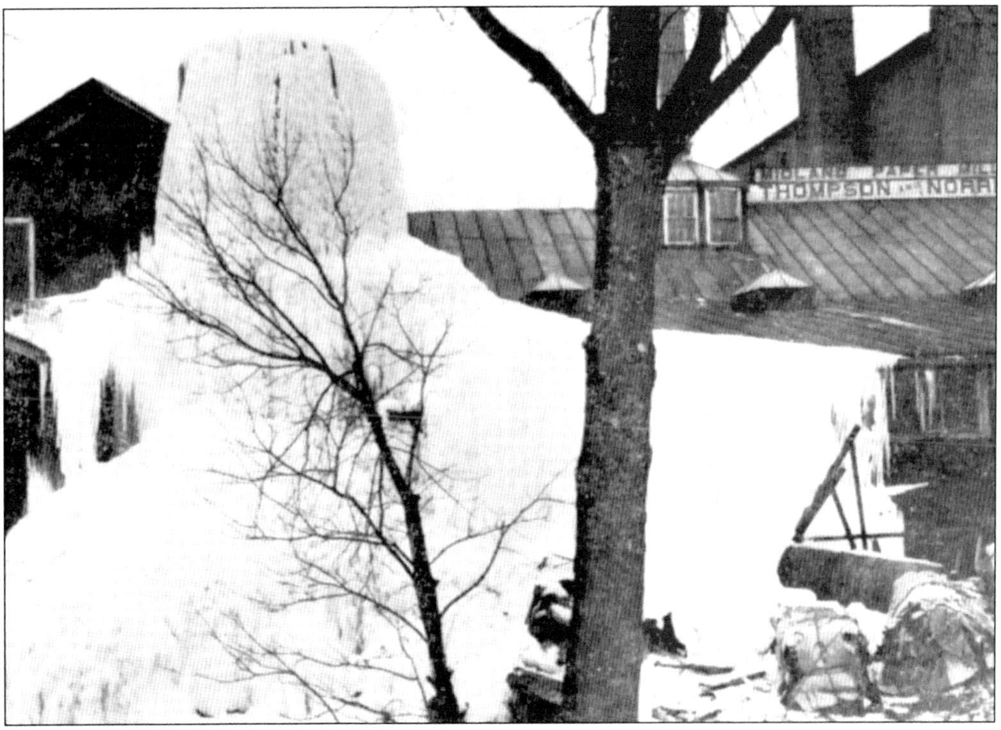

This card shows a sign that identifies this scene at the Midland Paper Mill of Thompson and Norris. The water tank was rendered useless by an early-1900s hard freeze. Since water was needed in the manufacture of strawboard, the plant probably had to shut down until the tank thawed and the damage was repaired.

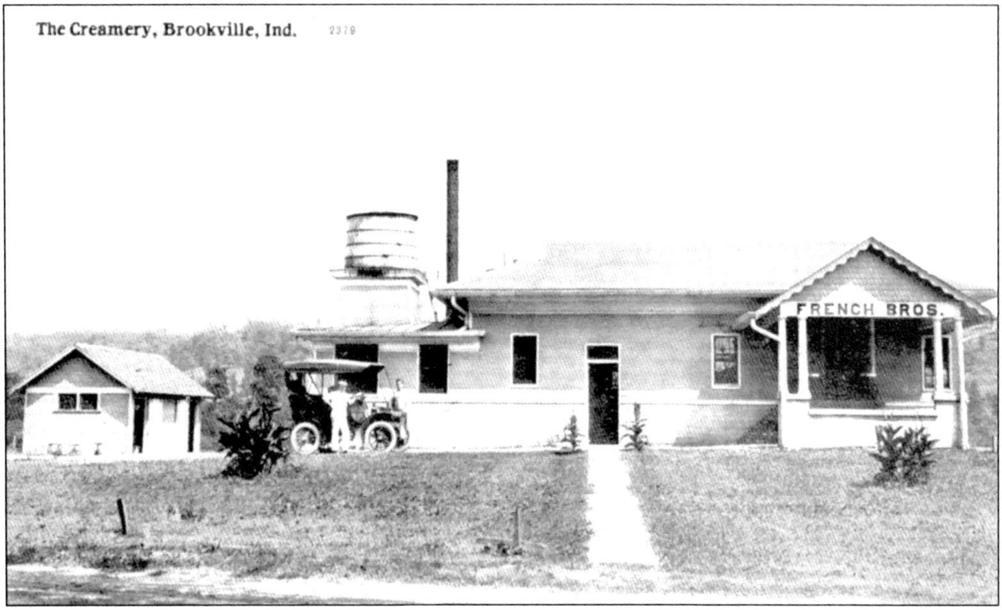

The French Brothers Creamery was located on Fairfield Avenue. The original building was built in 1900, damaged by fire in 1951, and then converted into a private home minus the water tower and smokestack. It has been owned by the Chappelow family since 1957. The sender wrote on the back of this card, mailed in 1908, "I watched them make sidewalks on one of the streets yesterday."

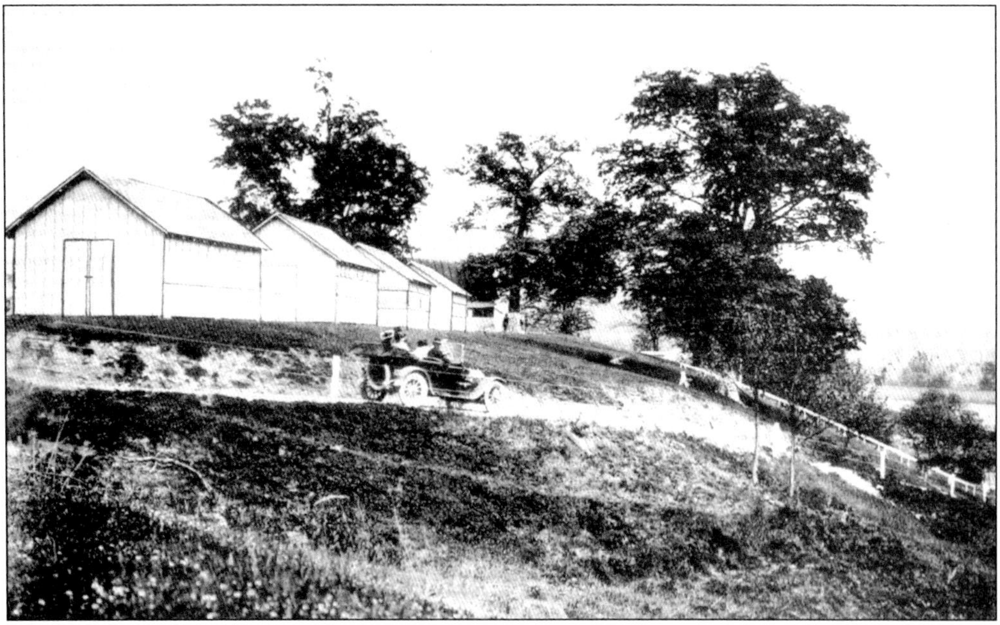

Magnesia Springs was a popular Brookville resort in the early 1900s. The resort was built on the site of a sizeable Native American village where there were nine mounds and a spring that was said to contain magnesium and have miraculous healing powers. There were cabins for overnight visits, a dining hall, and a dance hall. At times, special events such as political rallies and religious revival meetings were held there.

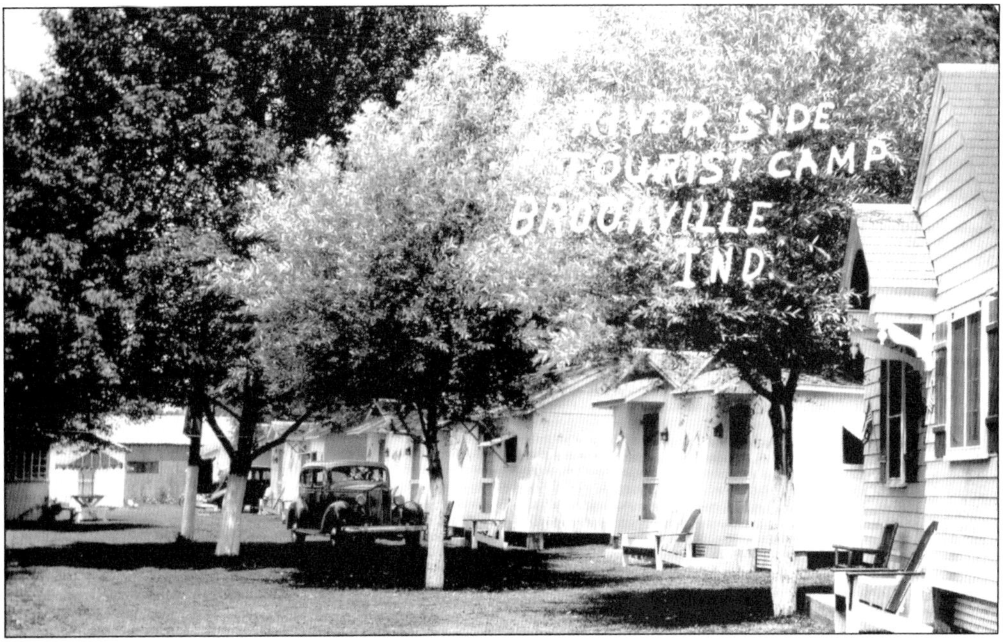

The Riverside Tourist Camp was at the south edge of Brookville before there were any commercial businesses south of the lower bridge across the East Fork. There was a saloon there that was a "last chance" and a "first chance," depending on which direction one was going. There is a small restaurant there now and one of the original tourist cabins. The card below calls the buildings the Scenic Valley Motel. That would seem to be an exaggeration; these buildings provided only the basic needs, a shelter from the weather (but no insulation or inner wall), a toilet and basin, and possibly a small kerosene stove. There are still a few of these cabins standing, and they are being used by a used automobile business. (Courtesy Schlesselman.)

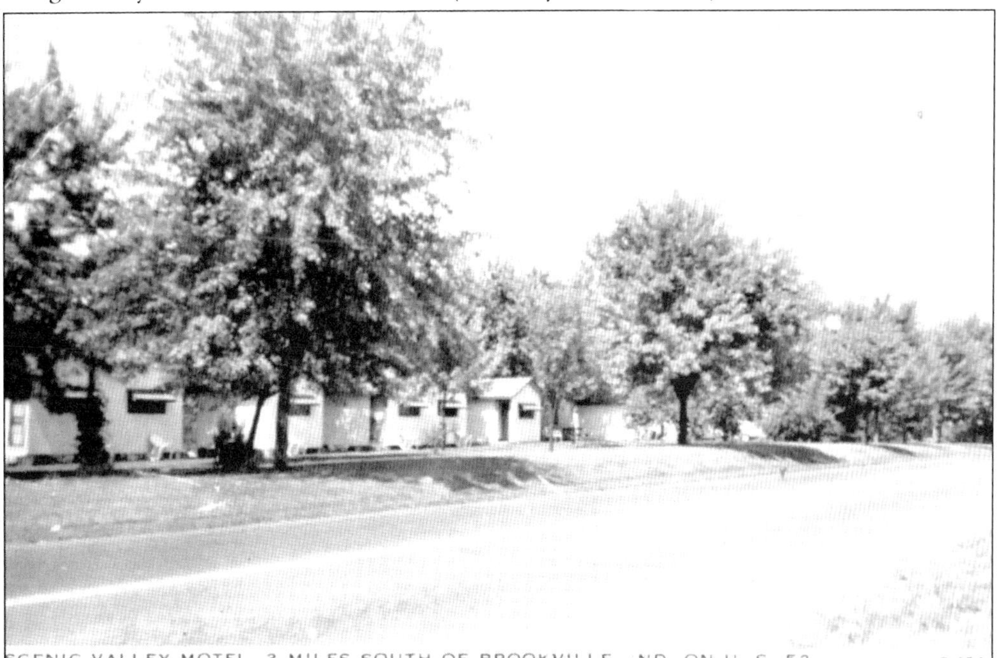

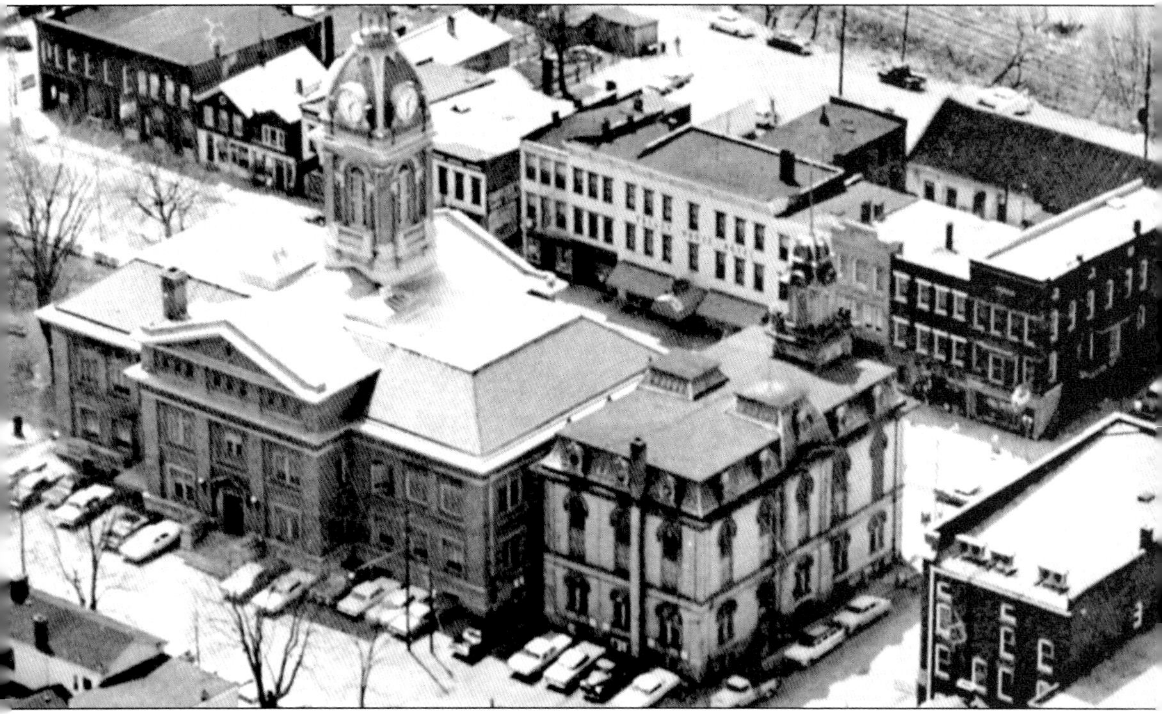

This aerial view of downtown Brookville, from around 1950, shows the east face of the Franklin County Courthouse and town building in the foreground and the 400 block in the background. This is a historic view since the south half (left) of the 400 block has been razed. In this time period, the first building at the south end of the block was the Corner Café, next door to the north was Bernhart's Grocery, then Hemke Dry Goods, Jones Wallpaper, Cappy Fohl's Restaurant and Bar, Public Service, and Swayzee's Drug Store. In the north half of the block was the 440 Café, Seible Sisters ladies' clothing store, Valley House Hotel (which was in operation then), Ferd Hubig's Barber Shop, Wissel's Clothing, Harry Waywood's Tire Shop, and the Rexall Drug Store at the north end of the block. In this photograph, Hertel's Restaurant was south of the Corner Café across West Fourth Street (upper left). The Kirschbaum Buick automobile agency was behind the Rexall Drug Store.

Two

County and Town Government Buildings

Formed in 1811, Franklin County selected Brookville as the county seat. At that time, Indiana was still a territory, becoming the 19th state in 1816. The first Franklin County Courthouse was a log building. The growing county soon needed a larger, permanent structure. In 1817, workers completed a brick building on the present-day courthouse square. It was simple in design, a square building of two stories resembling others of that period. That courthouse was destroyed by fire in 1852, along with many of the buildings across Main Street, including the Brookville Hotel where the fire started. In 1910–1912, county officials enlarged and modernized the 1852 courthouse. The earlier structure was entirely enclosed by the new front and back entrances and the additions on the north and south. This structure is still in use at this time, but it is being modernized again to include an elevator and new offices and courtrooms. Most of the county offices moved to the government center on Franklin Avenue in 2006. The judge, county prosecutor, and clerk of courts will be the only offices in the county courthouse on Main Street. Besides the town offices and functions, the Brookville Town Building was used by a number of organizations over the years, including the post office, American Legion, and a movie theater. In recent years, it has been used as a courthouse annex.

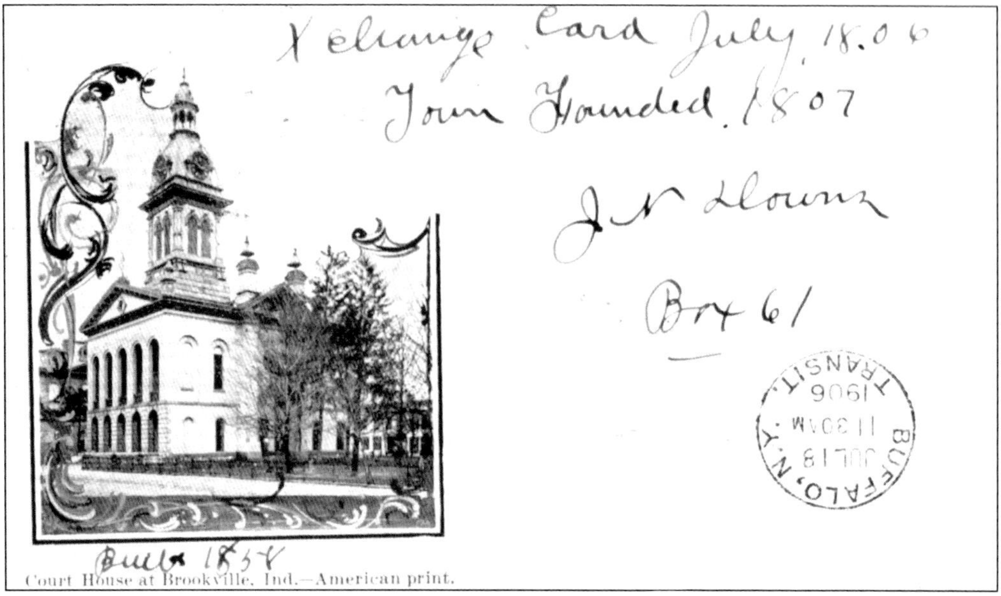

Court House at Brookville, Ind.—American print.

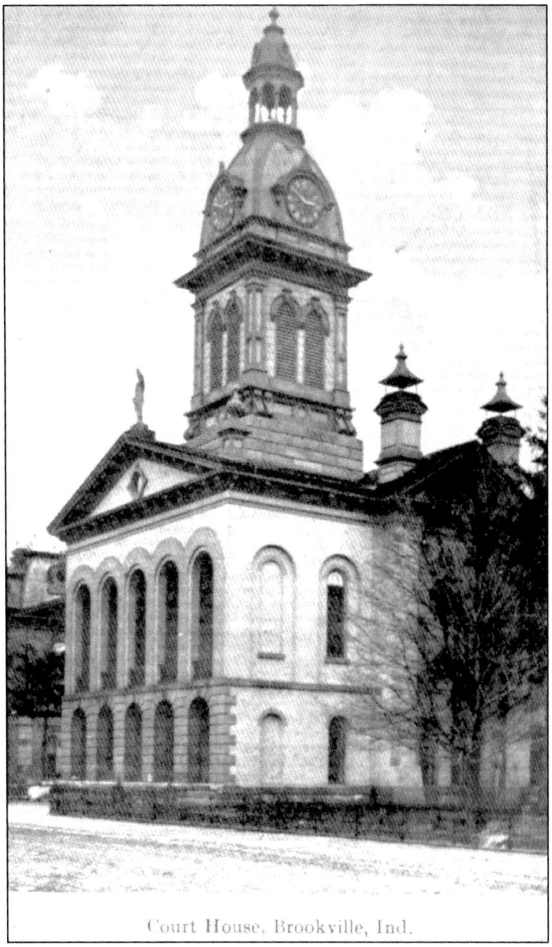
Court House, Brookville, Ind.

After a fire in 1852, a larger and more elegant structure was built on the same site as the earlier brick courthouse. The architect for the new building, Edwin May, later designed the Indiana statehouse at Indianapolis. The original tower may have been intended to house a clock, but early photographs show one was not installed. A more imposing tower was built in 1877, and a clock was installed around 1890. This top postcard of the Franklin County Courthouse, postmarked 1906, is one of the oldest in the book. In this case, the sender decided to include some historical notes—although incorrect. The town was actually founded in 1808 and the courthouse was built in 1852. "American print" along the bottom probably means that the card was produced in the print shop of the *Brookville American*.

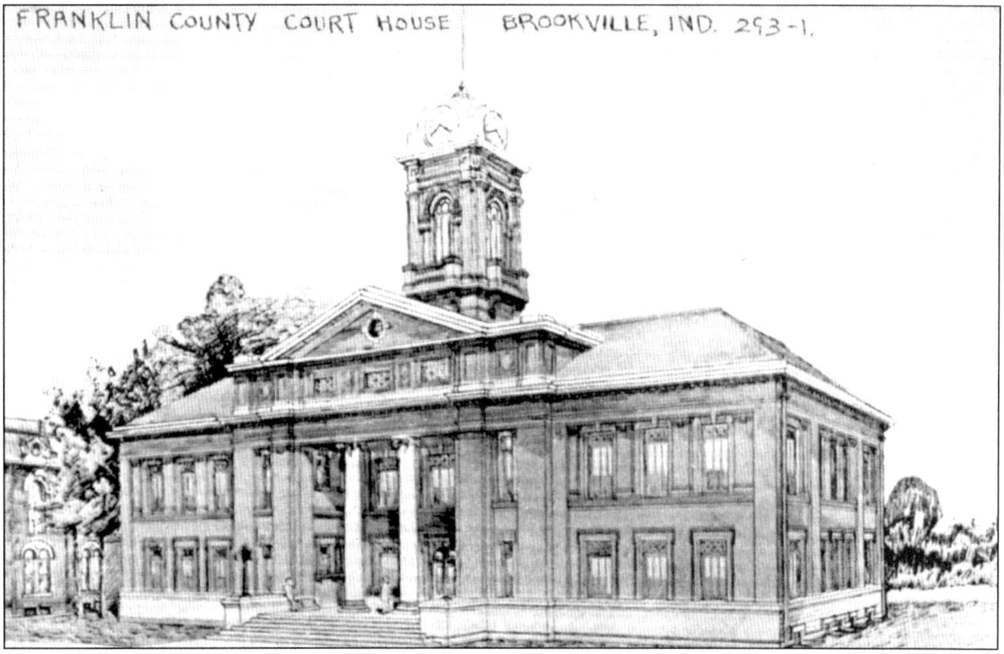

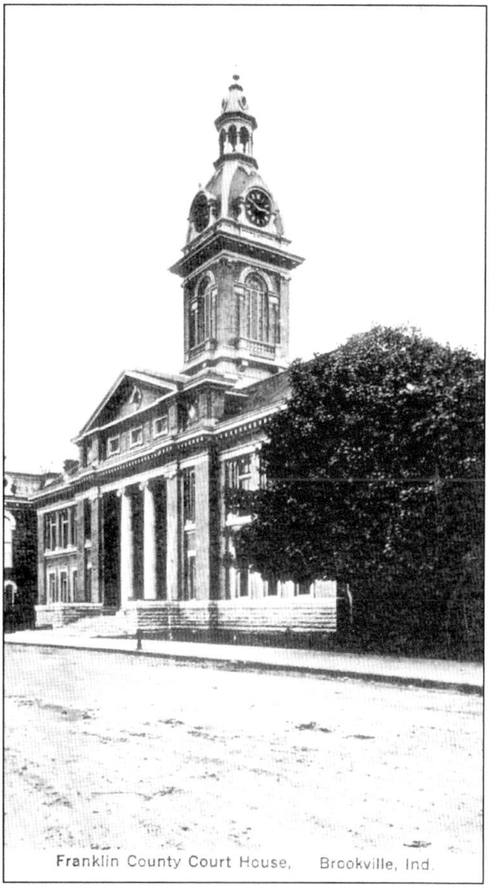

The unusual postcard above is an architect's rendering of a remodeled courthouse. This drawing appeared on the front page of the *Brookville Democrat* on March 3, 1910. In 1910–1912, county officials enlarged the 1852 courthouse by adding north and south wings to the old building, removing the two-level portico in front and replacing it with a massive two-story porch supported by stone pillars with Greek angular Ionic capitals at the top. They rebuilt the exterior of the clock tower but with little change in appearance. The interior entry and hallways of the remodeled building featured polished white marble throughout. The two public stairways were equipped with brass railings with the abbreviation FC. The administrative offices were located downstairs, and the court offices, including the judge's chamber and courtroom, were upstairs.

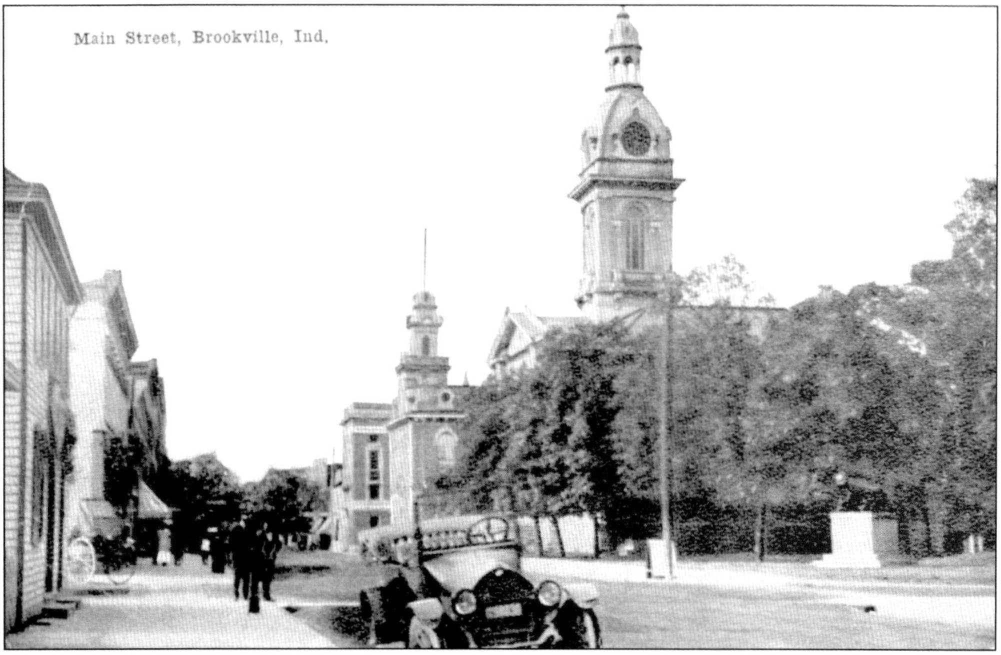

This view shows the heart of Brookville from Fourth Street at the pedestrian level. The Franklin County Courthouse, town building, and Franklin County National Bank, all on the right, make for a prosperous image of the town in the early 1900s. Automobiles have made an appearance, but the street is still not paved. At the far right, the old Civil War cannon is still on its perch. (Courtesy FCHS.)

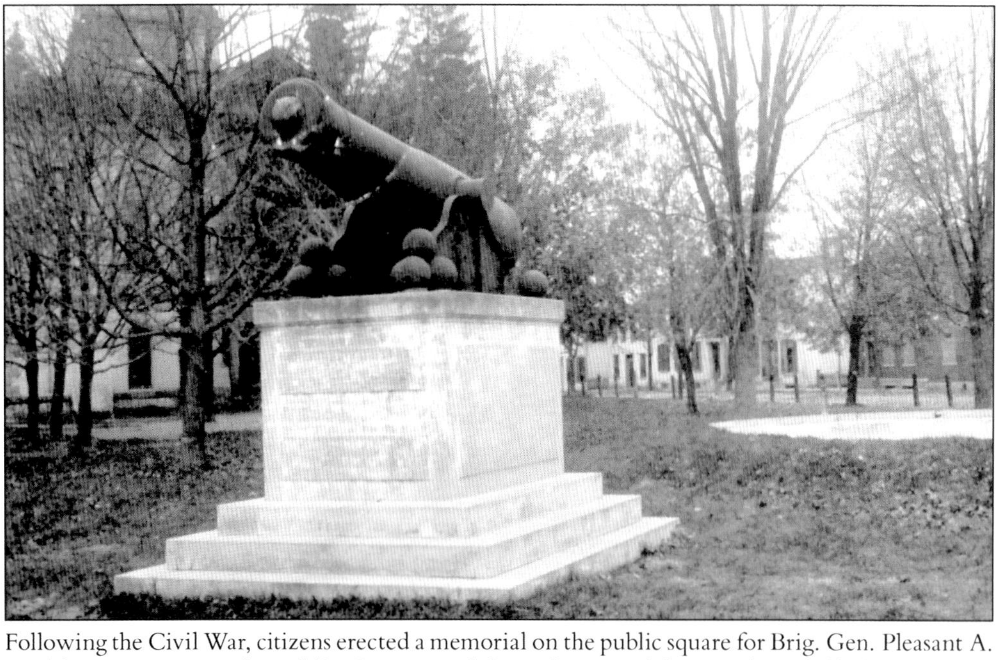

Following the Civil War, citizens erected a memorial on the public square for Brig. Gen. Pleasant A. Hackleman, a native of Franklin County and the only general from Indiana killed in the Civil War. The cannon was removed from its base in 1942 and donated to a World War II scrap drive. Some history lovers say this was a useless gesture as the metal was not suitable for further use.

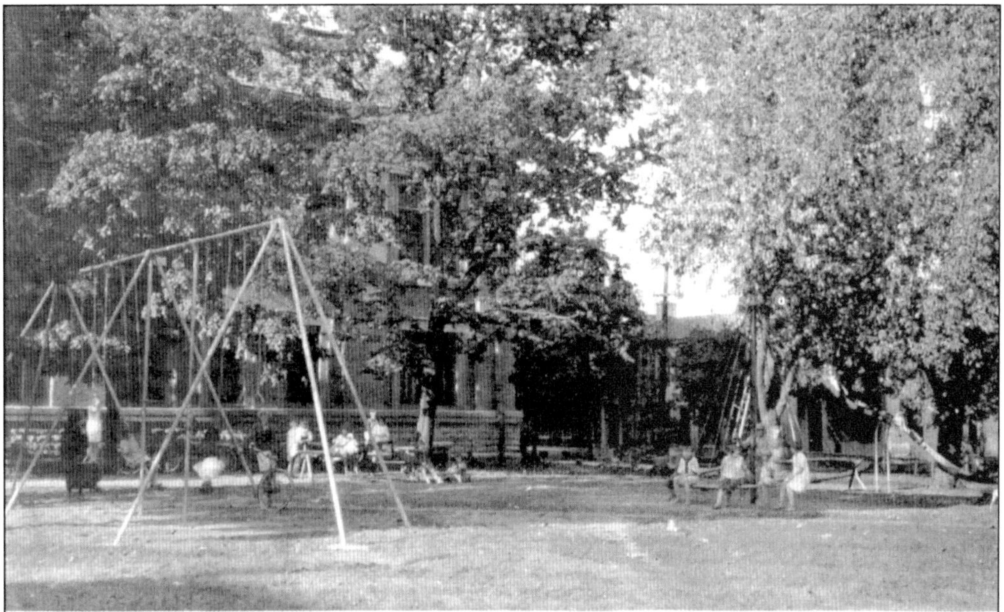

Playground in Court House Park, Brookville, Ind.

This card, postmarked 1928, shows a playground for children in the court yard. At one time there was a gazebo or bandstand nearby in the yard. Citizens used this public area for celebrations. There was a boy's band and a town band for adult men who probably performed here. While the adults were entertained, the children could enjoy the playground.

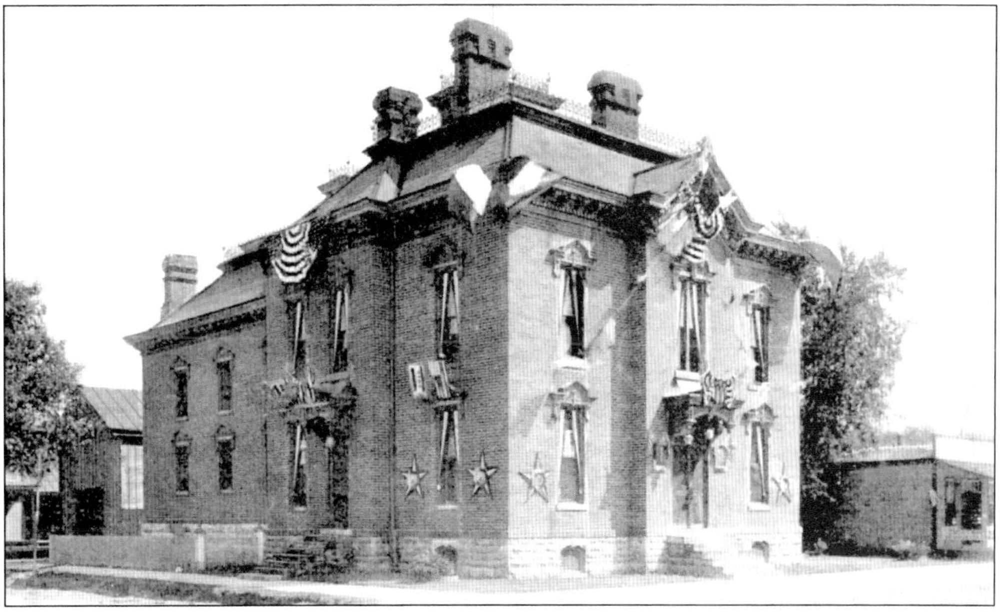

The home of the Franklin County sheriff, better known as the jail, is shown here decorated for the 1908 centennial. Built in 1883, the jail has been called "outstanding for its Italianate design." The sheriff had living quarters in the front, and the jail was in the rear of the building. A modern addition, known as the security center, was built on the south side in 1991–1993. (Courtesy Rowe.)

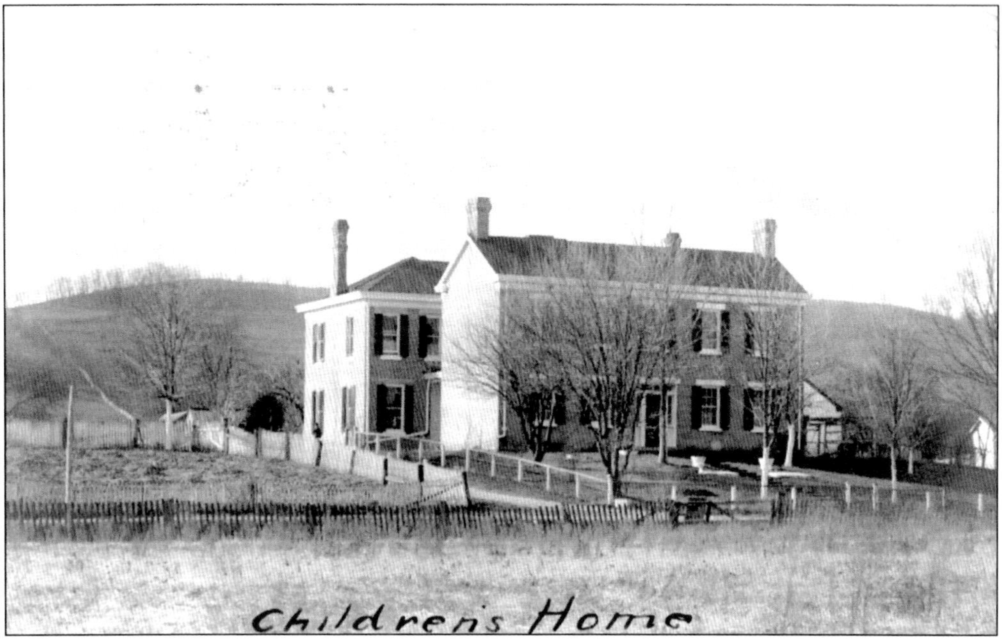

County commissioners purchased this house and 32 acres from Celia Wright in 1889. It was located adjoining the county infirmary, better known as the poor farm. The Children's Home was an orphanage established for the pauper children of the county. It closed in 1937. Today the house is a fine-looking residence on Blue Creek Road beside the county park.

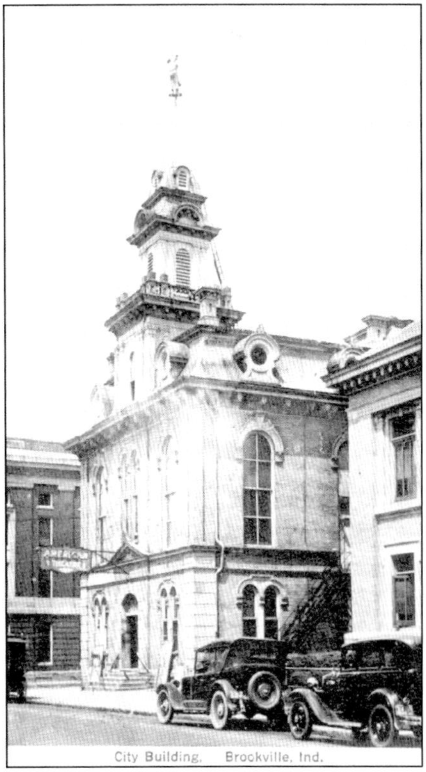

A brave workman is shown in this postcard painting the flagpole. The cornerstone for the town hall was laid in 1876. It was a rather elaborate-looking building, resembling other town halls of that time. The town hall has been used for a variety of purposes over its lifetime, and the sign in front says American Theatre. (Courtesy Hauberg/Quinton.)

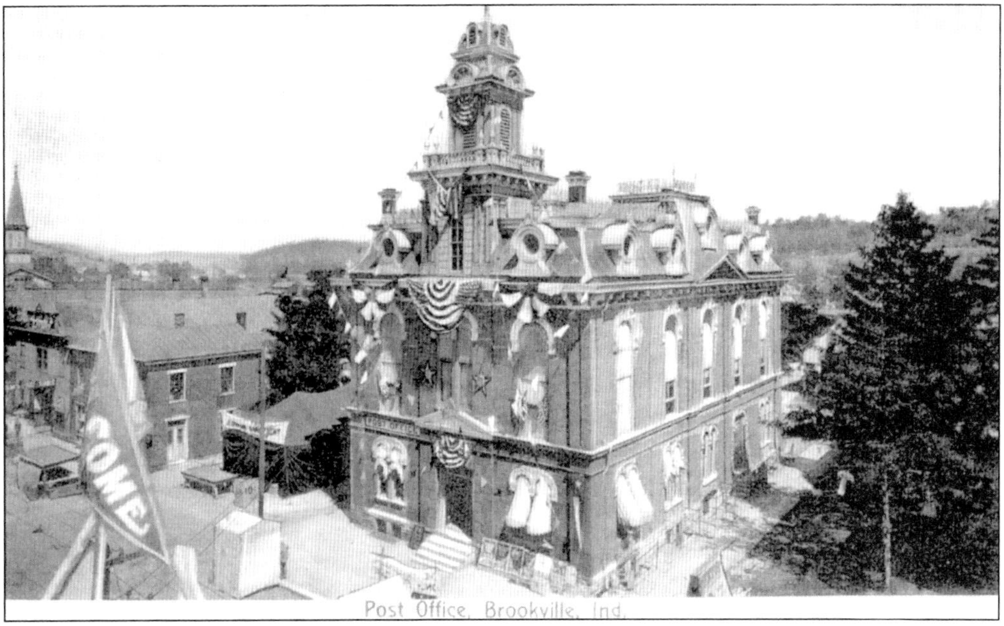

This postcard shows the town hall in 1908 decorated to celebrate Brookville's centennial. The north half of the first floor was being used as the Brookville post office at the time. The town board met in the building, and a large open room upstairs was used as an auditorium. Brookville High School held graduations there before the school had its own auditorium. The card at right shows how close the remodeled courthouse was to the town building on the right-hand side of the photograph. The awnings kept the summer afternoon sun from shining into the front rooms. Most of the businesses on Main Street had awnings to shade morning and afternoon sun. Windows were often open, and the awnings kept out rain while still allowing natural ventilation. (Courtesy Rowe.)

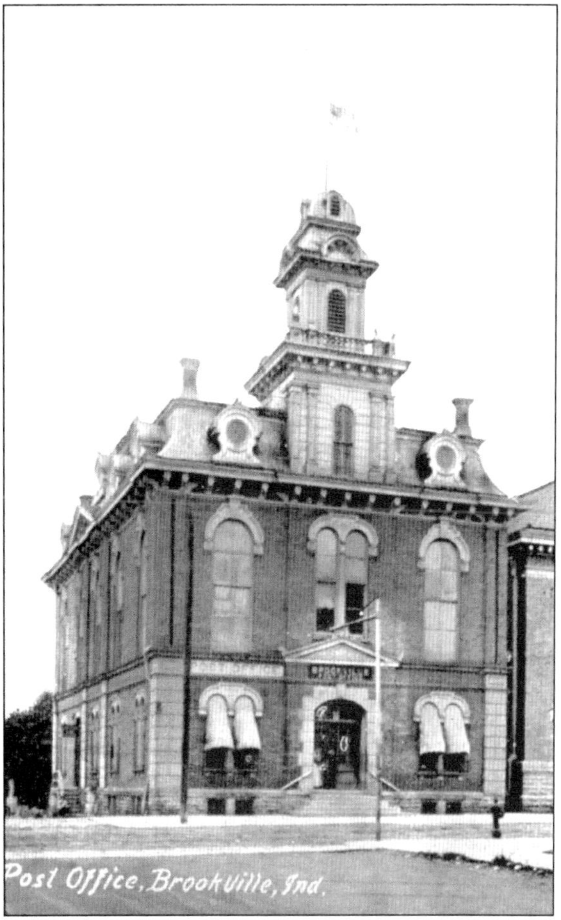

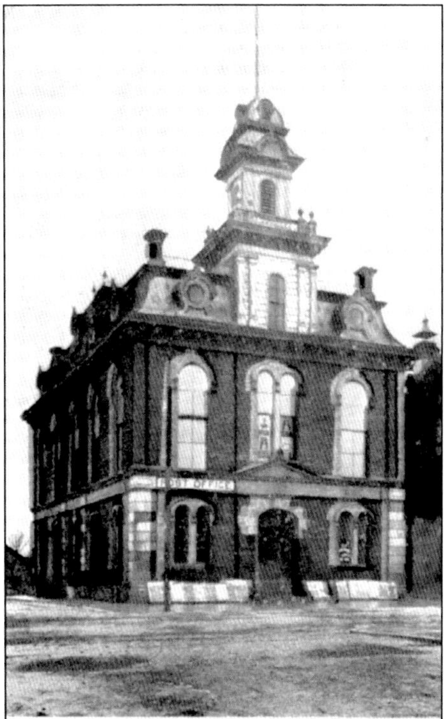

Post Office, Brookville, Ind.

Brookville civic organizations held meetings in the upstairs of the town hall, also called the Brookville Opera House or post office, as noted in the card at left. Posters along the front tell of coming events, often featuring Brookville talent. This place was also used as a movie theater. The Morin theater had its beginning here before building a new building on West Fifth Street behind the National Brookville Bank. In later years, the American Legion had its headquarters in this building. In 1974, it built a new building at the north end of the town park near the East Fork of the Whitewater River. Around 1973, the upper floor and tower of the building were torn down and a roof built over the now one-story building. For many years, it was something of an eyesore on Main Street, but recent repainting has improved its appearance.

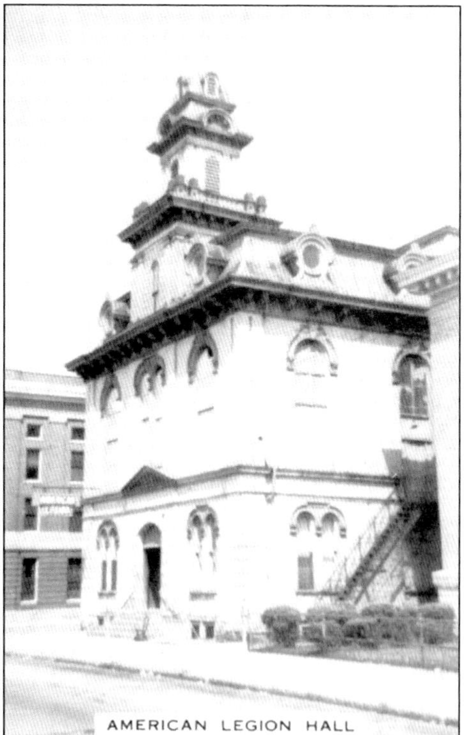

AMERICAN LEGION HALL
BROOKVILLE, INDIANA

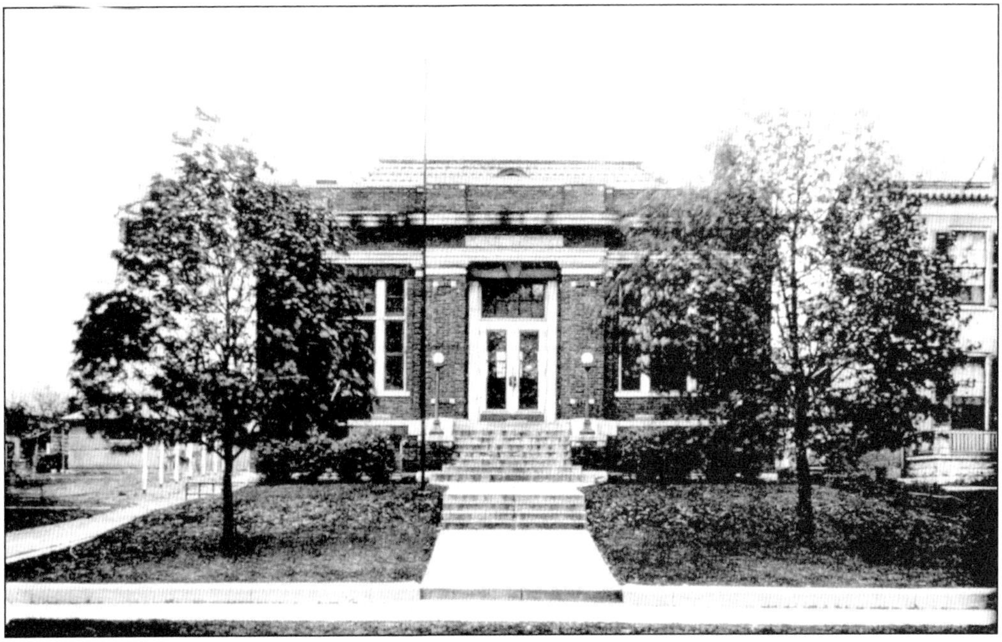

This is a good view of the public library, on a card postmarked 1927. Brookville's prominent banker, businessman, and civic leader John C. Shirk obtained a financial grant from Andrew Carnegie to erect a public library in 1912. It resembles other Carnegie libraries of that time. The library was and still is in the residential area of town. In the postcard below, the house on the left belonged to a Brookville merchant and was later converted to a funeral home, first Clevenger and now Cook. The house at the right dates from 1840 and once belonged to William W. Butler, son of the town's founder, Amos Butler. The semicircular portico shown here was added in later years. It is now one of the more beautiful and well-kept homes on Main Street. (Above, courtesy BPL; below, courtesy Houchin.)

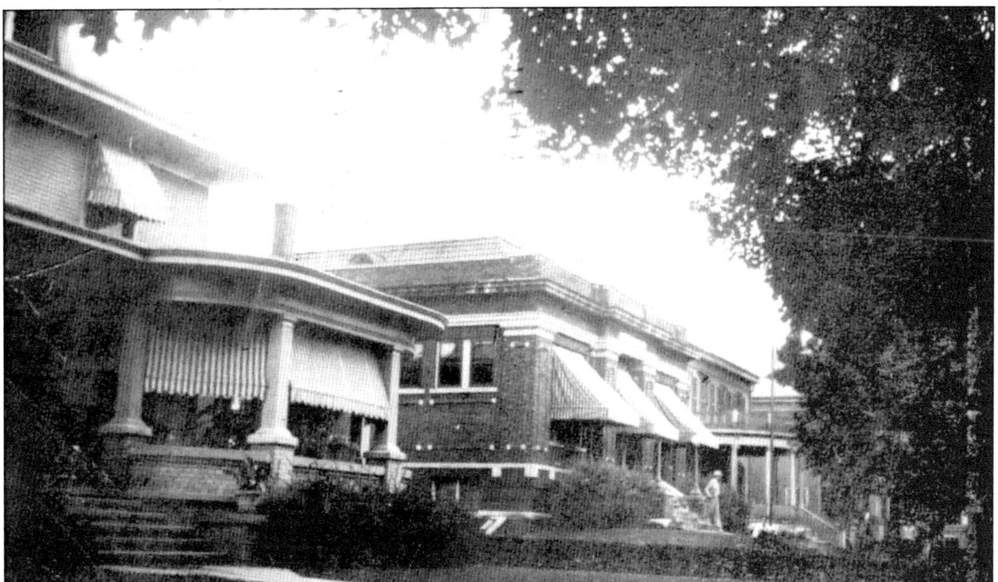

Public Library in Residential Section, Brookville, Ind.

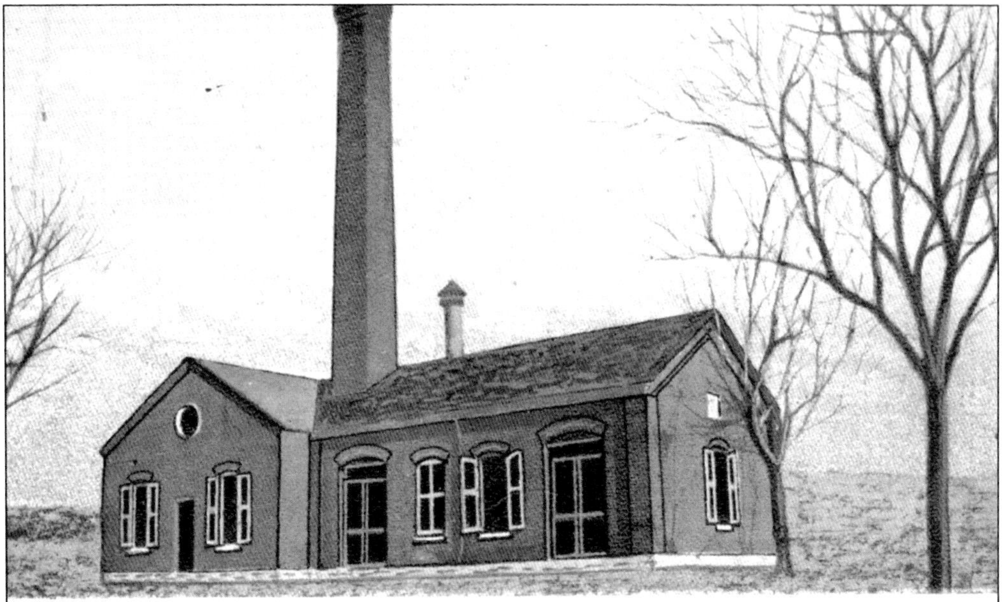

Water Works Pumping Station, Brookville, Ind.

In a special election in 1890, the citizens of Brookville voted to build a waterworks. When construction started in 1891, workers dug a well near the East Fork covered bridge and built the brick pump house shown on this postcard. The pumping engine was powered by steam. Water from the well was pumped to an elevated reservoir overlooking the town. The road leading to the reservoir is still called Reservoir Road. The postcard below shows how the reservoir resembled a swimming pool, and it was probably used for that purpose. Thus water was provided to the town water supply mains. This system was abandoned around 1920, when town officials had new wells dug near the West Fork and installed pumps in a building on Cliff Street. A storage tank was placed near the old open reservoir. (Above, courtesy Houchin.)

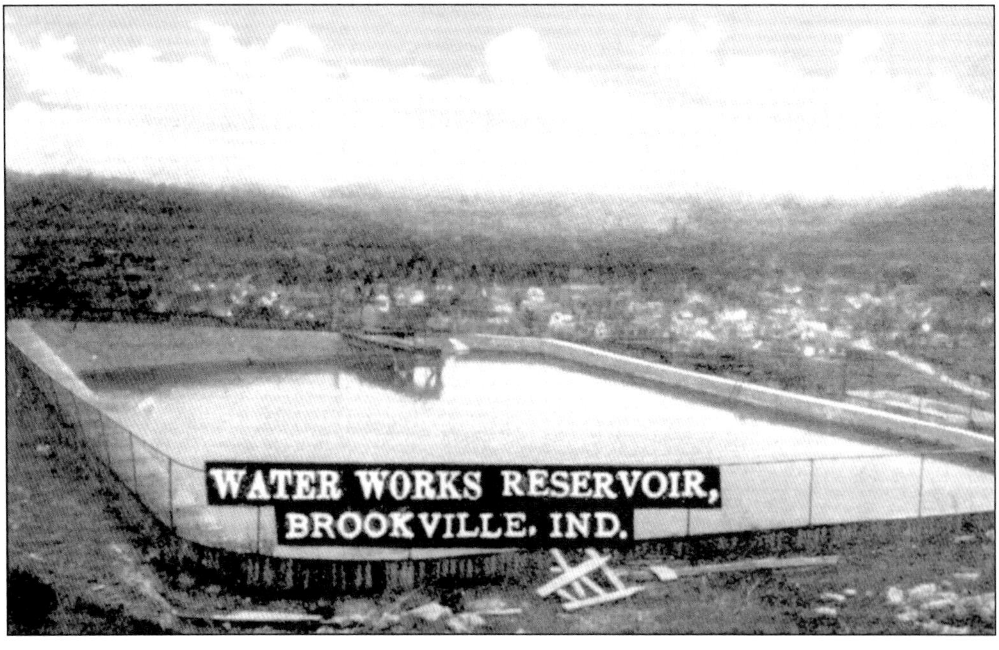

Three

Street Scenes

Brookville is what some have called a "one-street town." Nearly all the businesses and the county courthouse are along Main Street, and most traffic is on this street. Franklin Avenue is a parallel street through the residential area passing the town's churches. It connects with State Route 1 and State Route 101 at the north end and with the St. Michael square at the south end. It has many stop signs and many ups and downs. Brookville's cross streets, First through Twelfth, are largely residential, some with a steep slope into Brookville's valley, namely, East Fourth, Fifth, Sixth, Seventh, and Ninth Streets. East Eight Street does not connect with the valley but stops where it connects with Franklin Avenue in front of the Methodist parsonage. Sidewalks on both sides of most streets as well as large shade trees planted alongside the curbs make for a pedestrian-friendly town.

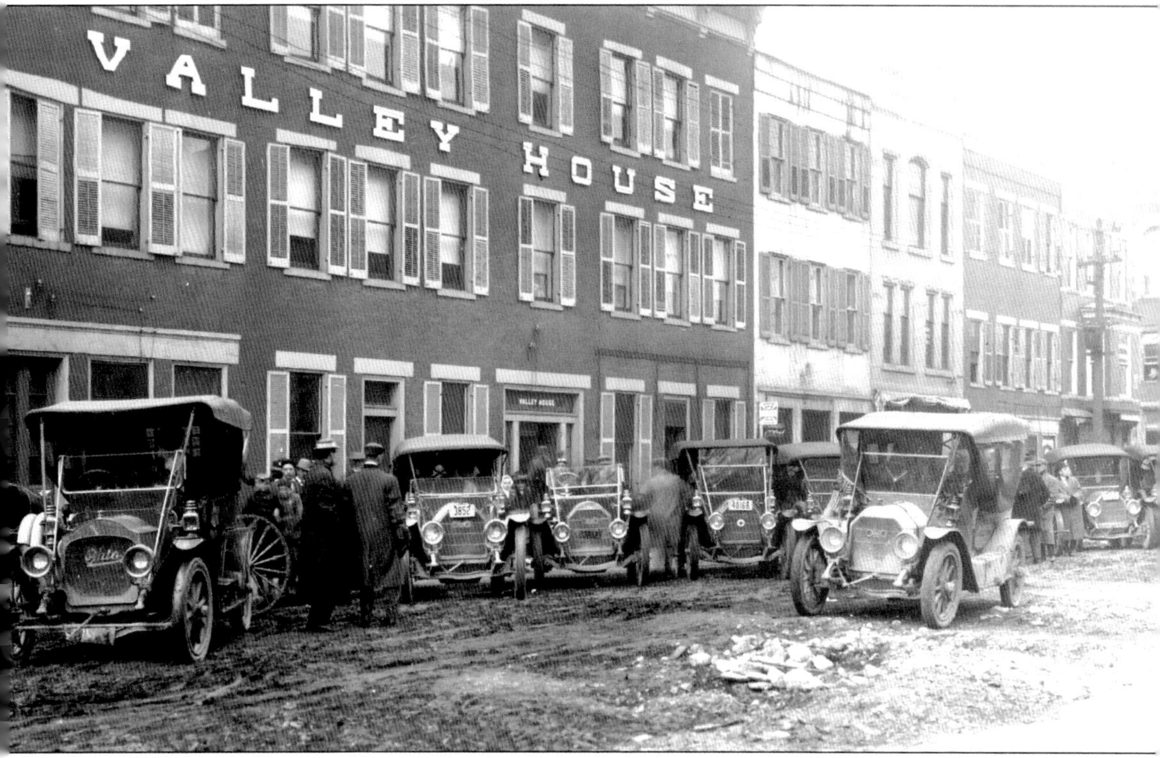

Ben Winans photographed this scene for this postcard on Main Street on December 2, 1911. The Cincinnati Automobile Club came to Brookville to meet the "Ohio Mud Hen." The Mud Hen carried Thomas W. Wilby and his wife on a coast-to-coast trip from New York to San Francisco and back. The Wilbys had a driver named F. D. Clark, and in other photographs Winans took of the traveling group, Clark always stood some distance apart from the Wilbys. Clark wore the classic duster, cap, and gloves and looked every bit the part of chauffeur. He also looked quite strong and stern, so he may have been their bodyguard as well. Brookville was on the route from Indianapolis to Cincinnati, and that route eventually became U.S. 52. Looking at the dirt street in Brookville, one wonders what the roads were like between the East and West Coast cities, especially when it rained or snowed. The Franklin County Courthouse was being remodeled, and that probably accounts for the stones lying in the street. (Courtesy Houchin.)

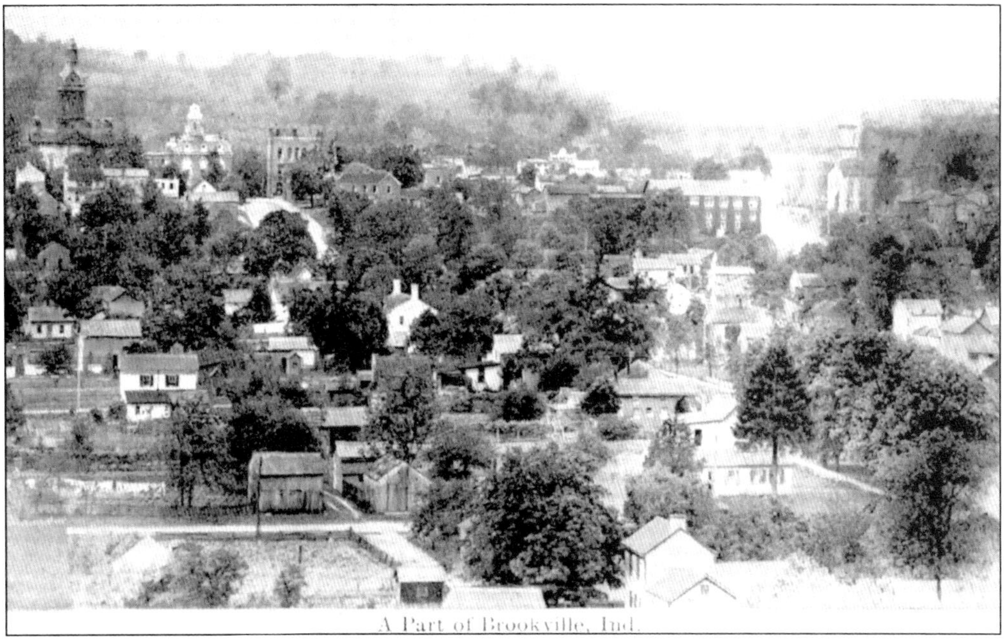

This card, "A Part of Brookville," was taken from an eastern hilltop. The valley residential area dominates the scene. The prominent buildings at the top are the county courthouse, the town building, the Shirk and Goodwin Bank, and the Presbyterian church at the far right. The street between the town building and the Shirk bank is Fifth Street. The building across Sixth Street from the church was a lumber mill.

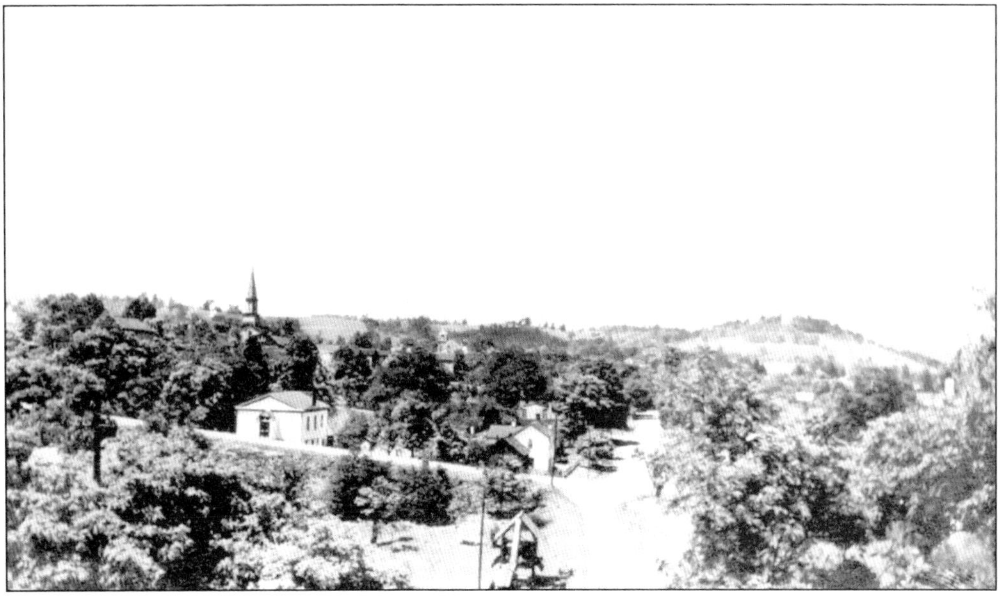

This postcard view is looking toward the north from Bracken Hill—the home of prominent Brookville lawyer and Civil War veteran William H. Bracken. The building in the foreground was a German Protestant church on Fourth Street, built in 1849. In the background is the Presbyterian church on Sixth Street, built 1852–1855. (Courtesy FCHS.)

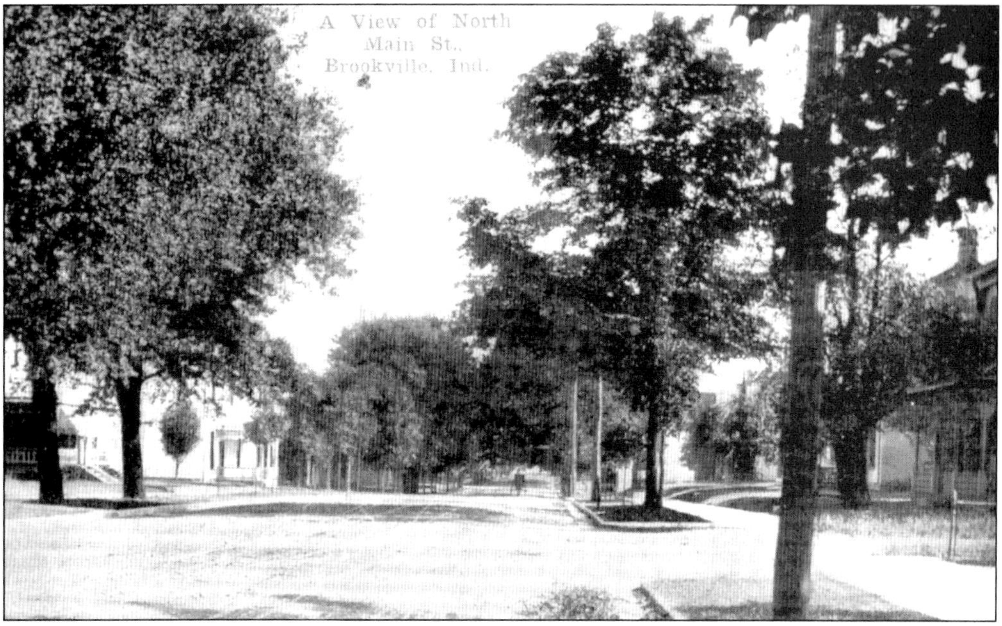

This card shows the residential section at the north end of Main Street. The view is looking south, and the street on the right is West Eleventh Street, which is offset from East Eleventh. The streets were not paved, and when it rained, they turned to mud. There were many trees along the street back then, forming a canopy over the street. The tiny speck is a horse and buggy, the mode of transportation of the time. The bottom view is looking down Connersville Avenue, which connected to the road to Blooming Grove and Connersville. This was before the connection between Main Street and Blooming Grove Road was constructed and before State Route 101 to Liberty was built. (Below, courtesy Smith.)

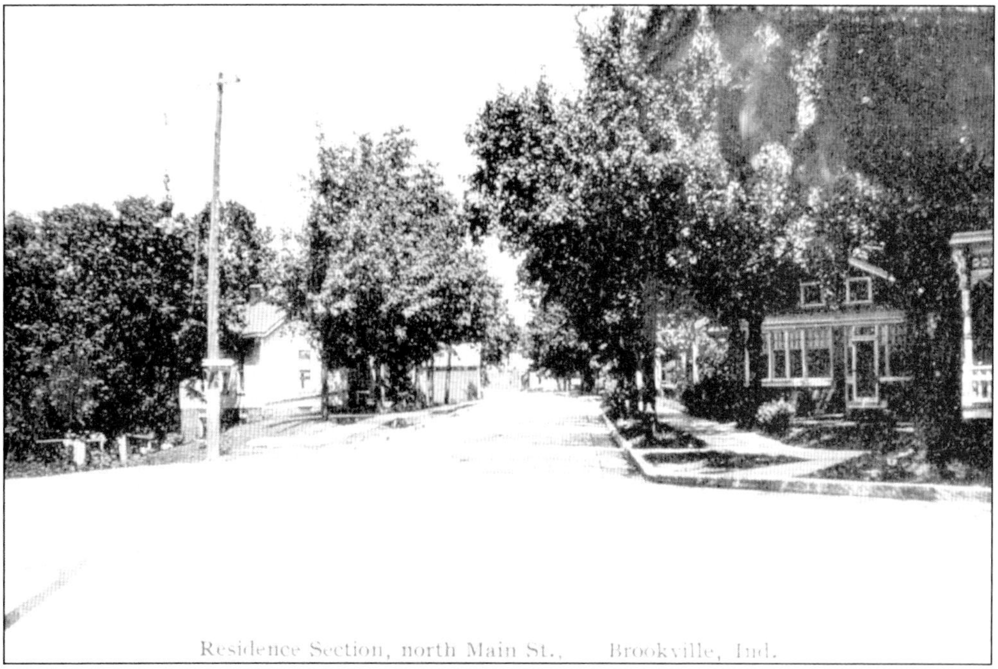

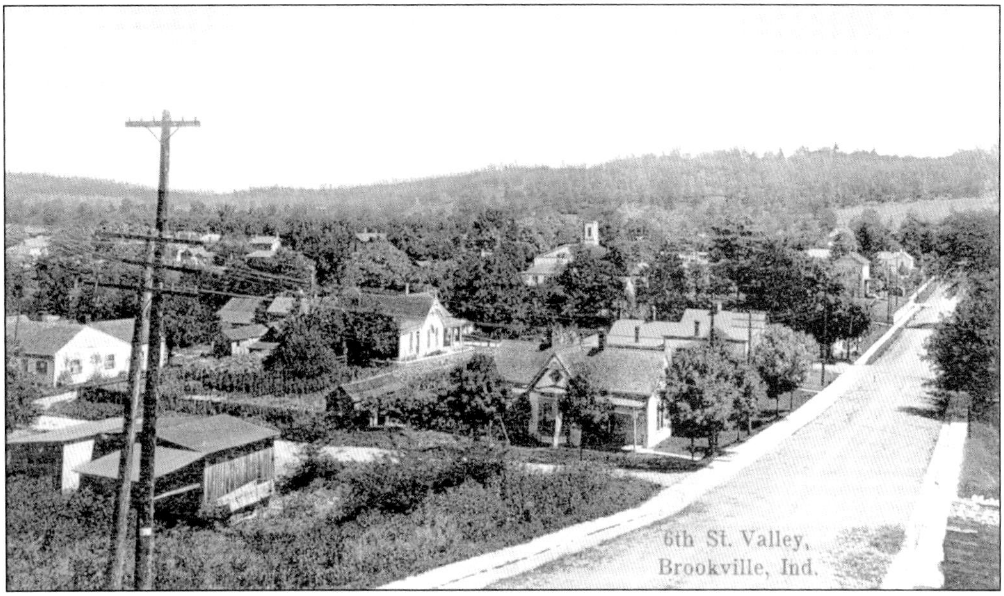

This image was taken from the Sixth Street hill in front of the Presbyterian church, looking east. Franklin Avenue crosses Sixth Street in the foreground. The belfry of the former Methodist church and then Christian church on Mill Street is slightly right of center. By this time, telephone and electric poles had made their unsightly, but necessary appearance.

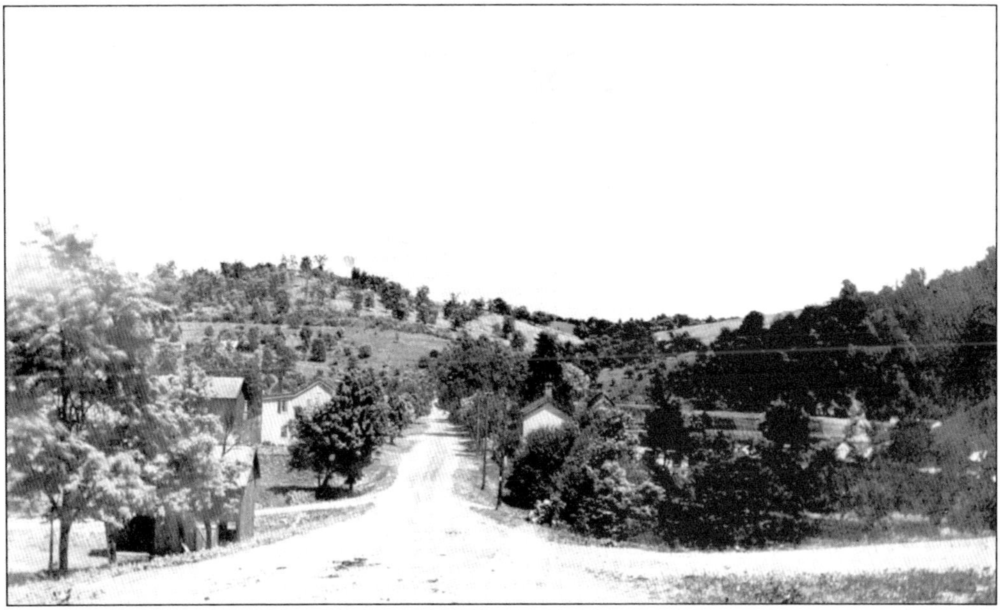

This card, postmarked in 1909, looks east down Fourth Street, which connected with a bridge across the East Fork and led to Palestine, Mount Carmel, and Scipio before passing out of Franklin County into Ohio. At Scipio, it split with one road going to Hamilton and the other to Venice (Ross) and Cincinnati, Ohio. These roads are old routes to the old Ohio cities. (Courtesy FCHS.)

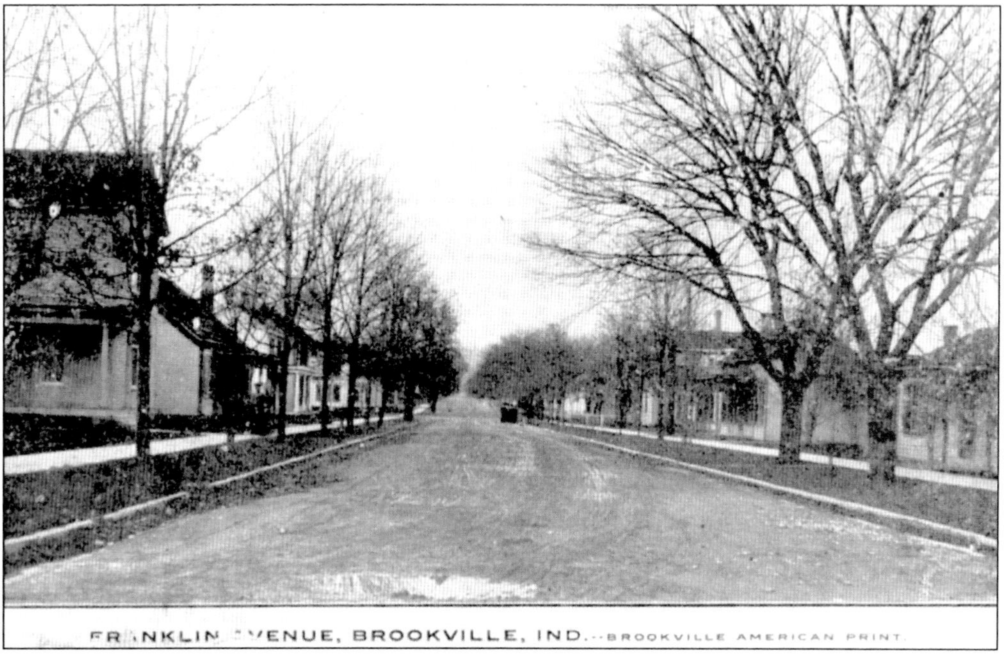

The top postcard view was taken by Ben Winans in 1906 and is looking north on Franklin Avenue from Eighth Street. Most of the buildings along this street are homes, and that section looks very similar today. The bottom view is two blocks north at Tenth Street and Franklin, also looking north. The public school grounds are on the far right. The building on the left is now the Phillips and Myers Funeral Home. The boy at the left is George Mullin, standing in front of his parents' house, according to his brother Jim. Concrete sidewalks and curbs had been laid, but the streets are still unpaved. (Above, courtesy Hauberg/Quinton.)

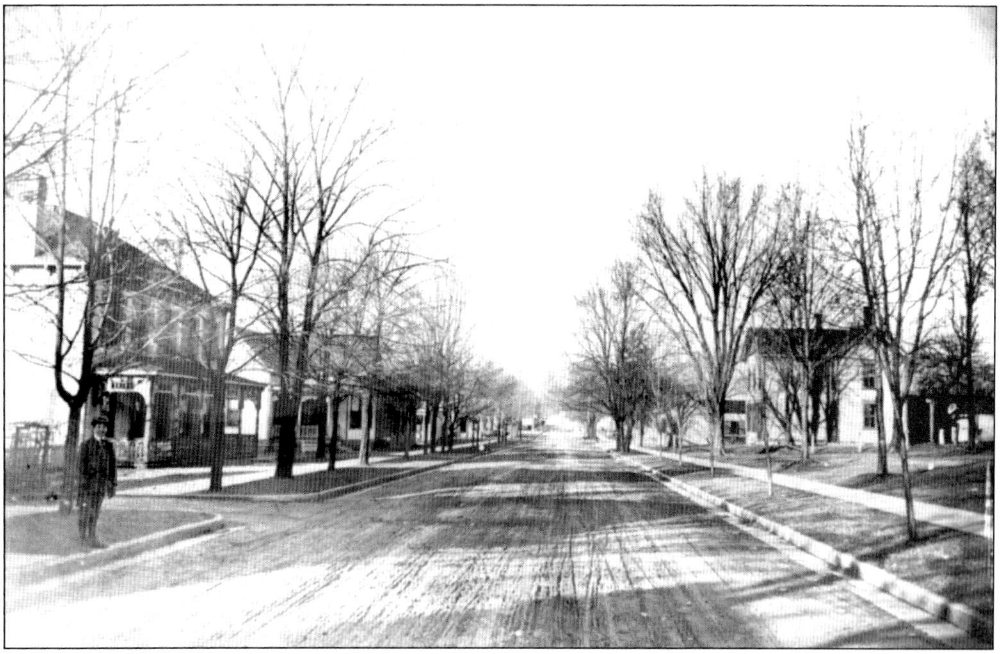

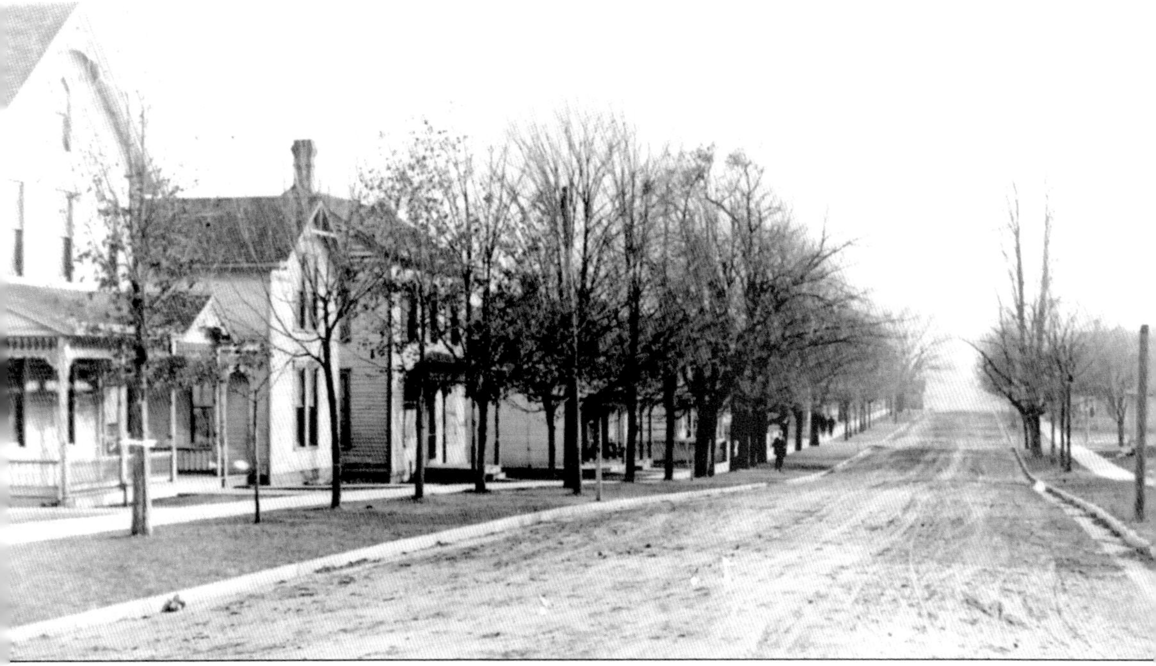

This card was postmarked in 1911 and shows Franklin Avenue looking south from Tenth Street. The three houses on the left are still standing. Many of the front porches of that period sported fancy trim and, over time, were not maintained and ultimately removed. Likewise many of the old houses have been covered with aluminum and vinyl siding, hiding the trim that gave them character.

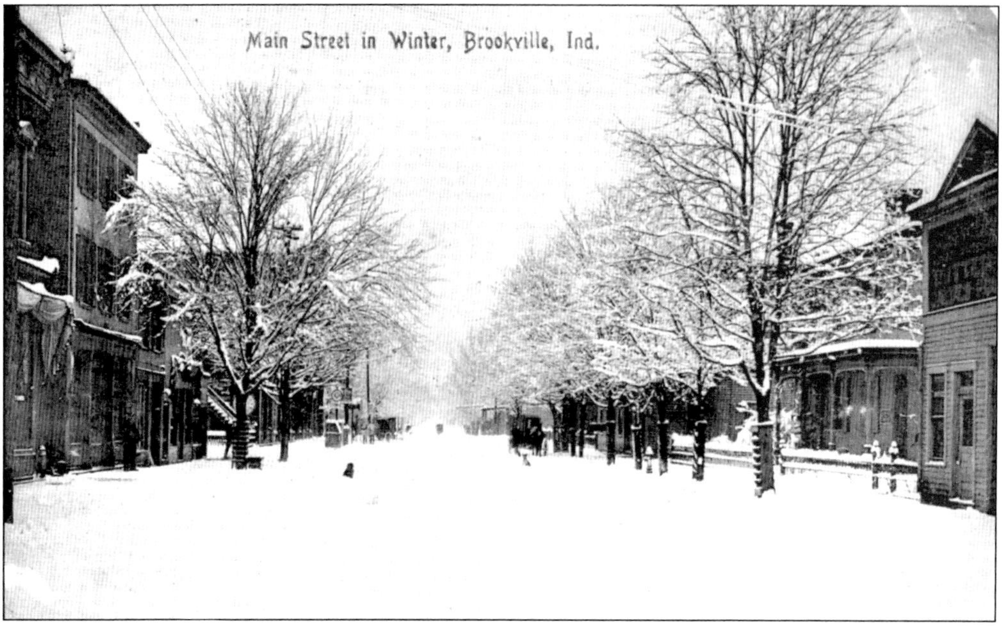

This view, capturing the beauty of winter, was taken from Sixth and Main Streets, looking north. The building at the far right was torn down in 1909 and Winans' Printery constructed there. Ben Winans's print shop has been converted to a fitness center, and the building next to it, which was Monroe Armstrong's dental office and home, is now the Finch Professional Building. (Courtesy Lamont.)

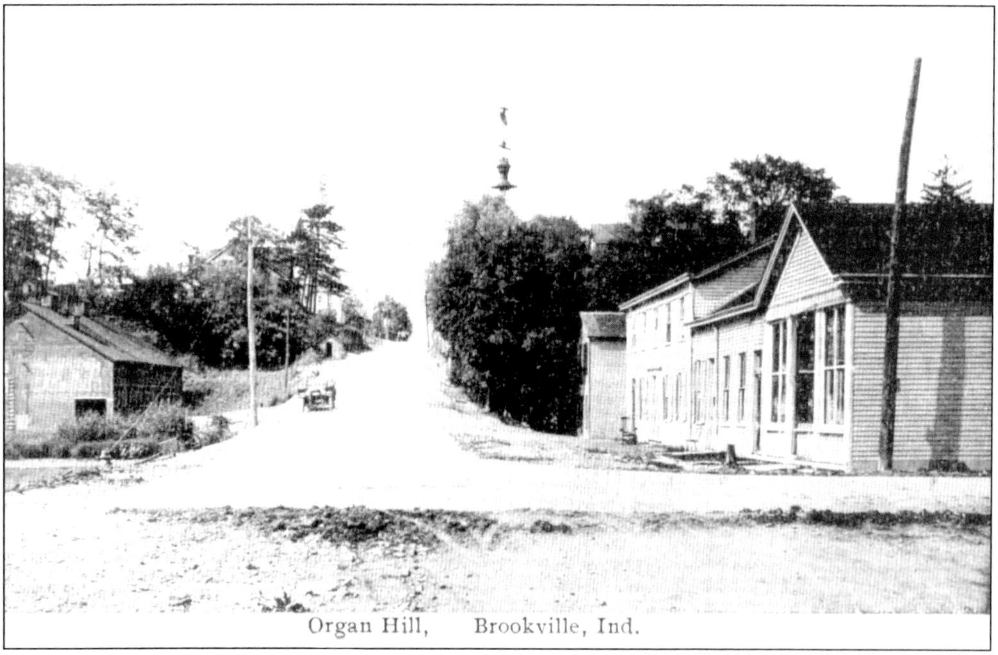

This view shows Oregon Hill, incorrectly labeled "Organ Hill." Oregon Hill received its name from the Oregon Hotel at the foot of the hill. The building on the left sat at the edge of the canal basin.

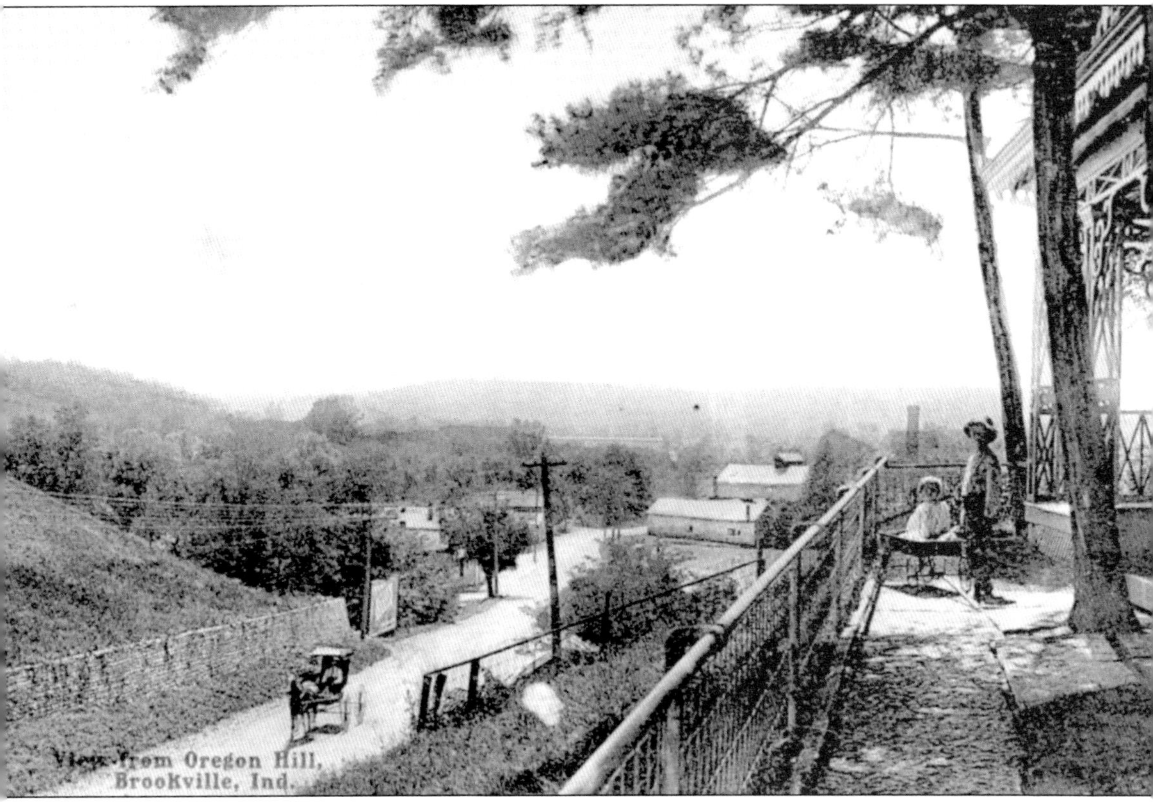

Much of Brookville sits on high ground with a valley on the south and east. When the town streets leading to the valley were built, workers dug through the hills and built stone retaining walls that are still in place today. This view shows Oregon Hill at the south end of Main Street, looking south. The terrace on the right with two children posing for the camera was part of an 18-room home that burned in 1948. The Anthony Geis family lost all of their possessions except the clothes on their backs.

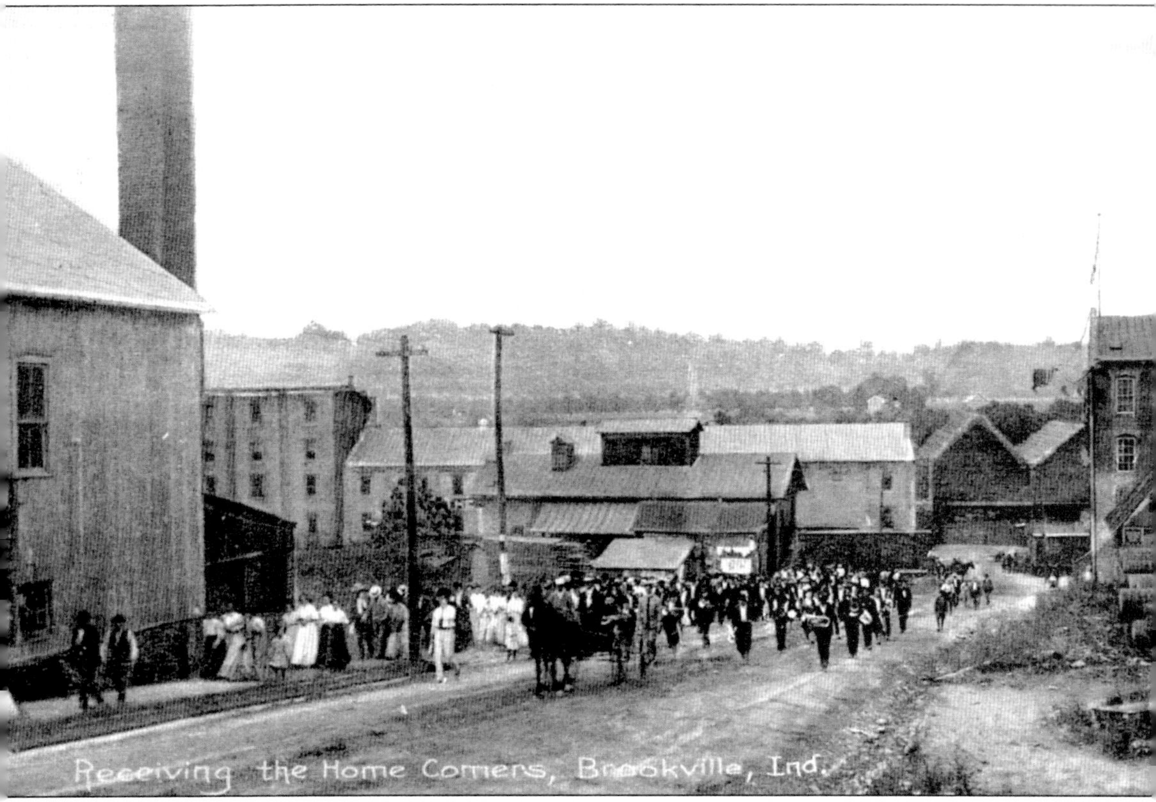

Someone important is being welcomed back to Brookville in this 1909 postmarked card. They are coming from the railroad station. The town band is marching up Eighth Street behind the carriage with lots of onlookers on the sidewalk accompanying the group. The people in the carriage may be John C. Shirk and his wife, Lura, returning from one of their many trips. (Courtesy Houchin.)

Four

Homes

Although the modern-day residential area on Brookville's Main Street is primarily on the north end of town, this was not always the case. Since the early to mid-1900s, the homes closer to the center of town have been torn down and replaced by businesses. The area from Eighth Street north is where most of the grand old homes of Brookville are located. In addition, there are some historic homes in the valley near the East Fork. The early homes of Brookville represented a variety of architectural styles, including fine examples of Italianate, Victorian, and craftsman bungalow. More modest but well-built examples of frame and brick homes still remain. The postcards of some of the more ordinary houses tell a story of "pride of place." In earlier times when wages and farm prices were low, many people's dream was to own their own home. Brookville of the 1950s was sometimes called a "retired farmers' town" as a result of the number of farmers who had prospered and enjoyed retirement in town.

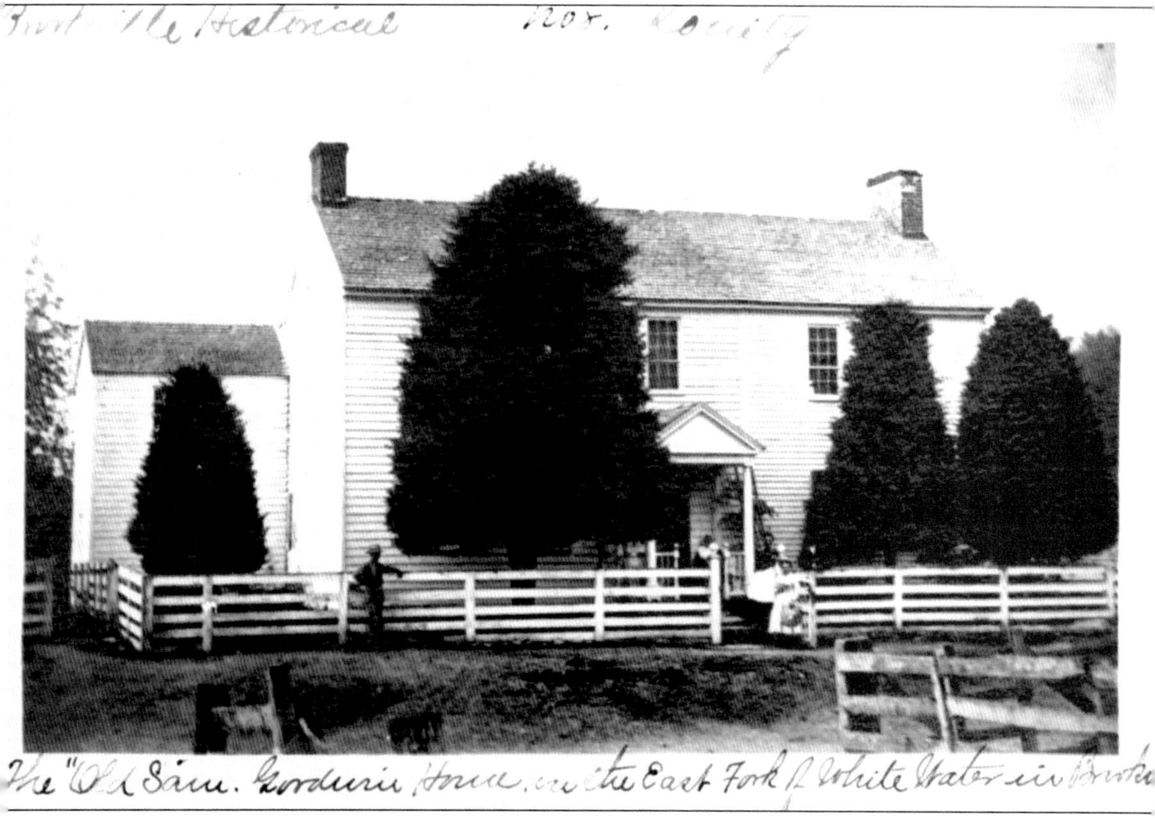

The leading spirit in building a Methodist church in Brookville was Samuel Goodwin. He came to Brookville in 1816 and has been called the "father of Methodism in Brookville." He was a tanner and lived at the east end of Fifth Street. His house is still standing. His family members were among the most prominent people in the town. (Courtesy BUMC.)

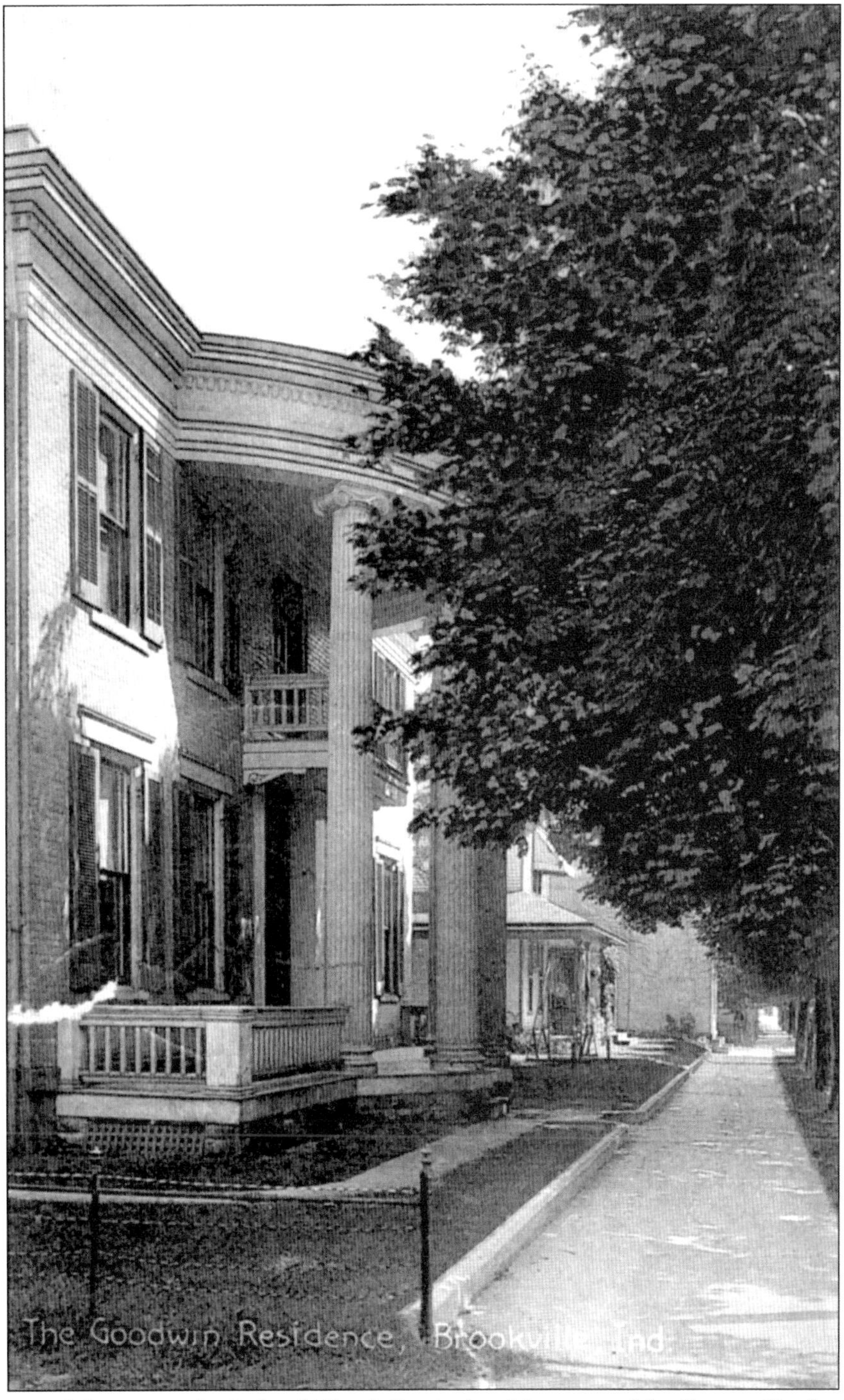

This postcard showcases the Federal/Greek Revival architecture of the former Charles Francis Goodwin home, built around 1856. Goodwin graduated from Brookville College in 1866 and from Asbury College—now DePauw University—at Greencastle in 1871. He was a banking partner with John C. Shirk in the National Brookville Bank. Shirk was also his brother-in-law. (Courtesy Rowe.)

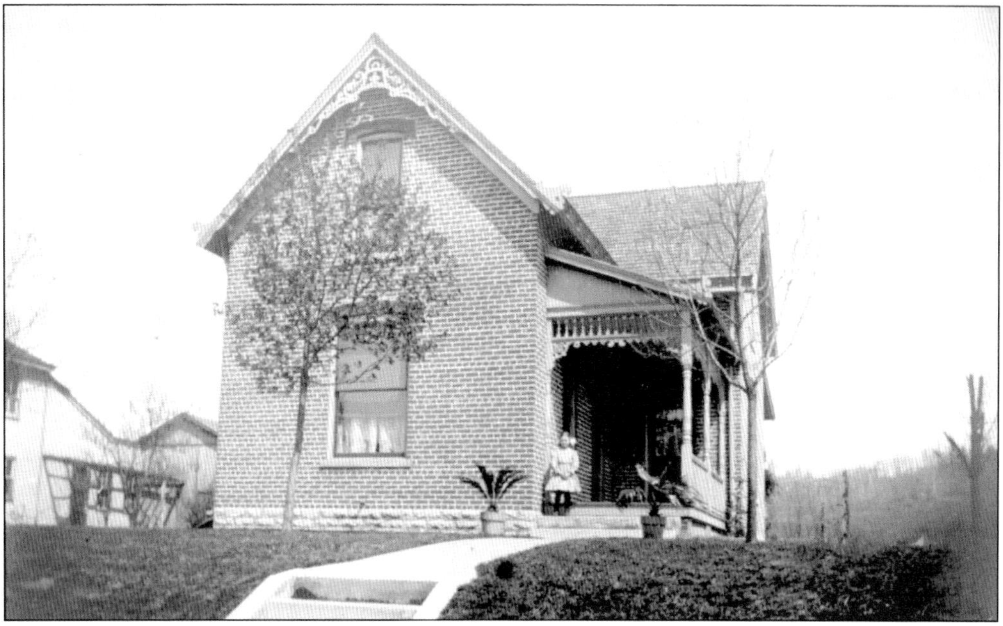

The house in this postcard is on Mill Street between Sixth and Seventh Streets. The little girl sitting on the porch is Hilda Geis, who was born in 1900. She was the daughter of William and Anna (Fries) Geis, who owned the house. Hilda became the wife of John Spaeth in 1923. The house was later sold to Emma and Charles Harrop and still belongs to one of their descendants. (Courtesy Fritz.)

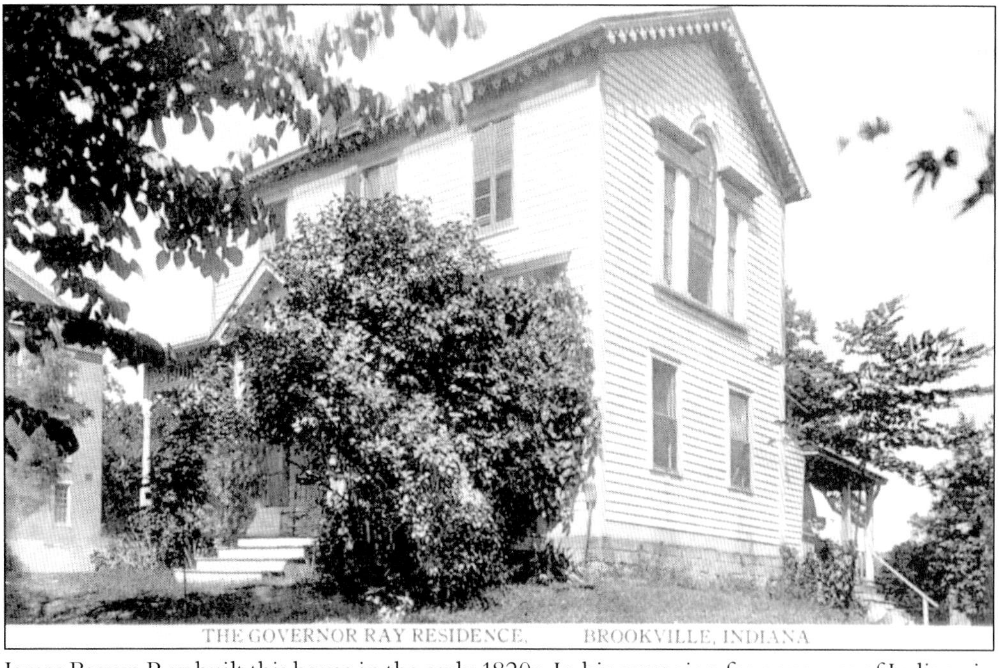

James Brown Ray built this house in the early 1820s. In his campaign for governor of Indiana in 1825, the ornate window on the south end of his house became a target by his opponents, who claimed it was extravagant. He won that election and a second term in 1828. The house is on Tenth Street and is being purchased by the Citizens for Historic Preservation. (Courtesy Smith.)

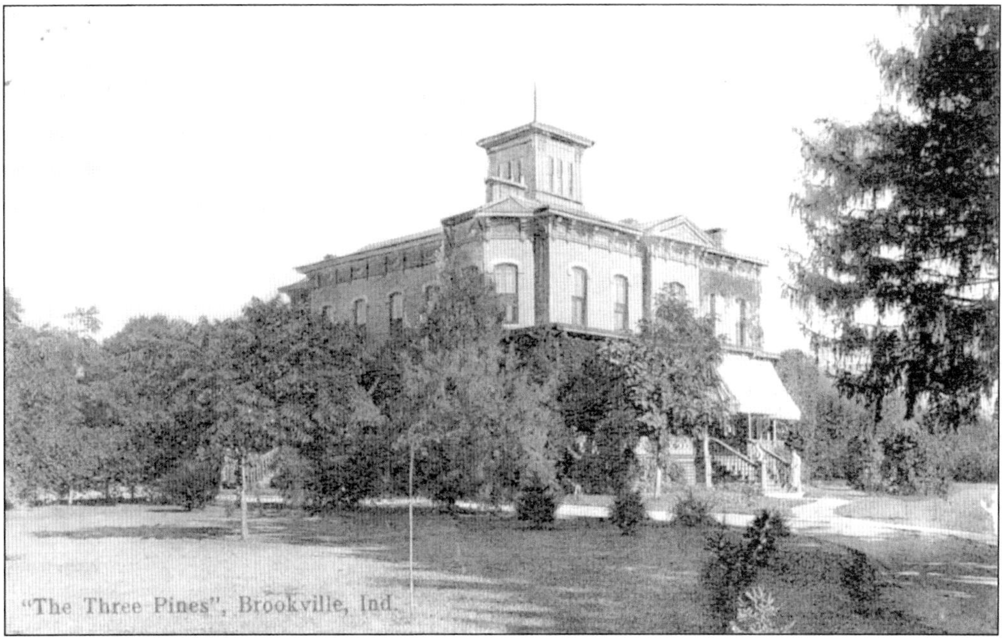

Frank Walz, a whiskey distiller, built the grandest house in Brookville in the 1870s and later went bankrupt. He died in 1874 at a young age, leaving a wife and children in dire straits. John C. Shirk purchased the house in 1900, and Three Pines became identified with that family. The house and grounds occupied an entire block. Shirk's primary occupation was that of banker, but other business interests included a furniture factory, telephone company, furniture store, and insurance company. He was also the town's most active civic leader. He led the effort to build Brookville's Carnegie library, erected in 1912. (Above, courtesy Rowe; below, courtesy Hauberg/Quinton.)

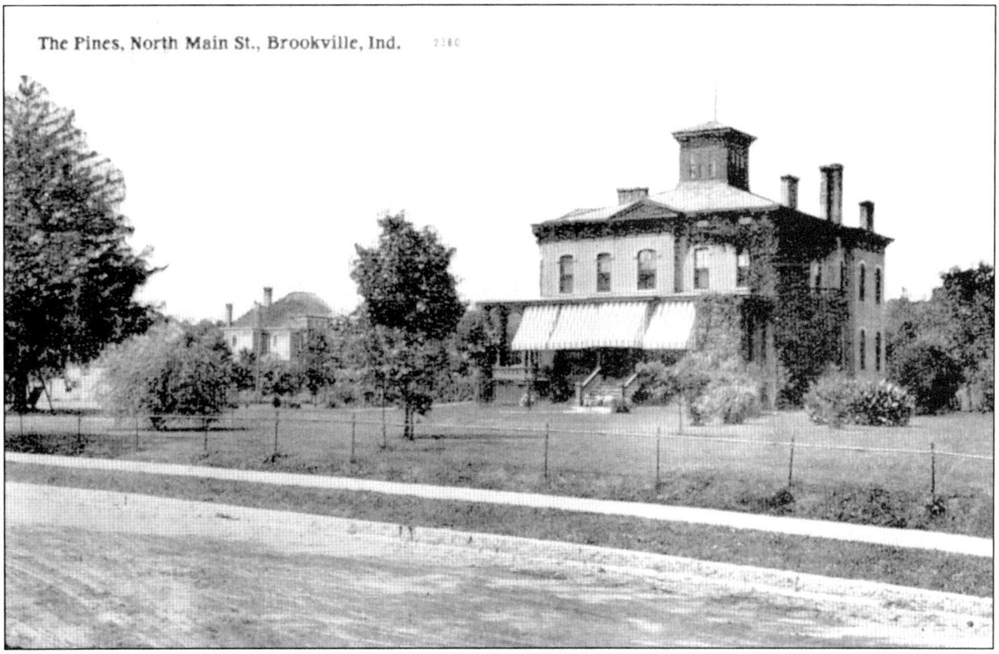

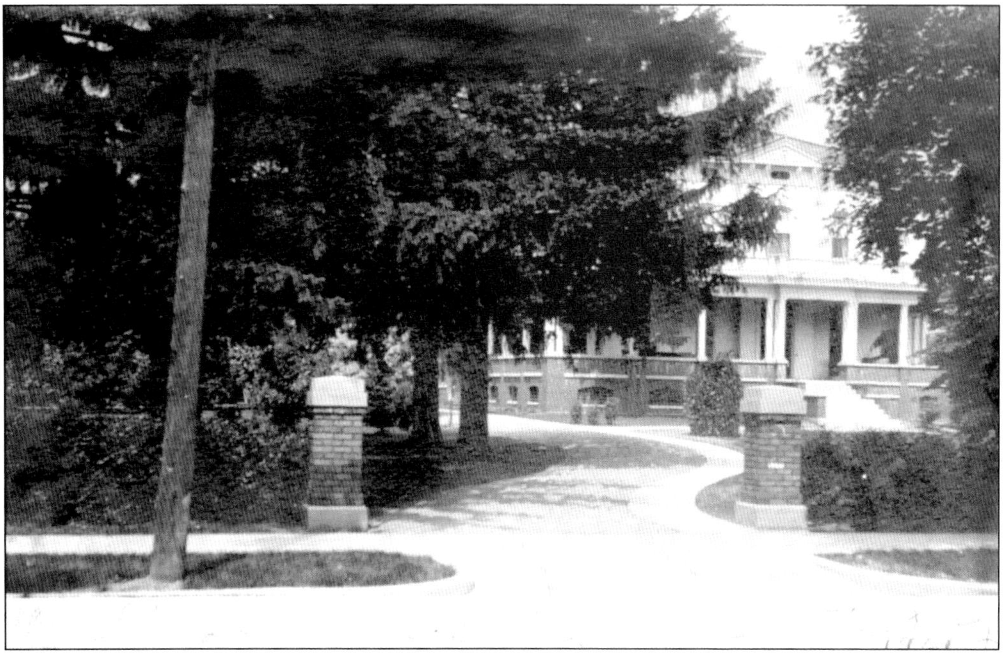

In later years, the Shirk house was painted, and most will remember it looking like this postcard. The house was torn down in 1961 to make room for commercial businesses. Today there is a CVS drugstore where the house sat with two other businesses on Main Street and a residence at the southwest corner of the lot. One of the Shirks' sons, Grovsner, lived there in his later years. (Courtesy FCHS.)

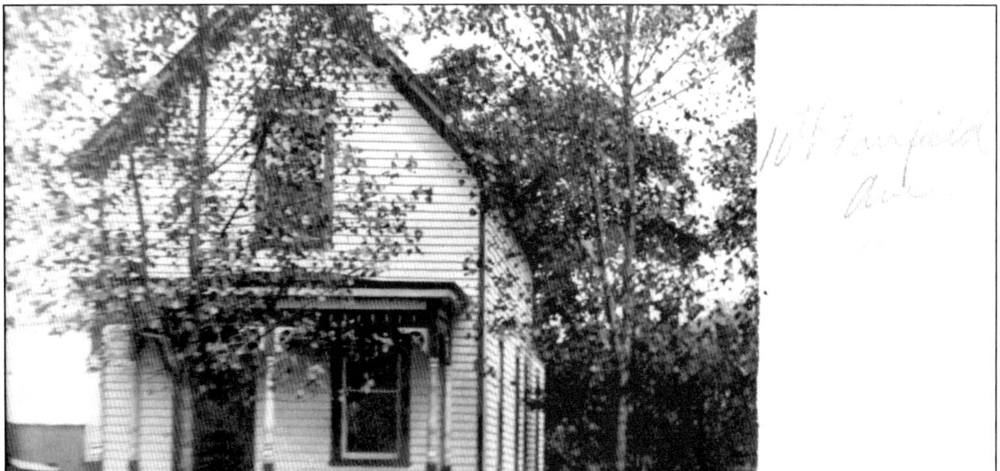

This house is on Tenth Street across from the old town cemetery. Am. Davis written on the bottom of the card refers to Abraham Davis. Many will remember Mary Johnson, who lived there in the late 1960s. Johnson raised 11 children after her husband died at a young age. (Courtesy FCHS.)

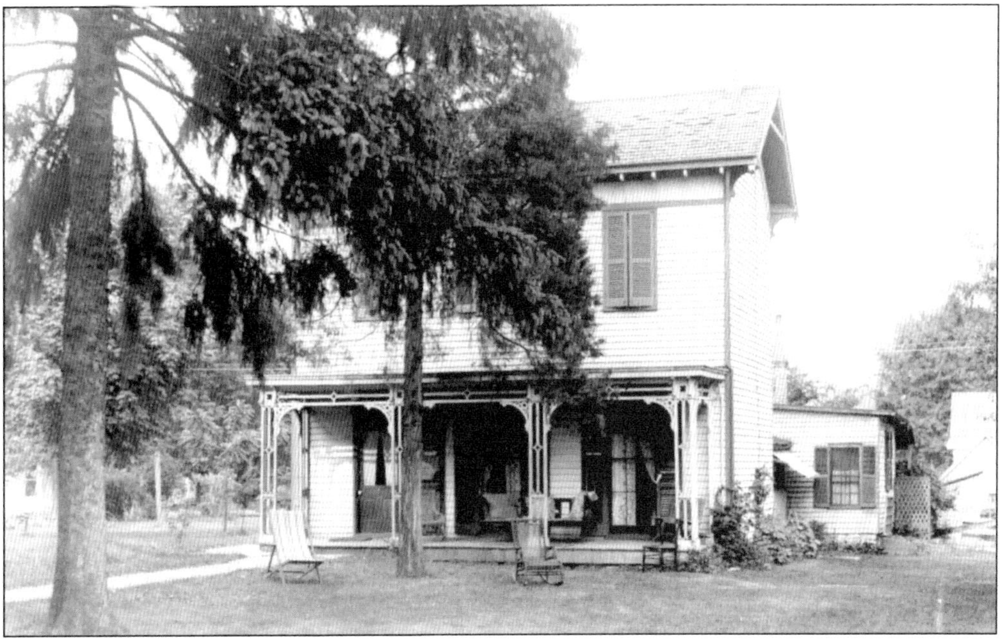

This house apparently no longer exists, but a handwritten notation on a similar card says it was the "King Home on North Main Street—parents of Ella Rockafellar." Rockafellar was a daughter of John King, a prosperous Brookville merchant who built a much larger and grander house at the corner of Eleventh and Main Streets in 1900. It is now the Brookville Inn. (Courtesy FCHS.)

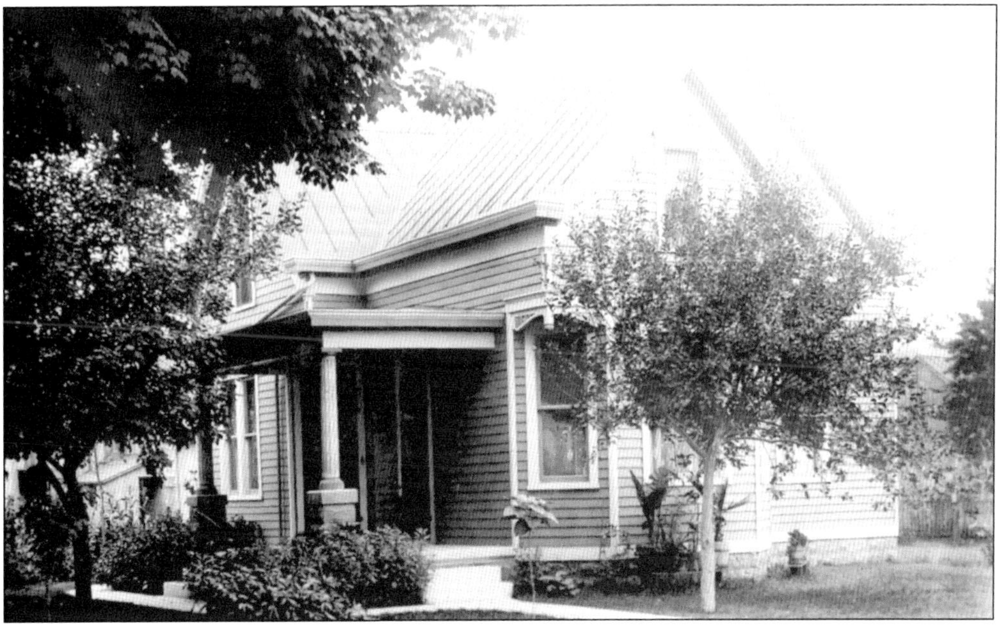

This card was sent from Mr. and Mrs. William Wolber Sr. to Emma Lanvermeyer, with this message: "This is our new home as it is to day, built 1910." William was a retired farmer whose farm was north of Brookville on present-day State Route 1. His great-grandson Calvin Finch lives there now. The Wolbers' town house is still standing and is located on Fairfield Avenue. (Courtesy Fritz.)

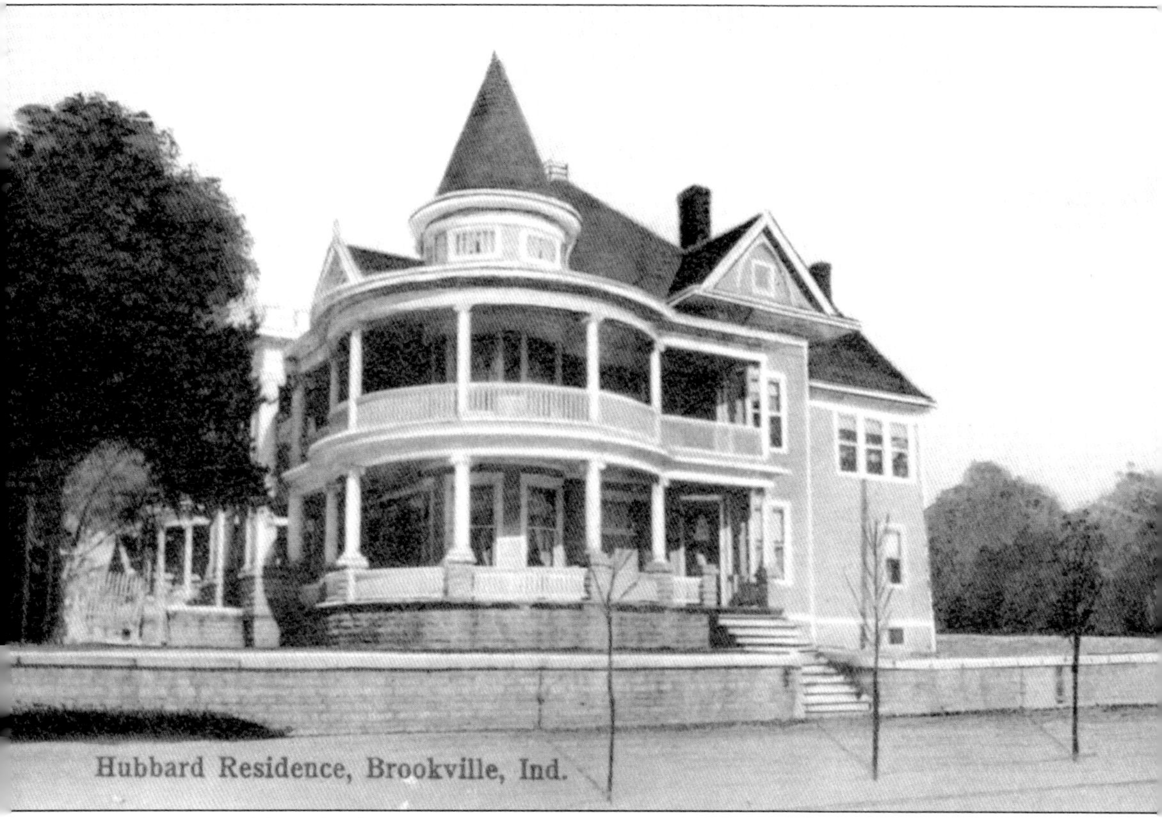

Milford P. Hubbard built this house at the corner of Ninth and Main Streets around 1900. Hubbard was a well-know lawyer and the second president of the Franklin County National Bank. The house became the office and home of Dr. Perry F. Seal and his wife, Mary, in 1946. Dr. Seal served the Brookville area for 47 years. He died in 1996. (Courtesy Rowe.)

Five

The Hermitage and Mills

The Brookville house with the most illustrious past is the Hermitage. One of the founders of Brookville, Amos Butler, first came to this area in 1804. He returned the following year and built a log cabin near the site where the Hermitage is located. In 1835, James Speer bought the property and built the original part of the house and also a paper mill. The mill was the first dry-roll paper mill west of the Allegheny Mountains. The ownership of the property returned to the Butler family in 1882. At one time, the Hermitage was the home and studio of two members of the famed Hoosier Group of landscape artists. J. Ottis Adams and Theodore C. Steele came to Brookville in 1898 and fell in love with the area. Steele stayed until 1907, but Adams stayed the rest of his life, living here at least part-time until he died in 1927. During this time, he produced many fine paintings of Brookville scenes, the old mills, and the river. Adams's wife, Winifred Brady Adams, was a fine artist in her own right. Steele's wife, Libbie, coined the name Hermitage because of its location at the edge of town. The home stands on the banks of the East Fork of the Whitewater River at the end of Eighth Street. It includes 19 rooms with a 112-foot-long veranda surrounded by six acres of grounds. Libbie Steele died in 1899, shortly after they moved into the old house. In 1907, Theodore sold his interest in the house to J. Ottis and moved to Brown County, where he remarried. There he built the House of the Singing Winds. Both men produced many great paintings in the Brookville area. The Hermitage is one of the properties in the town that qualified Brookville to be placed on the National Register of Historic Places. The Twin Forks Chapter of the Daughters of the American Revolution placed a historic marker on the property.

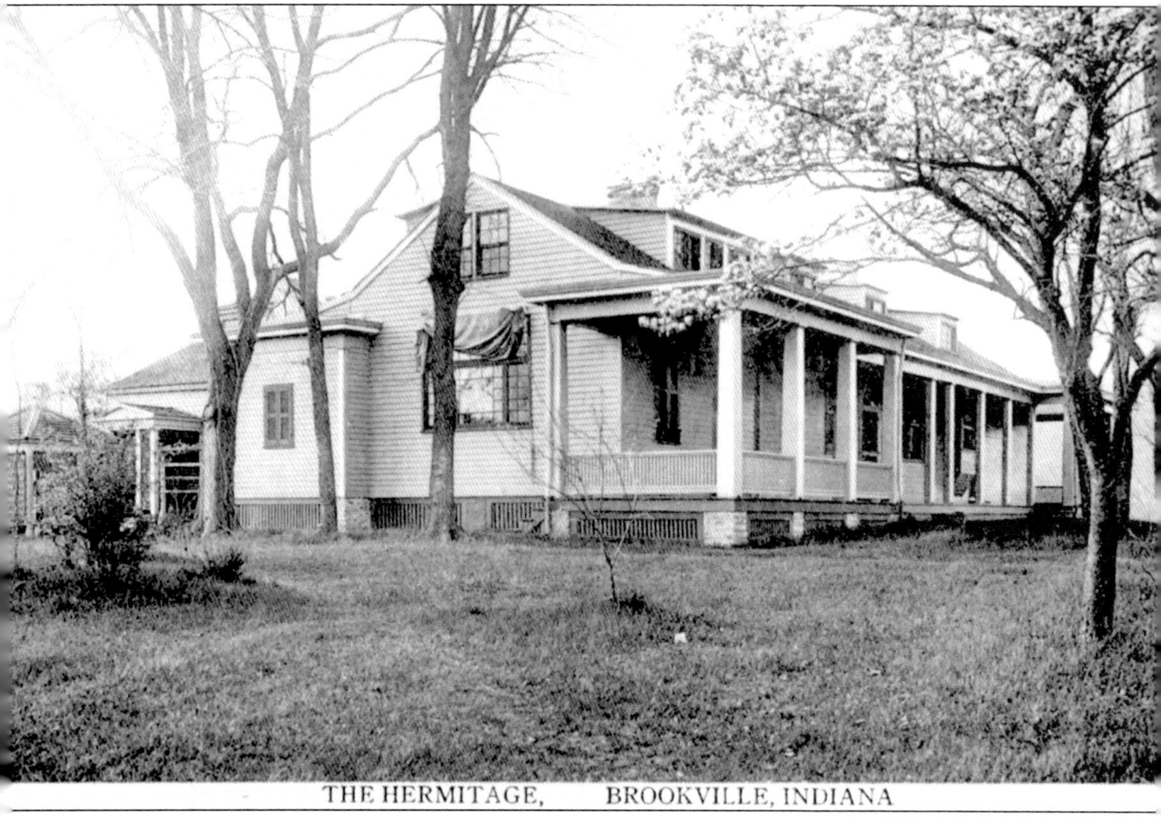

The Hermitage that exists today closely resembles this image made by Ben Winans in 1902. The veranda, which extends across the front of the building, is the defining characteristic of the old home. Theodore C. Steele used the south studio and J. Ottis Adams the north studio, which was at the opposite end of the house in this view. The rooms between the two are the oldest part of the house, built by James Speer after he bought the property in 1835. The living quarters for the two families were in an addition at the rear of the house. (Courtesy Smith.)

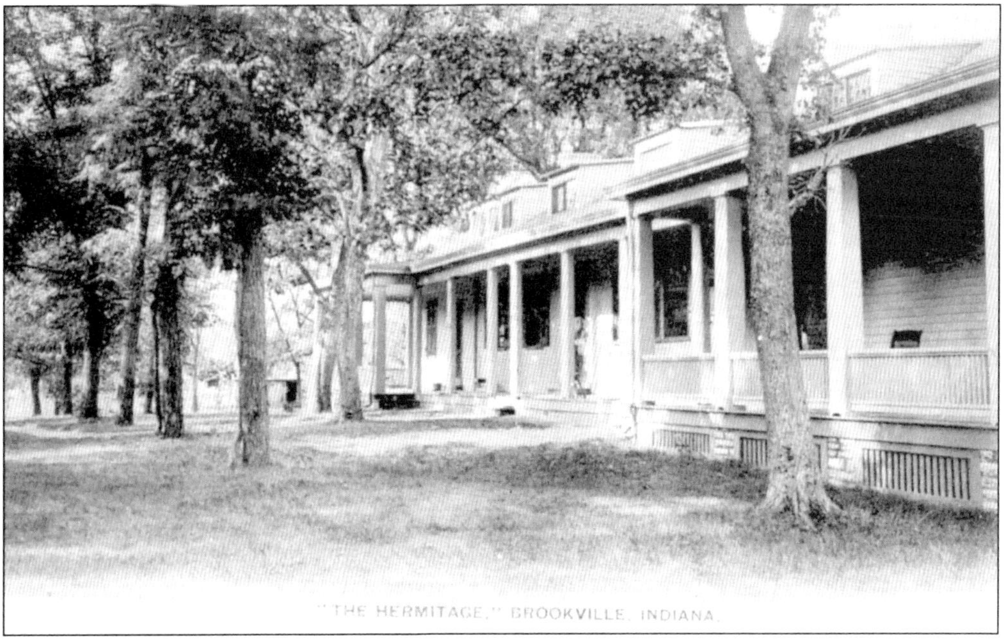

The top postcard shows the front porch from the opposite end as the previous card. The bottom postcard looks like an impressionist painting, but it was made from an undated photograph by Ben Winans. It seems likely that it is merely a view from farther back showing remnants from an earlier time. The old gates and fence may have been left over from the previous owner, William Butler, son of Brookville's cofounder, who probably needed it to contain his cows, pigs, and chickens. (Courtesy Shea.)

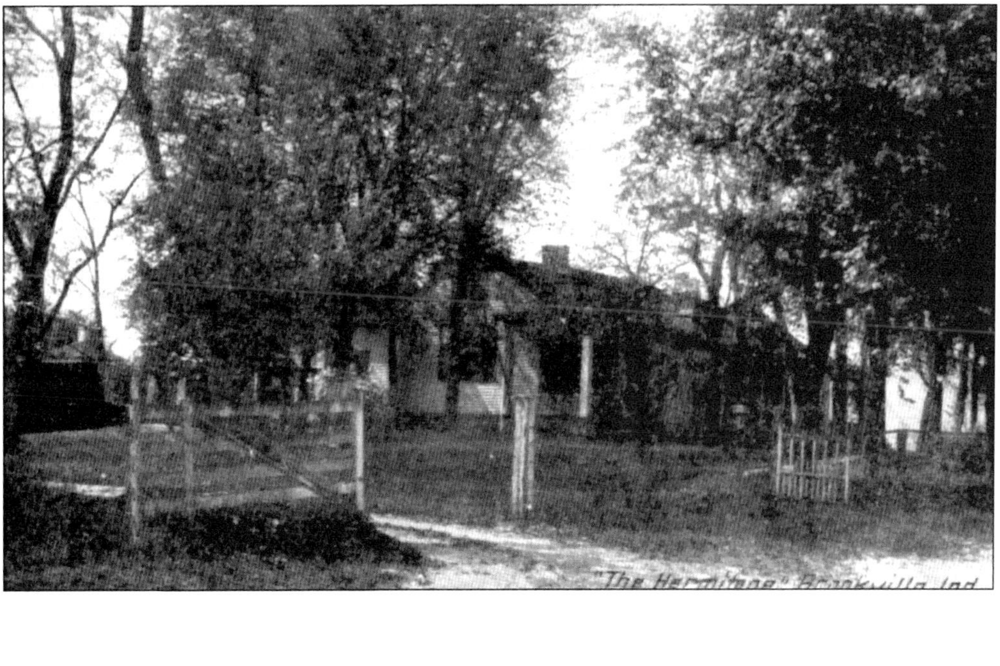

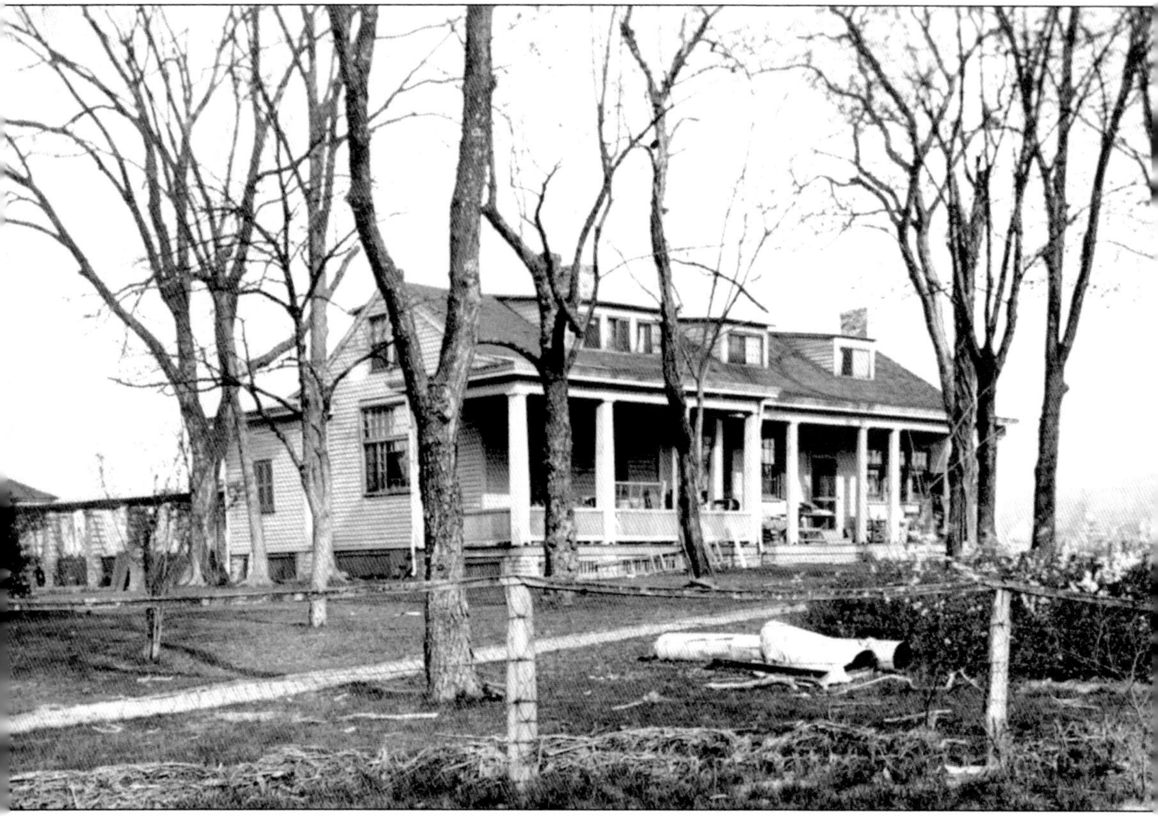

At first glace, the frontal view in this postcard of the Hermitage might not show the damage done by the March 25, 1913, flood. But the north studio, the one used by J. Ottis Adams, was destroyed by the rushing waters of the East Fork. (Courtesy Shea.)

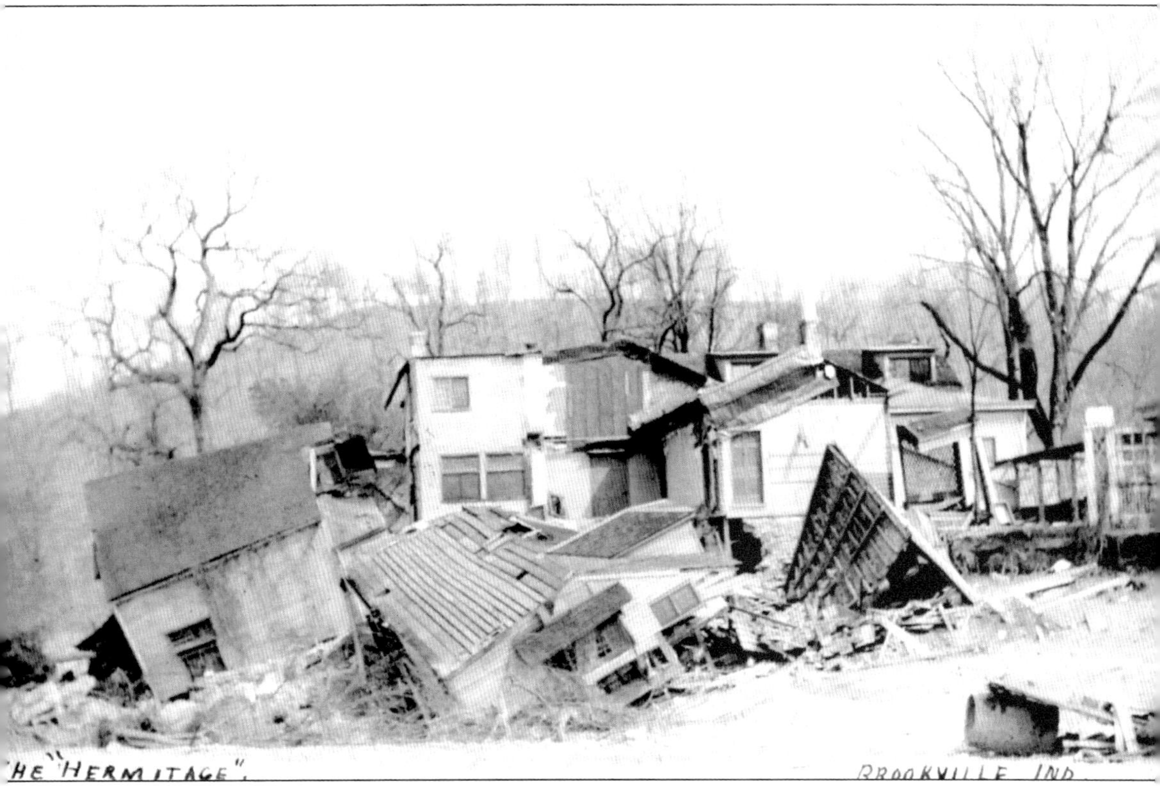

Looking at the artists' home from the rear in this postcard tells a far different story than the view on the previous page. The rear addition, which served as the living quarters, was likewise destroyed. It has not been possible to learn what the original rear addition looked like. A drawing made by Winifred Brady Adams of a proposed replacement was never built. J. Ottis Adams decided to rebuild the north studio and the living quarters and finished this task around 1916. (Courtesy Shea.)

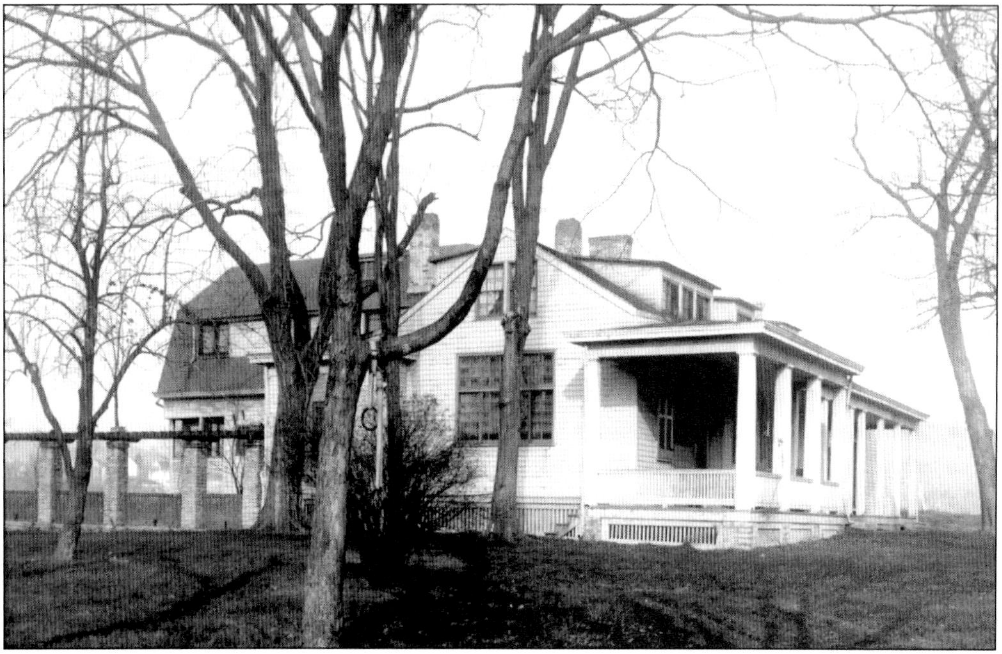

The top postcard was made from an image by Ben Winans in 1916 after the rear addition had been replaced. It does not appear that the north end of the veranda and the north studio had been replaced at that time. The bottom postcard, which is a modern view, shows the north end of the veranda at the right with its extension toward the front. In 1989, a windstorm knocked down 192 trees, including a 287-year-old oak tree, and changed the character of the six-acre Hermitage grounds. The Hermitage is on East Eighth Street and is now a popular bed-and-breakfast business. (Courtesy Shea.)

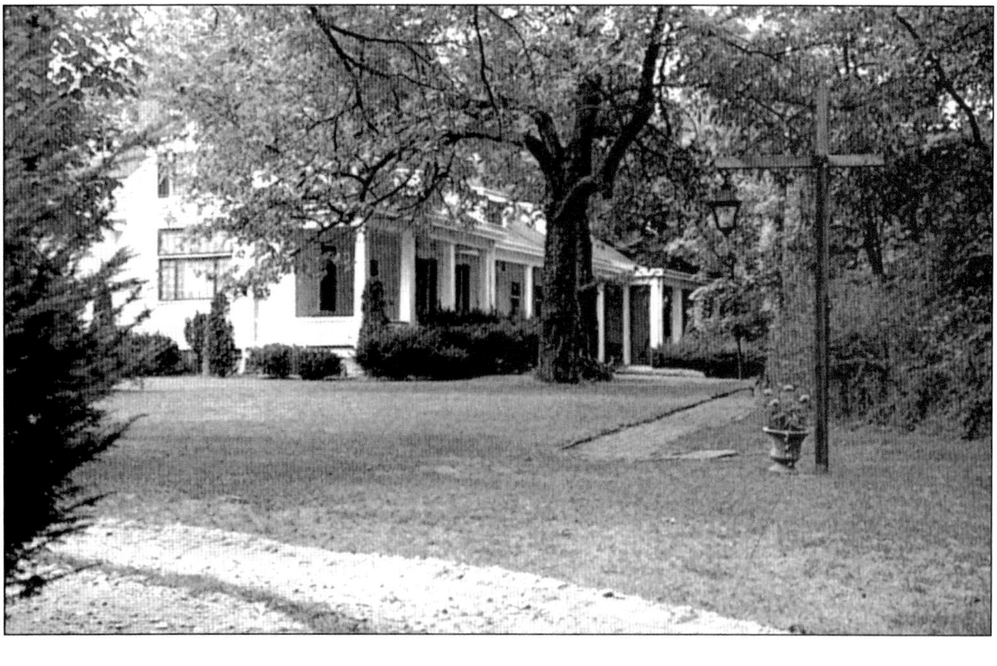

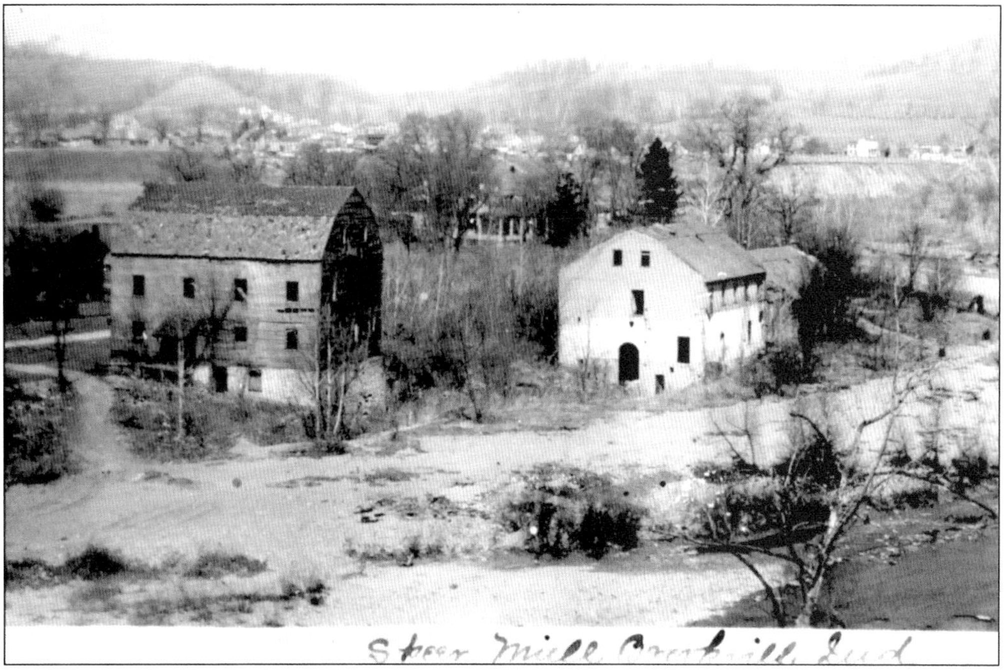

The abandoned gristmill (left) and paper mill (right) near the Hermitage in these photographs were favorite subjects for several members of the Hoosier Group of artists who lived and visited the artists' home and studios. J. Ottis Adams painted a scene similar to this in his 1900 painting *In the Whitewater Valley* and again around 1900–1902 in his painting *The Old Mills of Brookville.* Winans and his camera did not have the artistic license of the use of arrangement and colors in oil to capture the beauty of the scene from an elevated perspective across the East Fork as did Adams. The Hermitage can be seen centered between the two mills in the top card and the north end of Brookville on higher ground in the background. (Above, courtesy BUMC; below, courtesy Hauberg/Quinton.)

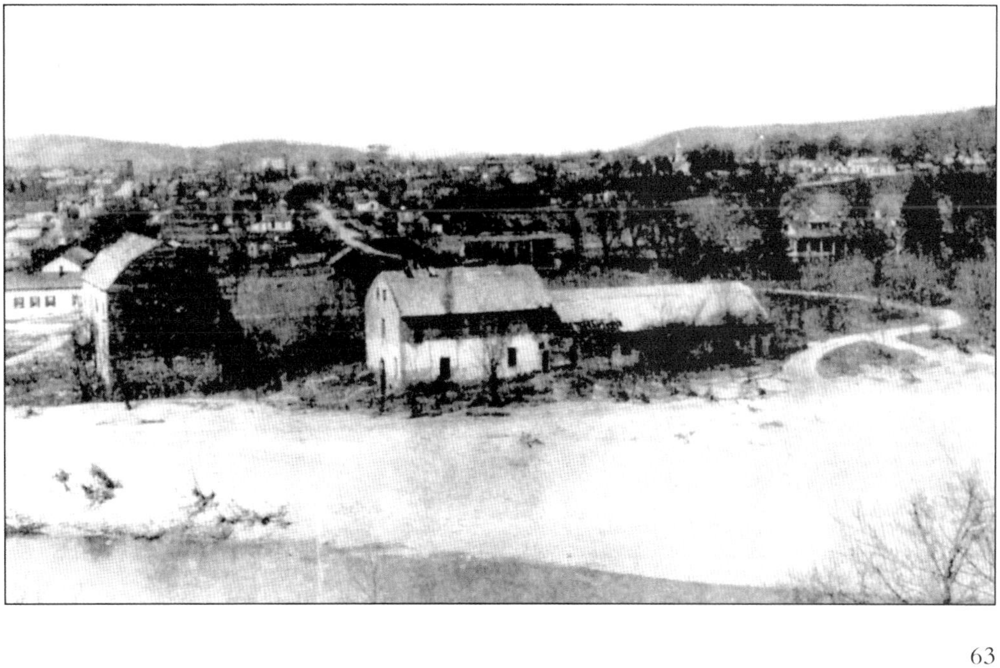

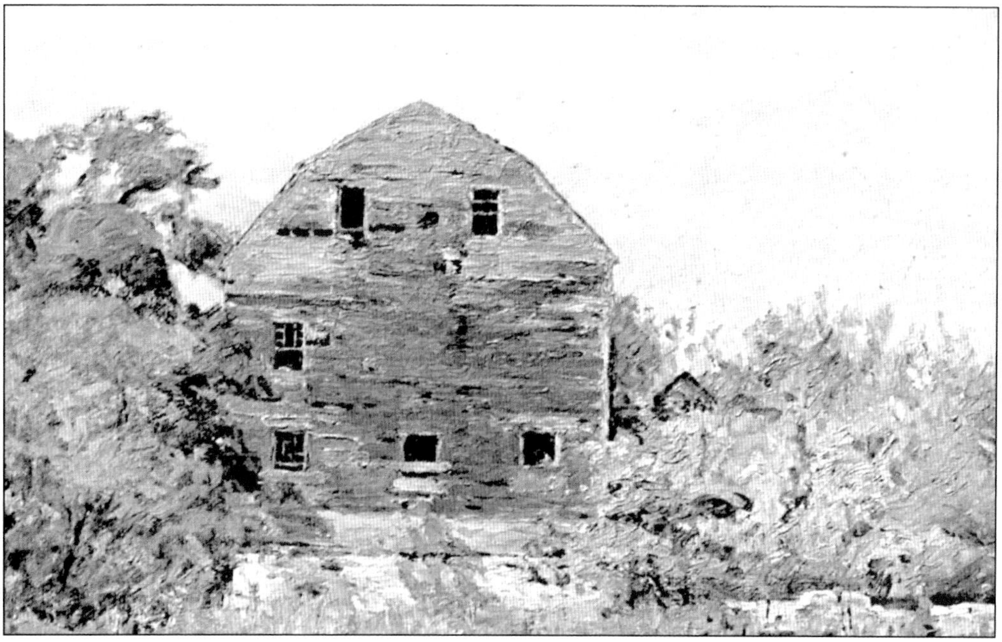

The old gristmill was captured in oil on canvas by J. Ottis Adams, Theodore C. Steele, and William Forsyth. Adams's and Forsyth's show it in profile, but Steele's version was an end view done sometime before he left Brookville in 1907. The work of these artists can be enjoyed in the book *The Passage*. (Courtesy Shea.)

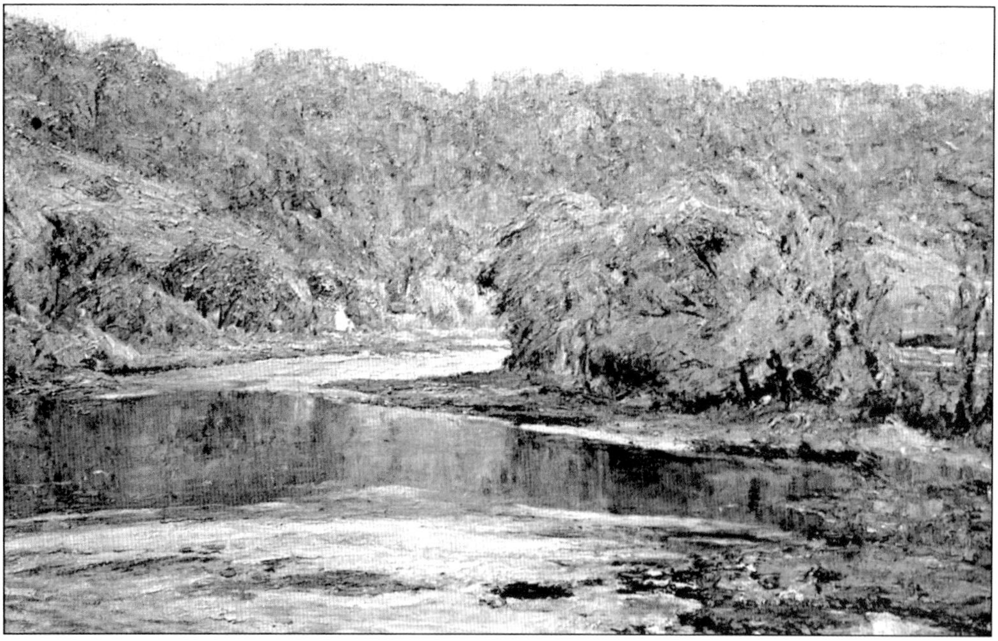

This view of the painting *Whitewater River Valley* by Theodore C. Steele may have been done a short distance north of the Hermitage. The riffles in the river, the bend in the river, and the trees closely lining the riverbank look familiar. This scene is easy to spot in Brookville's wonderful town park in the low ground north of the Hermitage. (Courtesy Shea.)

Six

Churches

The religious history of Franklin County can be traced to 1805 with the arrival of the Baptists. They built their church three miles south of Brookville in 1812 and had two ministers, Rev. William Tyner and Rev. Lewis Deweese. Tyner was a traveling minister who would go to other communities on horseback. The Little Cedar Grove Baptist Church is the oldest church in the county and is owned and preserved by the Franklin County Historical Society. The Methodists made their first appearance in the area in 1806. It was not until 1816, when Samuel Goodwin and his wife came to Brookville, that the local Methodist church became organized. Goodwin was called the "father of Methodism in Brookville." He and a circuit-riding preacher named Allen Wiley were the leaders in building the first church in Brookville in the old town cemetery. The early Methodists were served by circuit-riding preachers who traveled over a large area and visited each place only about once per month. The rest of the month, people like Goodwin served the congregation as "class leaders." Initially the Brookville Methodist classroom was at the Goodwin residence on East Fifth Street. The first Presbyterians came to the county in 1822 and to Brookville around 1839. They were to have an important impact on the early education of children in the town. The Catholics, mostly German in ancestry, came to Brookville in 1838. While St. Michael got its first church in 1845, it did not have a resident priest until 1863. The early Brookville parish was served by the priests from Catholic churches in the western part of the county. Later the Brookville priest served to establish a church at Cedar Grove. The Lutherans, who like the Catholics were German in origin, came to Brookville in the 1830s. Initially they were served by ministers from Klemme's Corner, Cincinnati, and Hamilton. In 1848, they bought a share in the old church in the cemetery from the Presbyterians, and a German Lutheran pastor began holding regular services.

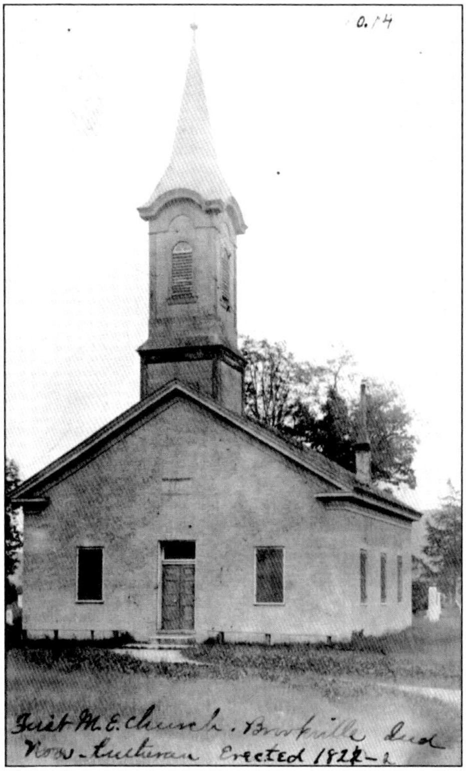

The Methodists built the first church in what is now Brookville in 1821 in a cemetery that was outside the town limits. Today the old church is still standing and is located on Tenth Street. The Methodists used the church until 1839 when they built a new church on Mill Street. The Presbyterians bought this church and occupied it until 1852. In 1848, the Lutherans purchased a share of the church. They used it until 1924, when they moved to their newly built church on Franklin Avenue. The church was abandoned until it was purchased by the Baptists in 1953. They built a modern church in the valley in 1964. The old church has been restored and maintained by the Franklin County Historical Society since 1966. (Above, courtesy BUMC; below, courtesy FCHS.)

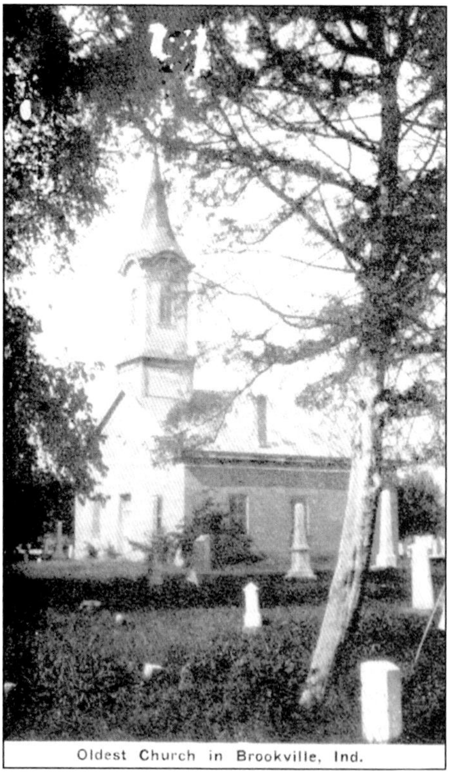

Oldest Church in Brookville, Ind.

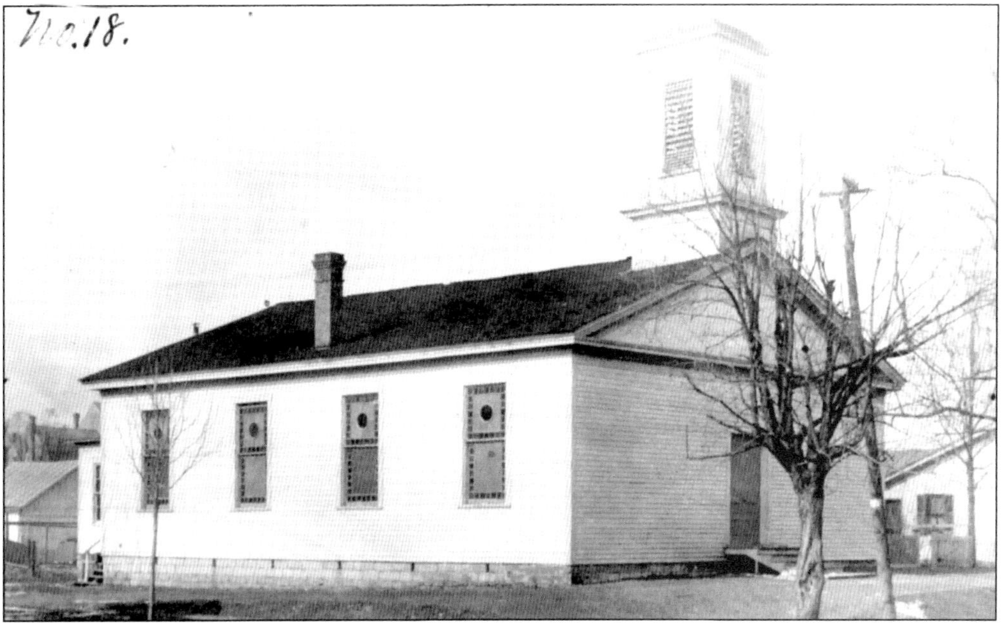

In 1839, the Methodist built a new frame church on Mill Street near Seventh Street. This location was closer to town, and the ladies would not have to wade through the mud as they did at the old brick church in the cemetery. The Christian Church bought this building in 1884 and used it until it built a new church on Tenth Street in 1917. This church is no longer standing. (Courtesy BUMC.)

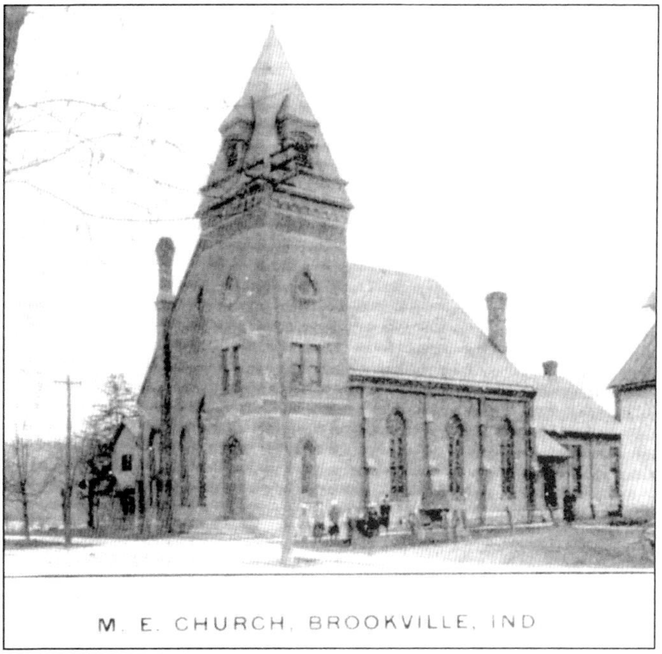

The Methodists began construction of a new building on Eighth Street in 1883 and held their first services there in March of the next year. At the time, the denomination was called Methodist Episcopal. In 1968, the Methodists and Evangelical United Brethren merged to form the United Methodist Church. The Brookville United Methodists are still using the 1883 church.

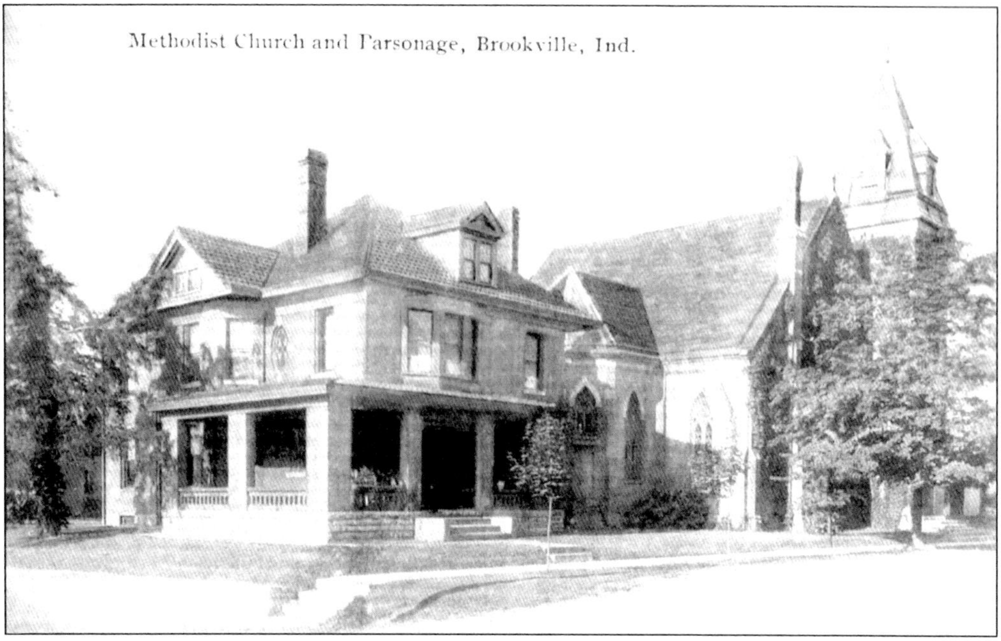

This view shows the Brookville Methodist Episcopal parsonage and the church when it still had its steeple. Around 1924, the steeple was replaced with a less-attractive tower. The old chimney is gone along with the stove, which provided heat in the sanctuary in the early days. The parsonage was built in 1907, replacing an old house that had been used since the church was built. The bottom card shows three ministers: John H. Carnes, Enoch H. Wood, and James E. Fisher in September 1909. Fisher was the Brookville minister, and Carnes and Wood were former ministers. The lady is probably Mrs. Fisher. On the back of this card, postmarked 1910, the sender wrote, "Town is out of N. Year cards so I send you this."

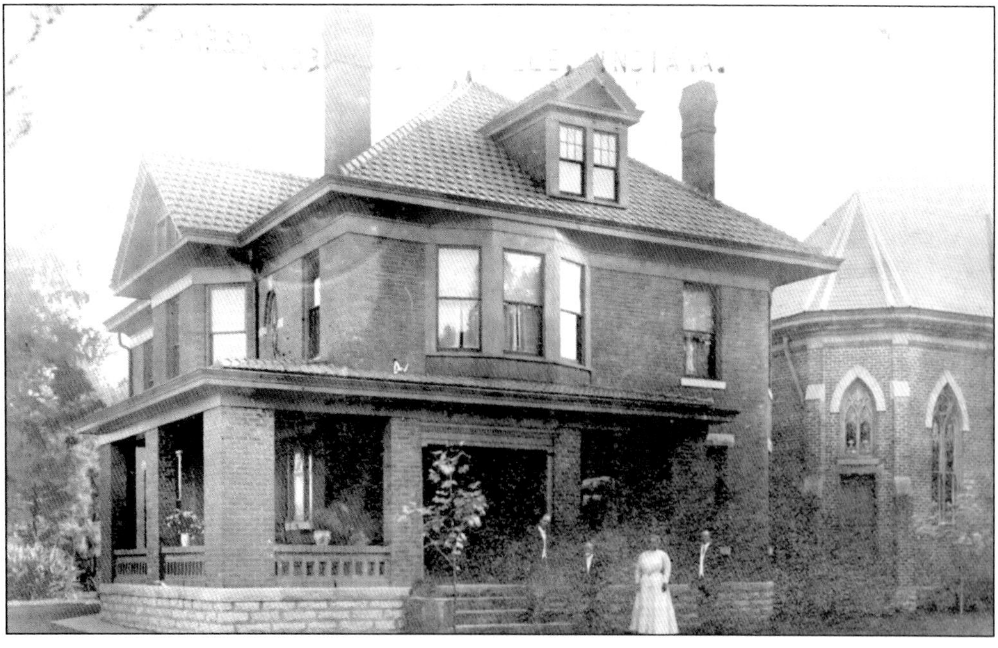

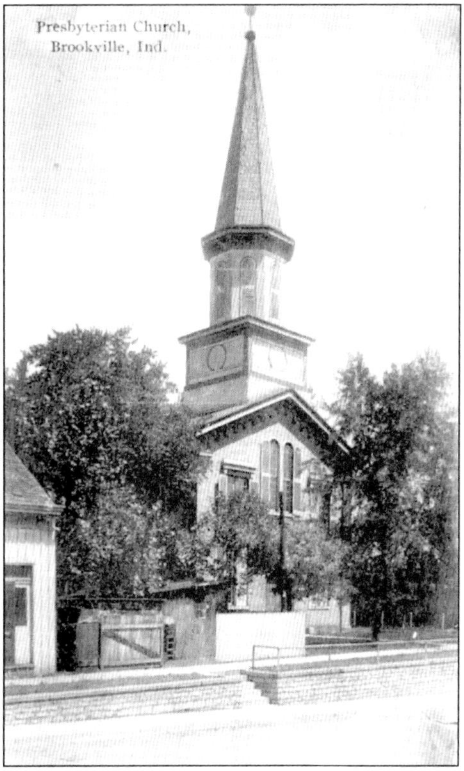

The Brookville Presbyterian Church was built on Sixth Street in 1852–1855. The congregation may have moved into the church basement when it was completed and remained there until the upper levels were finished. The sanctuary was on the second floor and dining and meeting rooms on the entry level. The church's handsome steeple was blown down in 1932 and replaced by a bell tower. This church was closed by the presbytery in 1959, and the Christian Church purchased the building. That group eventually disbanded, and many of the members joined the United Methodist church on Eighth Street in 1982. This church was being used by the United Pentecostal Church in 1993, when it was destroyed by a fire set by an arsonist. Nothing has been built on the site. (Courtesy FCHS.)

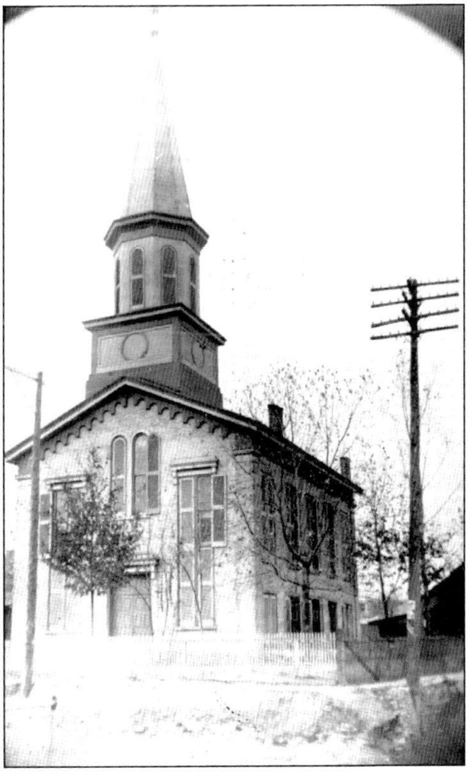

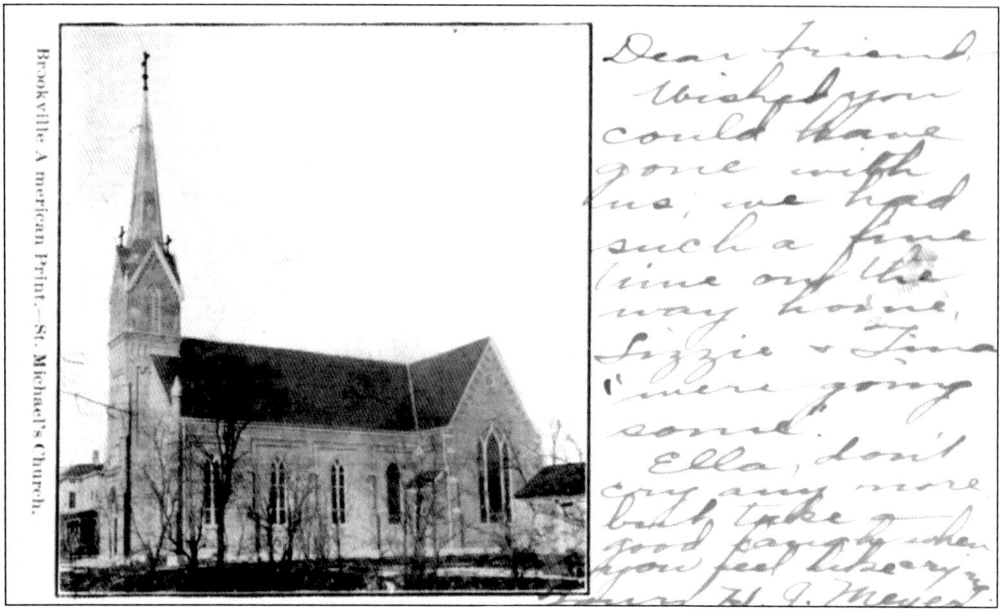

The first Catholics came to Brookville in 1838 but did not have a church until 1845. They purchased a small brick building, which they used until they built the present St. Michael Catholic Church, beginning in 1858 and completed in 1863 or 1864. In this vintage postcard, the original building is at the far right. (Courtesy Smith.)

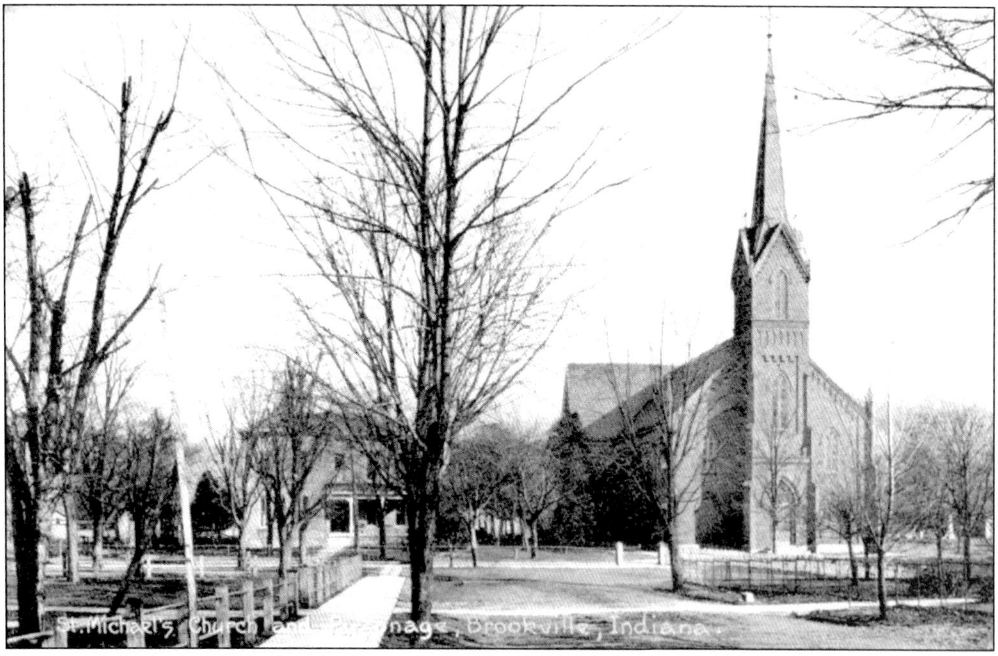

The first St. Michael Church rectory was the former home of the Noble brothers: James, Lazarus, and Noah. The present church rectory was built on the site of the old Noble home in 1883. The Catholic burying ground was beside and behind the church when this photograph was taken. There is a memorial beside the church to the early Catholic pioneers. (Courtesy Smith.)

Perhaps the most impressive feature of the St. Michael Church is its bell tower and steeple. As intended, it can be seen from distant points. Of the early Brookville churches, only the St. Michael Church and the old brick church in the town cemetery still have their original steeples. (Courtesy Lea.)

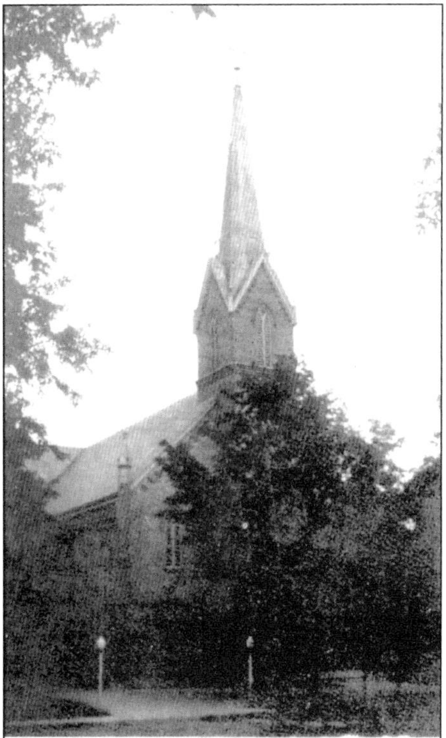

St. Michael's Church, Brookville, Ind.

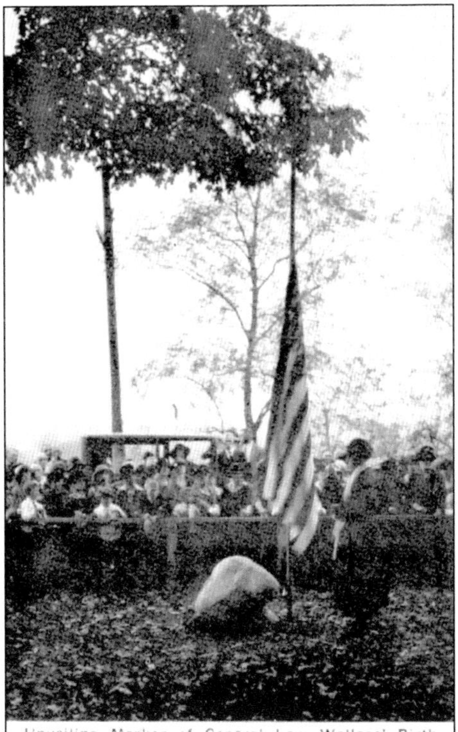

Unveiling Marker of General Lew Wallace' Birth-place in Brookville, Ind.

Lewis (Lew) Wallace, noted author, Civil War general, and diplomat, was born in Brookville in 1827. In October 1924, the Brookville Kiwanis Club placed a large boulder with a bronze plaque in the yard where the Wallace home had been. When the St. Michael Church built its parish activity center in 2003, the Wallace commemorative boulder was moved to the rear of the new building. (Courtesy Smith.)

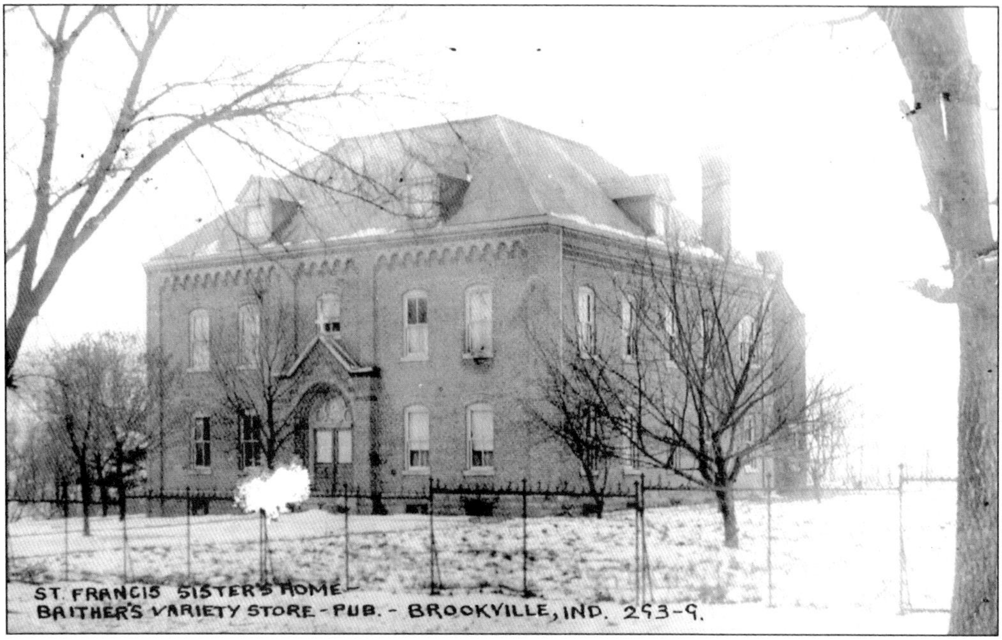

A new home for the Franciscan Sisters at Brookville was built in 1867. The sisters were sent by the Franciscan Order at Oldenburg to teach the children of the Catholic families at the St. Michael school. The building and its grounds are located on the south side of the square facing the St. Michael school. The church and rectory face the school on the east side. Prior to the building of this brick home for the sisters, they lived in an old house on the site. Those students who lived too far away to return home each evening were allowed to have room and board in the new sisters' house. There are no longer resident nuns at St. Michael. The building is now administrative offices for the church. (Below, courtesy Houchin.)

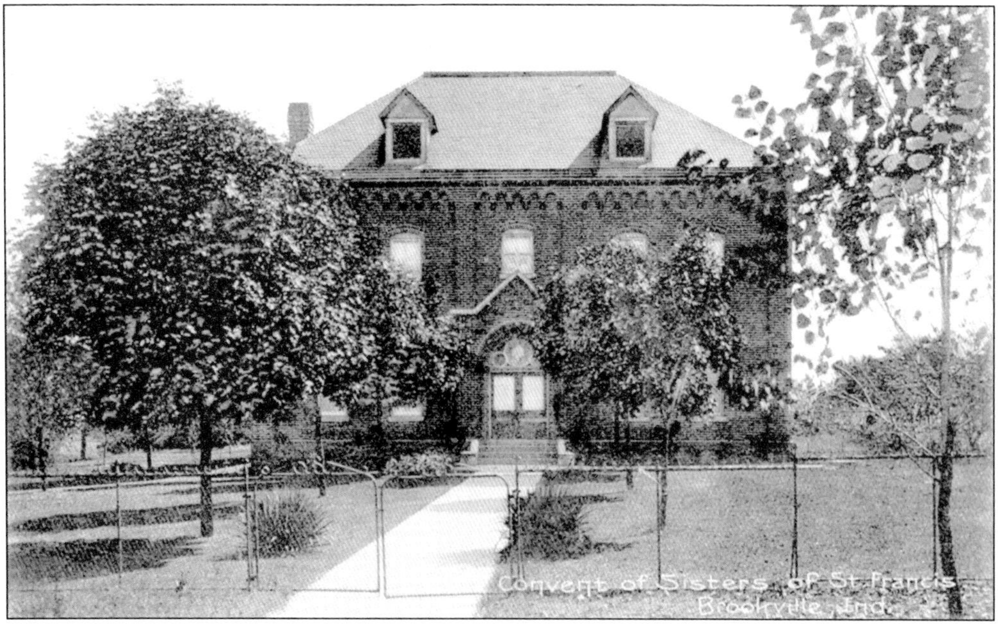

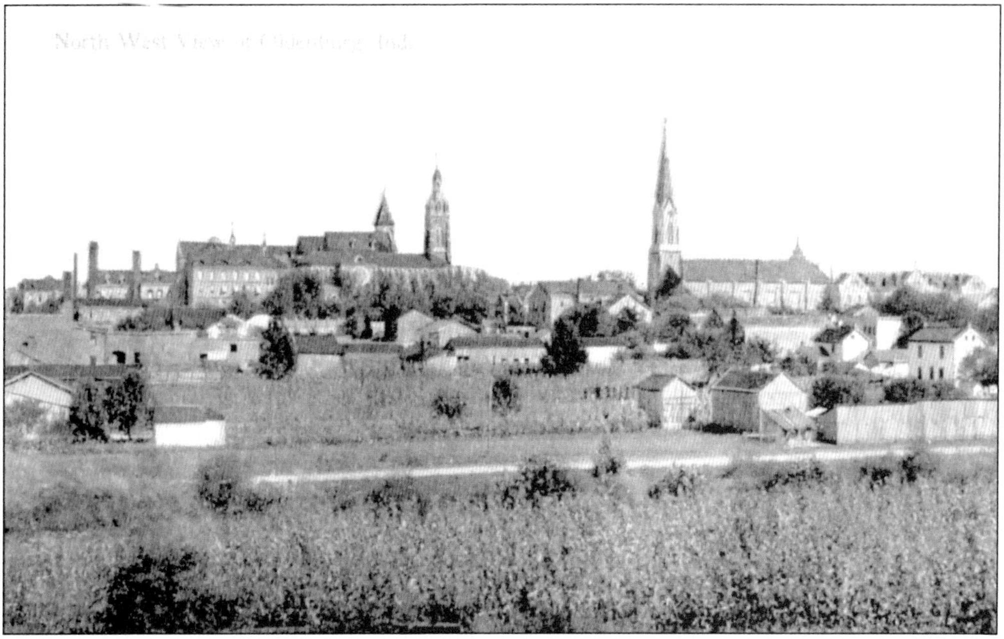

Oldenburg is in Ray Township in the southwest corner of Franklin County. It is a very picturesque little town and is called the "Village of Spires" because of its churches and religious educational institutions. The principal institutions located there now are the Sisters of St. Francis Convent, the academy (school), and the Holy Family Church. (Courtesy Schlesselman.)

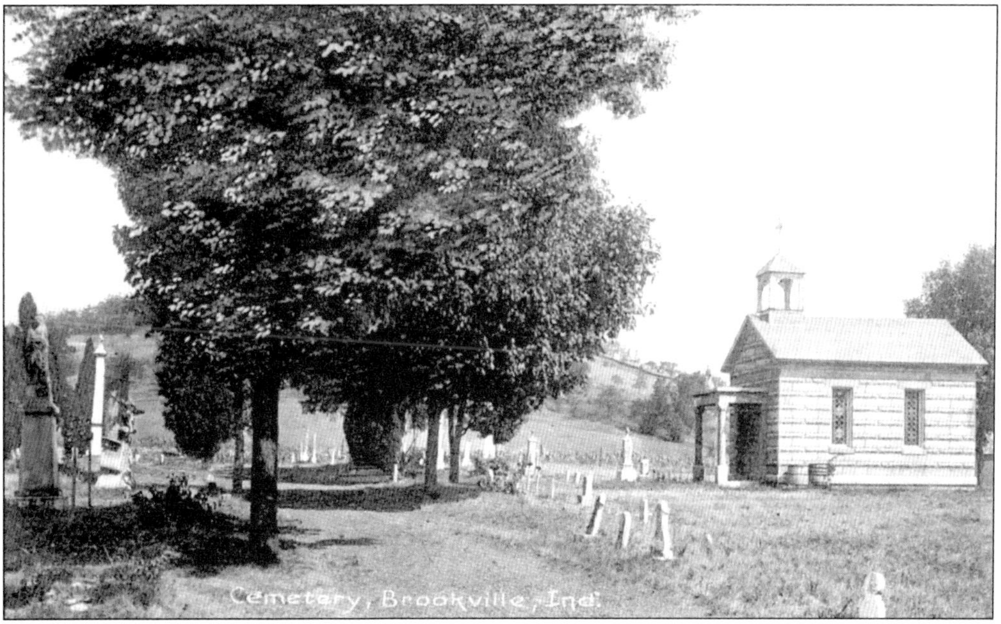

With the building of the St. Michael Church in 1863–1864, the cemetery in the churchyard was no longer adequate. Church officials purchased a new site in 1869 at the north end of town. Additional land was purchased from 1911 through 1915. Altogether, St. Michael Cemetery consists of nine acres of burial grounds. The votive chapel shown was built in 1906 and completed in 1916. (Courtesy Rowe.)

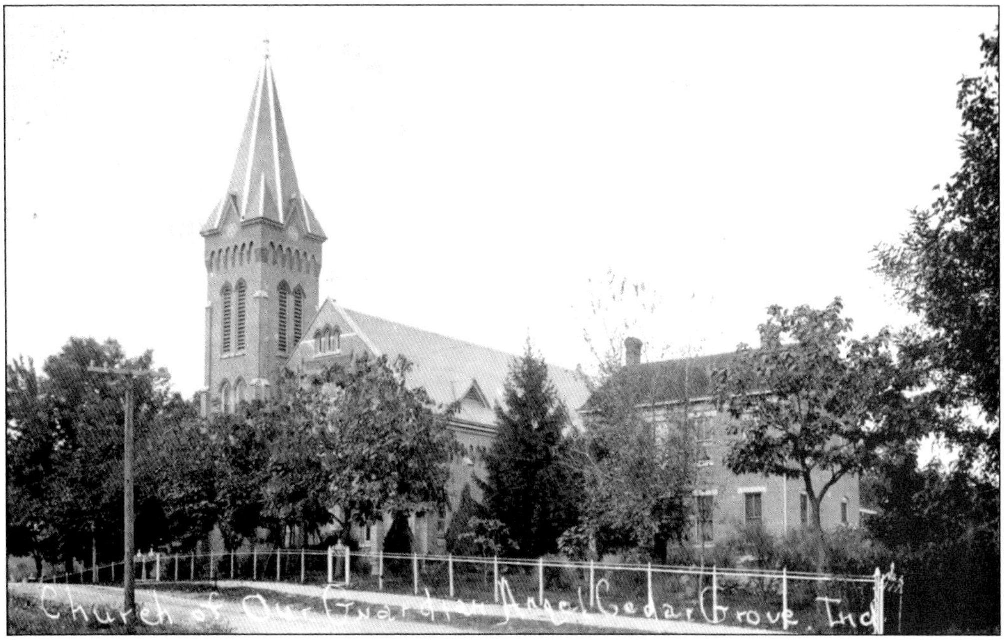

By 1872, there were 20 Catholic families in and around Cedar Grove, which was part of the St. Michael parish. Some of the families attended services at St. Peter and St. Leon. They decided they wanted their own church and petitioned their bishop. The priest at Brookville was appointed to organize the group, and in 1873–1874, a church dedicated to the Holy Guardian Angels was erected in Cedar Grove. By 1894, the congregation needed a larger church building and started construction that year and completed it in 1895. The earlier building was then used as a school. The priest's residence was completed in 1884. The bottom postcard shows the unusual and beautiful design with its vaulted ceiling. (Courtesy Smith.)

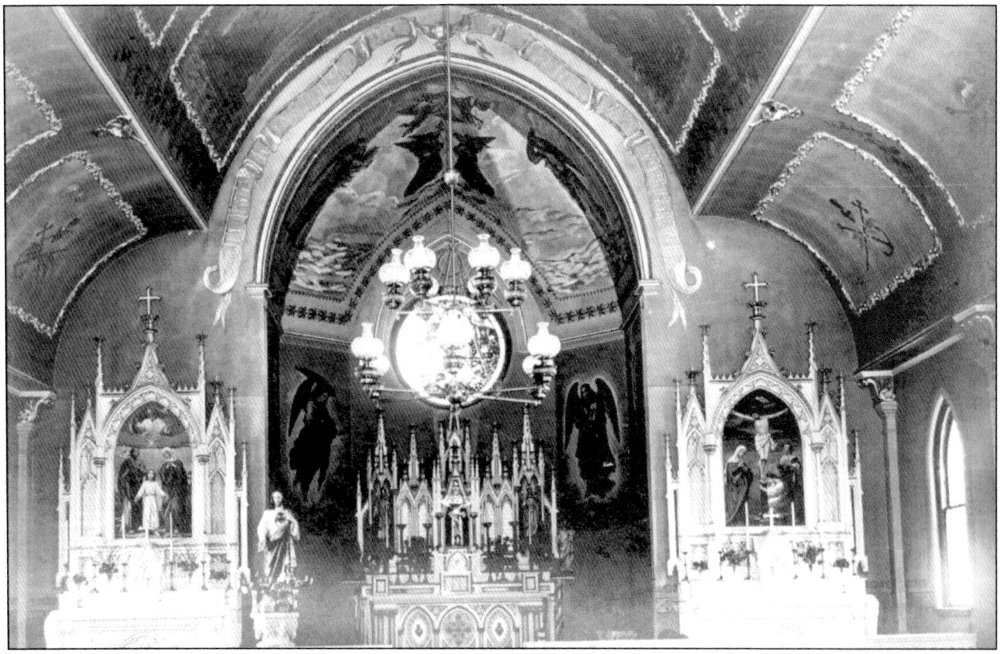

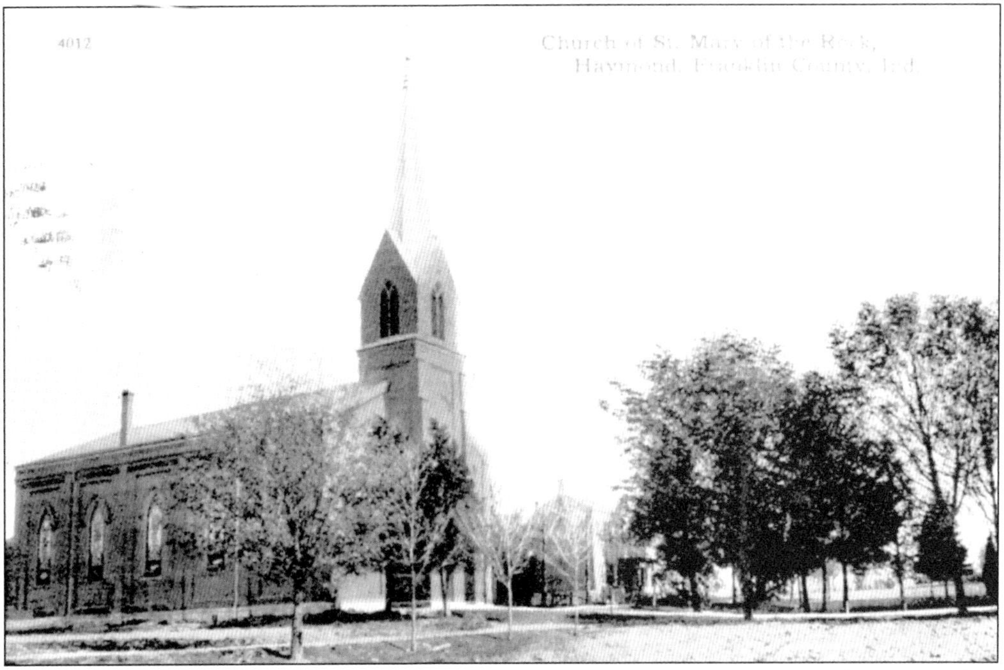

While the members of St. Michael got their first church in 1845, they did not have a resident priest until 1863. The Brookville parish was served by the priests from St. Peter, St. Leon, and St. Mary of the Rock. The first church at St. Mary was a log building built in 1844. Started in 1859 and dedicated in 1862, the brick church still stands today. (Courtesy Smith.)

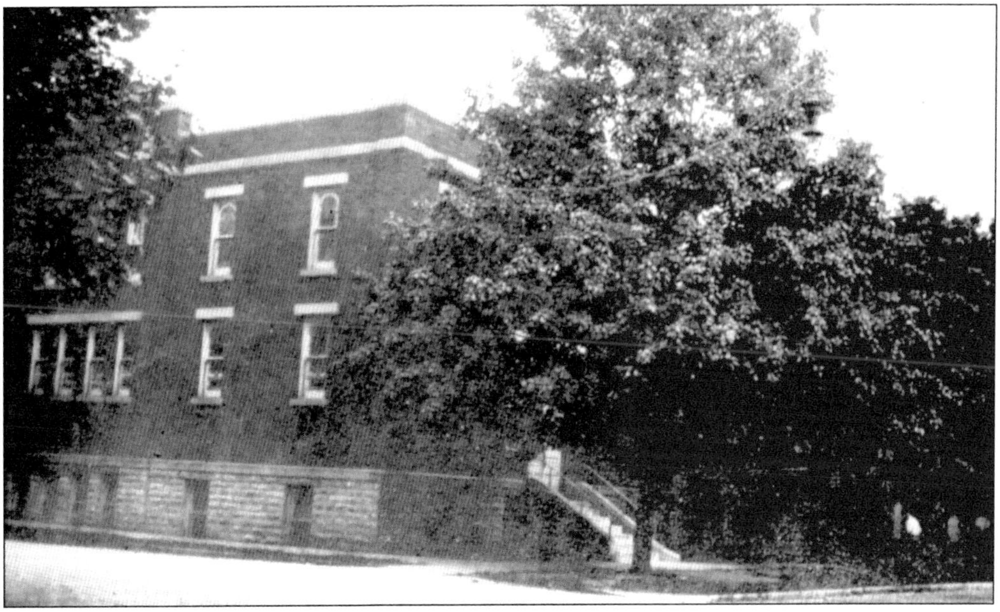

The Christian Church built a new church on Franklin Avenue in 1917 and moved out of the valley. By then it was able to finance a more substantial building on higher ground where it would not be threatened by Brookville's frequent floods. This church is now owned by the Church of Christ. The church was built in front of the James Brown Ray home on Tenth Street. (Courtesy Hauberg/Quinton.)

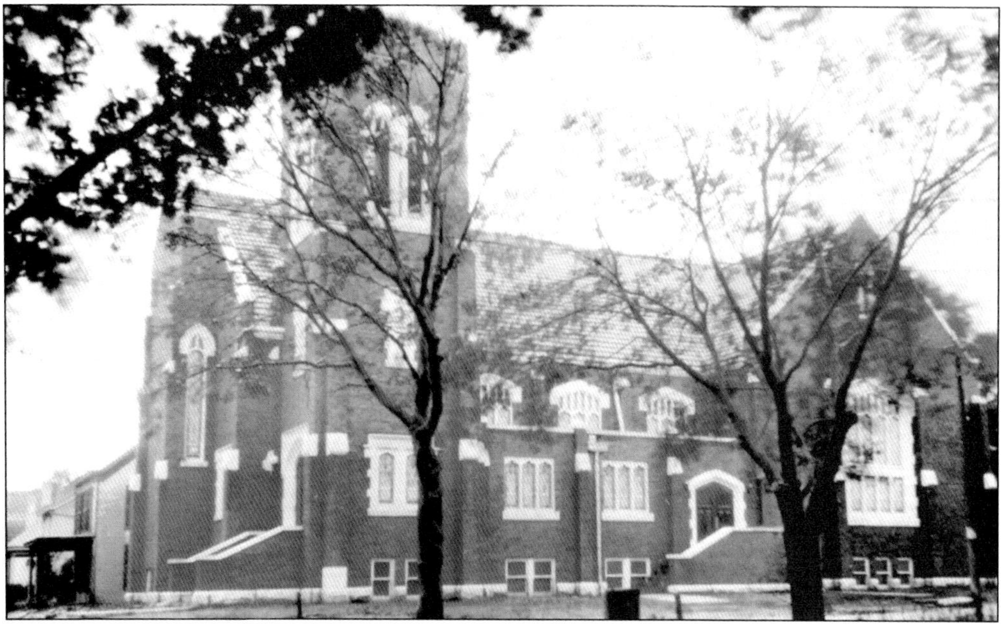

The German Lutherans used the old brick church in the cemetery from 1848 to 1924. Until 1921, the worship services were conducted in German. In 1922, they began construction of a new church at Franklin Avenue and Ninth Street. In 1924, they moved into their new church where they remain today. (Courtesy Houchin.)

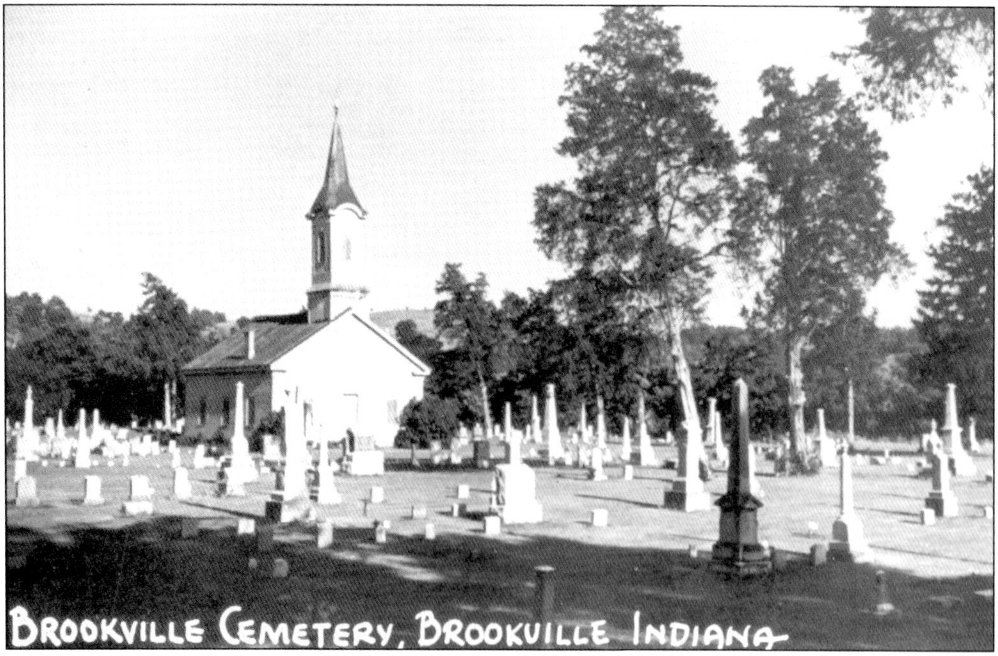

Four Revolutionary War veterans are buried in the old town cemetery. There are also two veterans of the War of 1812 and 29 Civil War soldiers known to be buried here. Some of Brookville's pioneers and other notable people are buried here, including a state supreme court justice and a signer of Indiana's first constitution. (Courtesy Fritz.)

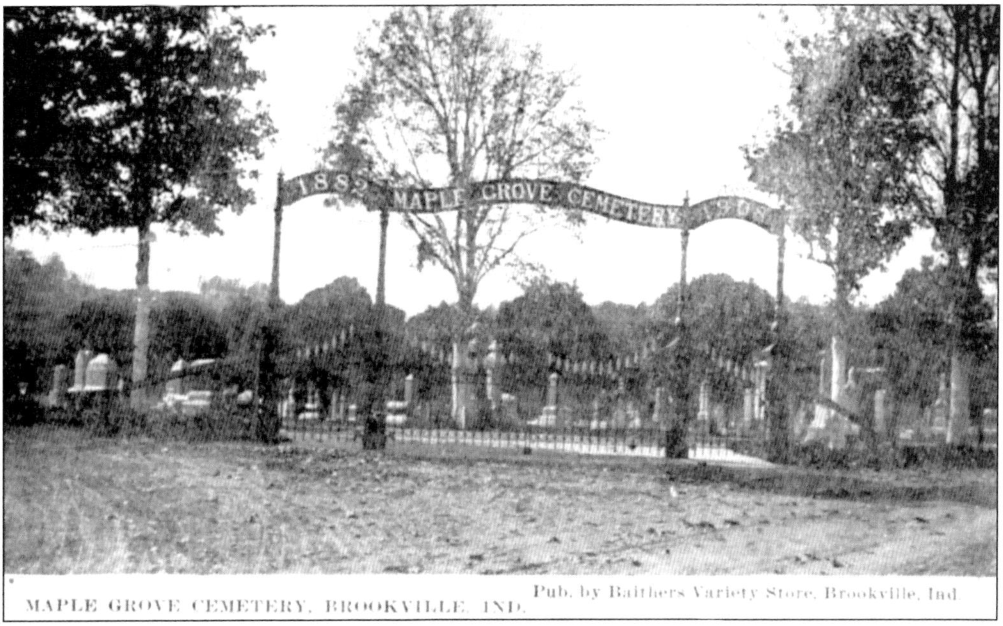

The gates to the main entrance to the Maple Grove Cemetery read, "1882 Maple Grove 1908." The cemetery is located west of Brookville on St. Mary's Road. It was originally property of the Stoops family, which pioneered this area. Brookville's Penn Lodge No. 30 Independent Order of Odd Fellows purchased 30 acres sometime after 1880 and laid out the cemetery. The first burial was in 1883.

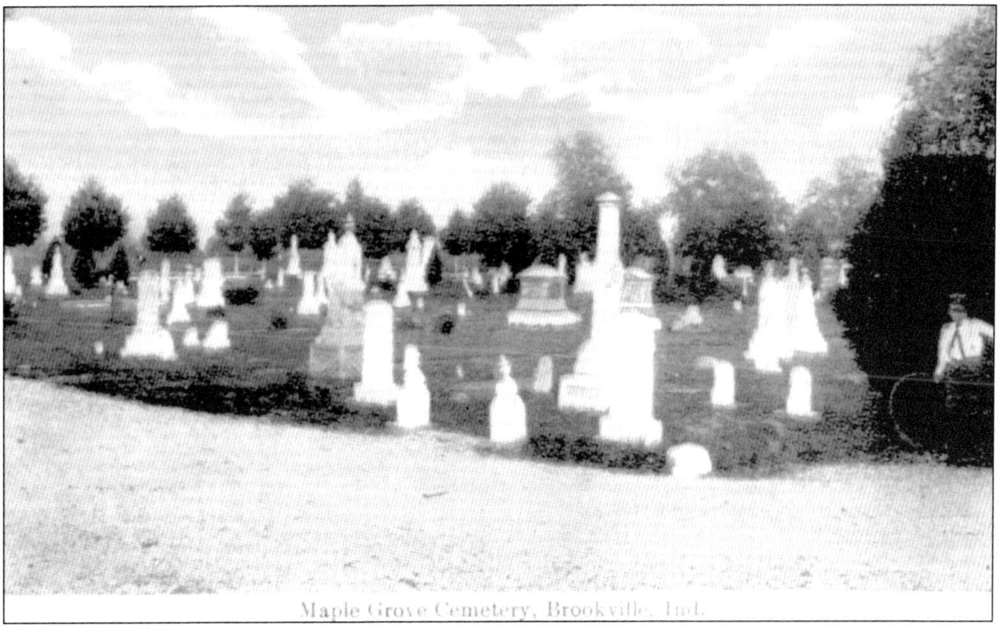

This image was taken in June 1902 by Ben Winans and clearly shows the maple trees for which the cemetery was named. American flags decorate the graves of Civil War veterans. A small boy, possibly Albert Lindsay, Winans's stepson, leans on his bicycle in the lower right corner. The gleaming white tombstones are marble, which suffers from the effects of time and the elements.

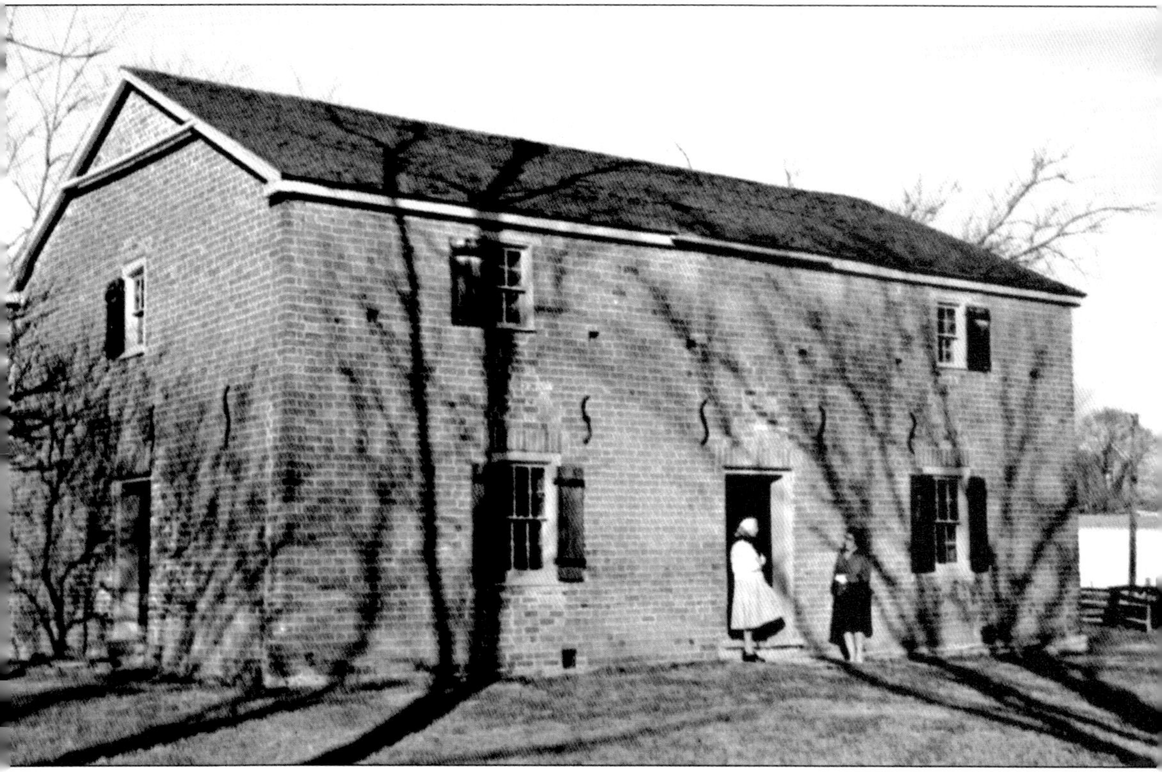

The Little Cedar Grove Baptist Church is three miles south of Brookville on U.S. 52. The church was built in 1812 and is said to be the oldest church in Indiana still on its original foundation. It was restored in 1955 with monetary assistance from local and state organizations. The most recent threat to its survival is the erosion by Little Cedar Creek behind the church.

Seven

Schools

The school system in Franklin County evolved from many small one-room schools in the 13 townships to three township schools and then to the present county-wide system of three elementary schools, a middle school, and a high school. Indiana's first constitution, written in 1816, provided for the organization of county seminaries. These were subscription schools for general education and not for religious training. In 1830, the Franklin County Seminary was opened in Brookville. In 1851, Indiana adopted a new constitution that provided for a system of free schools and the seminary closed that year. Public schools were mandated by Indiana's new constitution, and the seminary building was used for that purpose. Brookville had a college supported by the Methodist Church; it was located on Franklin Avenue and operated from 1852 to 1872. Following that, the college building was used by the public school from 1873 to 1912, when a new building was built. Until 1922, Brookville had the only four-year high school in the county. Since students from outside the town had to come to Brookville to get their high school diploma, most of them did not. This building on Franklin Avenue is no longer used for school purposes but is now the Franklin County Government Center. The present school system—elementary, middle school, and high school—is on a large campus on the east side of the East Fork between the Riverview and Hidden Valley subdivisions.

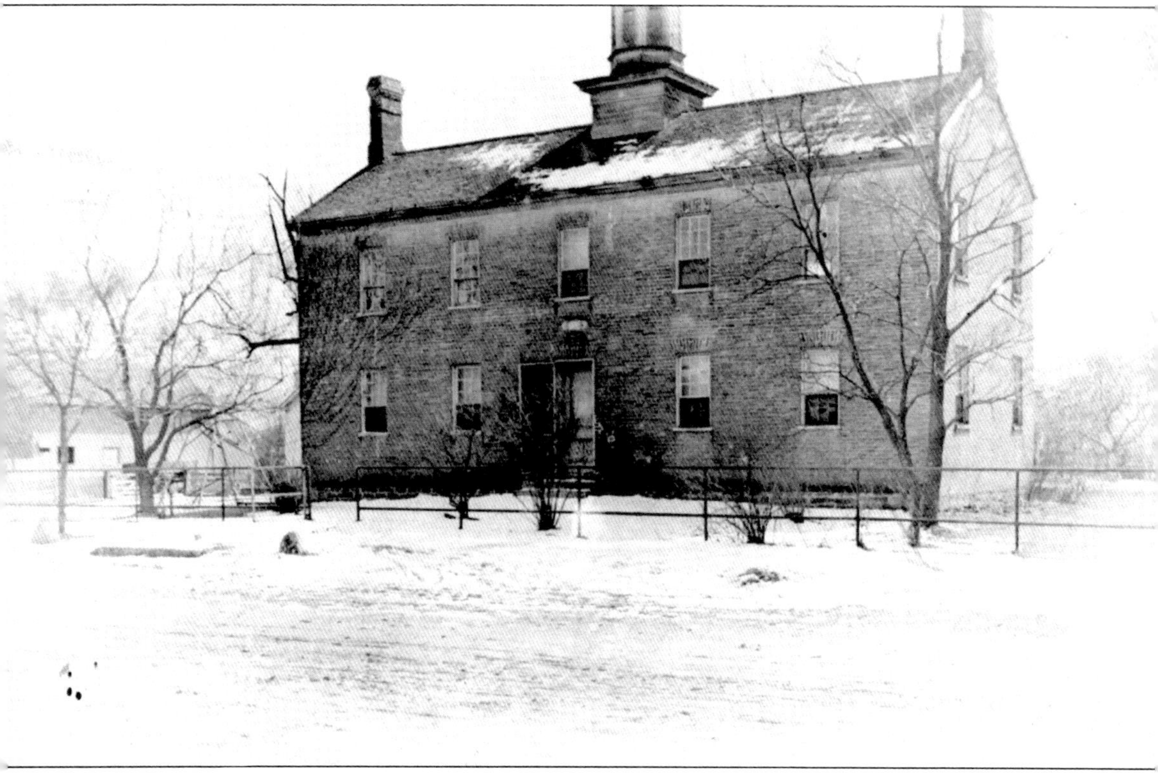

The Franklin County Seminary located at Fifth and Mill Streets was built 1828–1830 and was used for that purpose until 1851. It was then used by the Indiana High School for two years and then by the town as a school through 1873. It then became a private residence until 1968, when it was purchased by the Franklin County Historical Society, which restored the building in 1979–1981 as a museum.

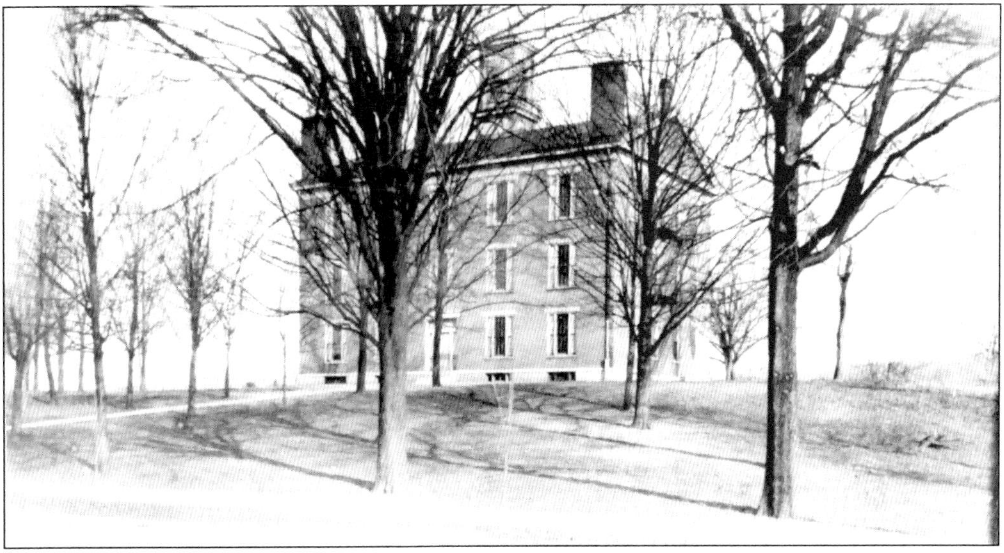

The Methodist Episcopal Church built Brookville College in 1852–1853 on a hill north of the old brick church in the town cemetery. The local Methodist Episcopal minister and some of the leading families of Brookville felt that an institution of higher learning was needed to replace the seminary. The college did not attract sufficient students and was closed in 1872. The building was purchased by the Town of Brookville in 1873 and used as the Brookville Public School for grades 1 through 12. The high school's first graduating class was in 1877. The old college building was used until 1912, when it was torn down and a new school erected on the same location on Franklin Avenue between present-day Tenth and Eleventh Streets. (Above, courtesy Hauberg/Quinton; below, courtesy Fritz.)

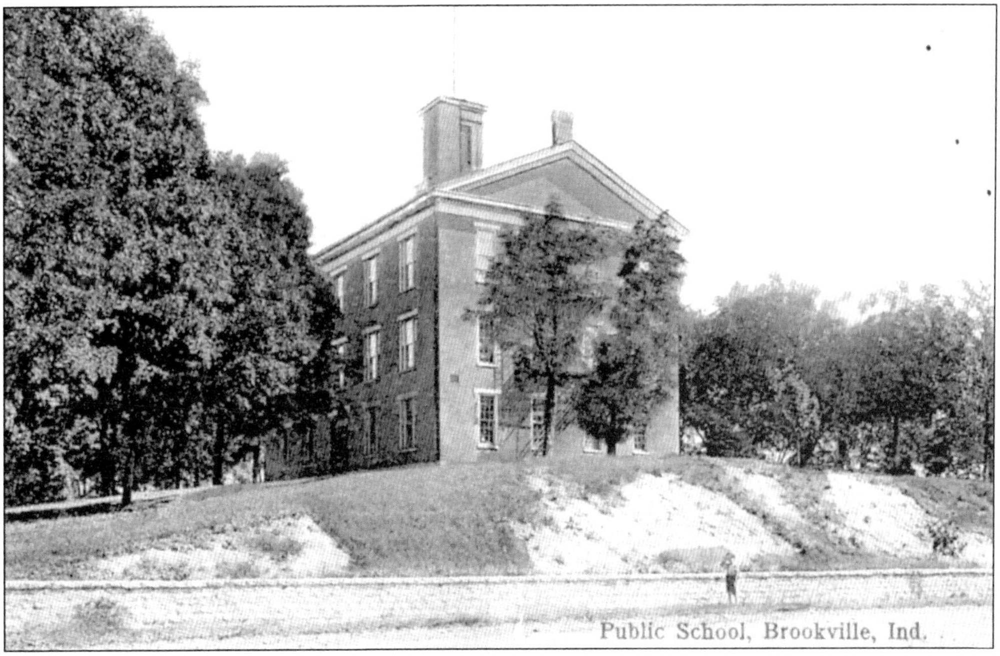

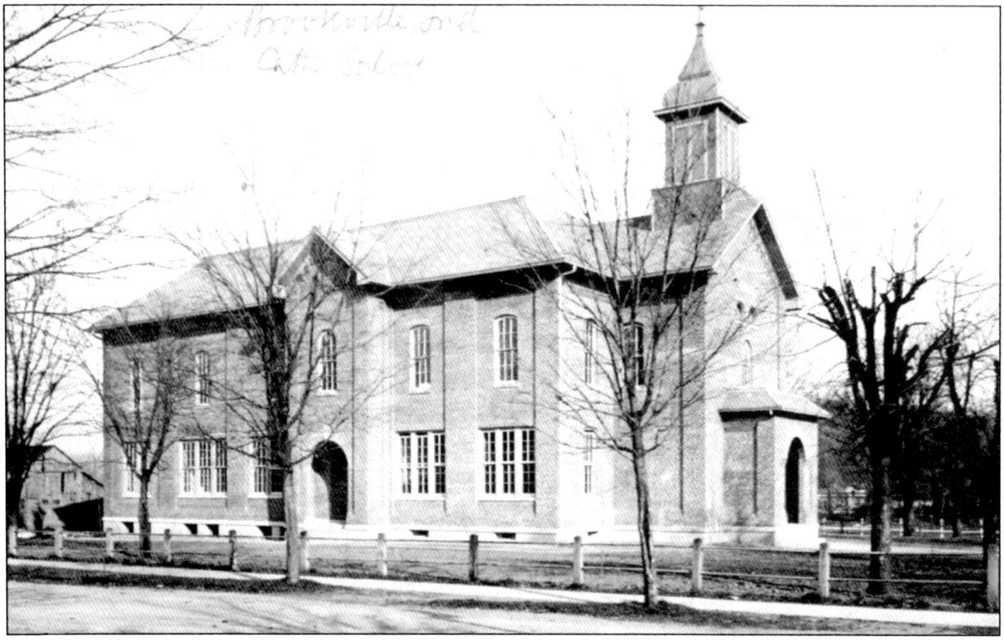

The first grade school for Catholic students of the Brookville area was established in 1855, probably in the old building that was used for church services until the present church was built. In 1873, a new school was built near the church. The school was rebuilt in 1912, as shown in this postcard. Since then, there has been extensive remodeling of the old building and two additions. (Courtesy Smith.)

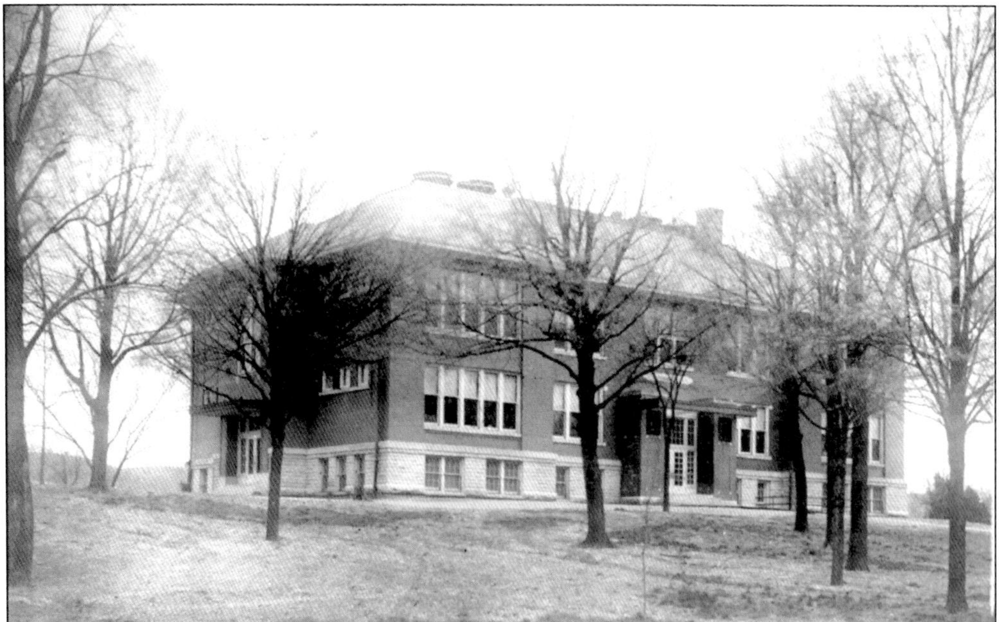

As noted, the old Brookville College building facing Franklin Avenue was torn down in 1912 and this new Brookville Public School erected on the site. This new school had 33 rooms with a gymnasium in the basement. All 12 grades used this school until 1931, when the town built a new elementary school and gymnasium nearby. (Courtesy FCHS.)

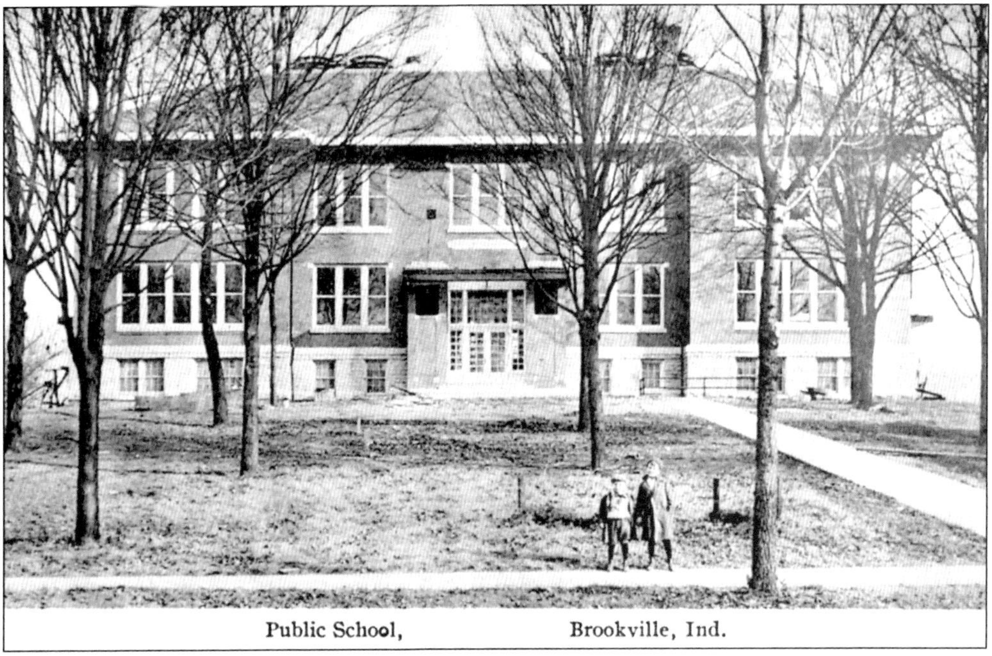

Public School, Brookville, Ind.

Times change but apparently student sentiment does not. The message written on the back of the top card says, "Here's my prison. The walk comes straight down from the door now. This is the walk for the old building. It has been changed. I have been on top of this building." The young boys in the postcard above are James and George Mullin, whose family lived across the street from the school. The bottom card shows the sidewalk after it was moved to the center of the building.

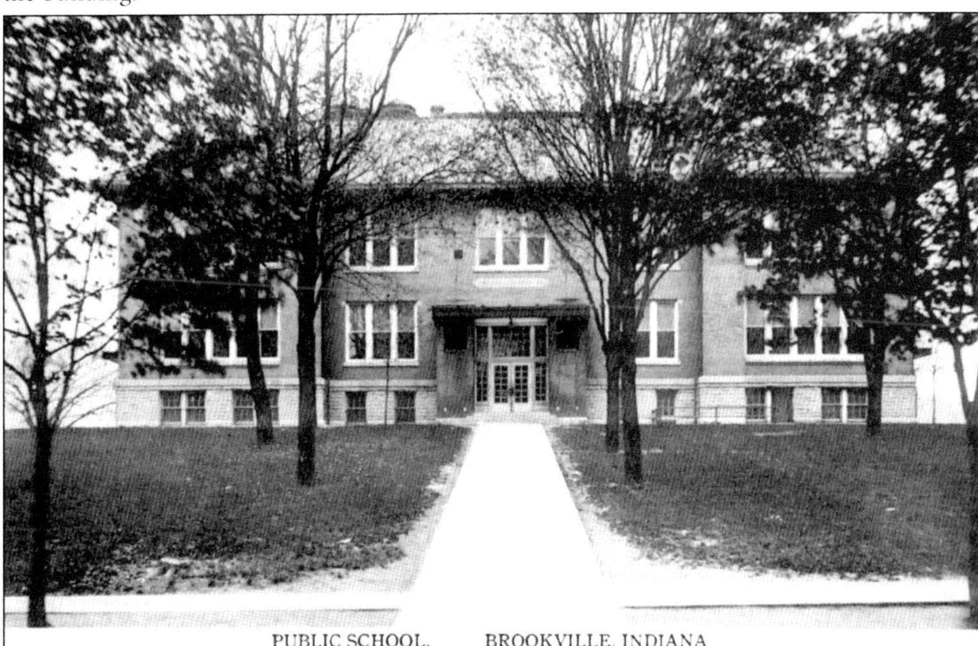

PUBLIC SCHOOL, BROOKVILLE, INDIANA

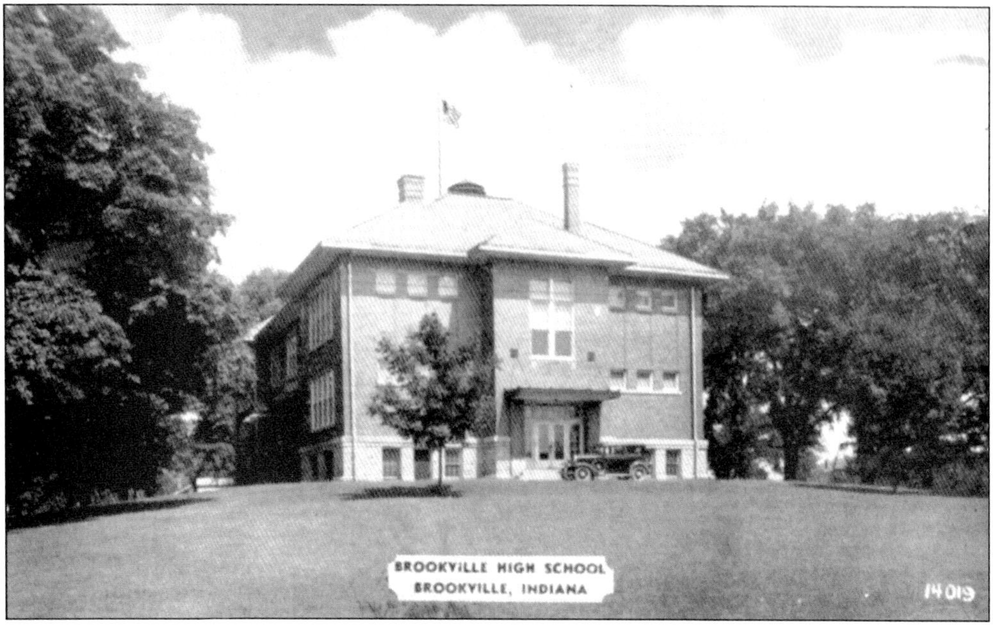

These views show the north end of the school. From 1912 to 1989, Brookville High School was in this building, but it was not until 1961 that it was used exclusively for high school students. In 1989, a new Franklin County High School opened across the East Fork, and all high school students (including those from all the other former township high schools) went there. (Above, courtesy Houchin; below, courtesy FCHS.)

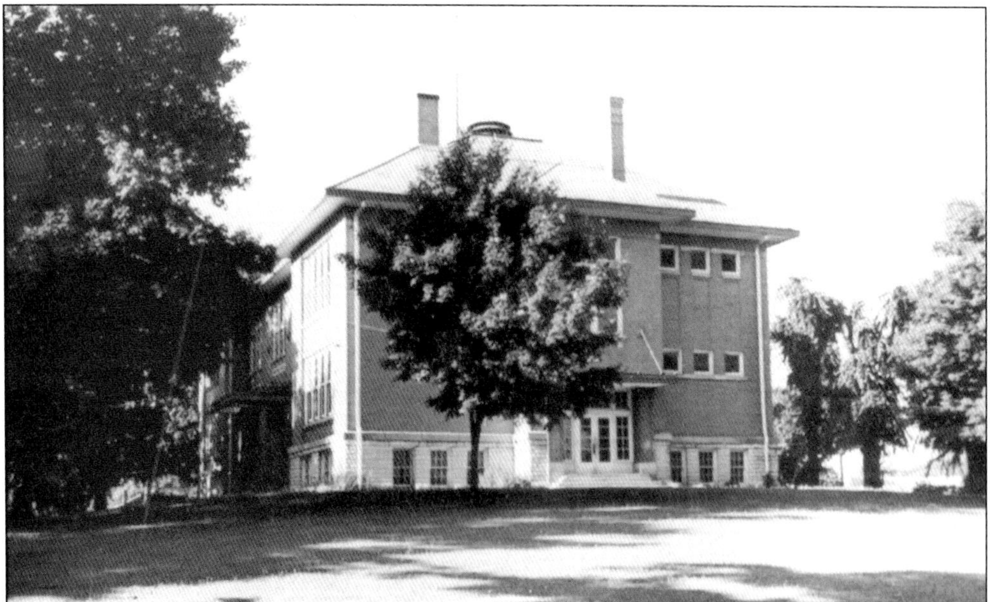

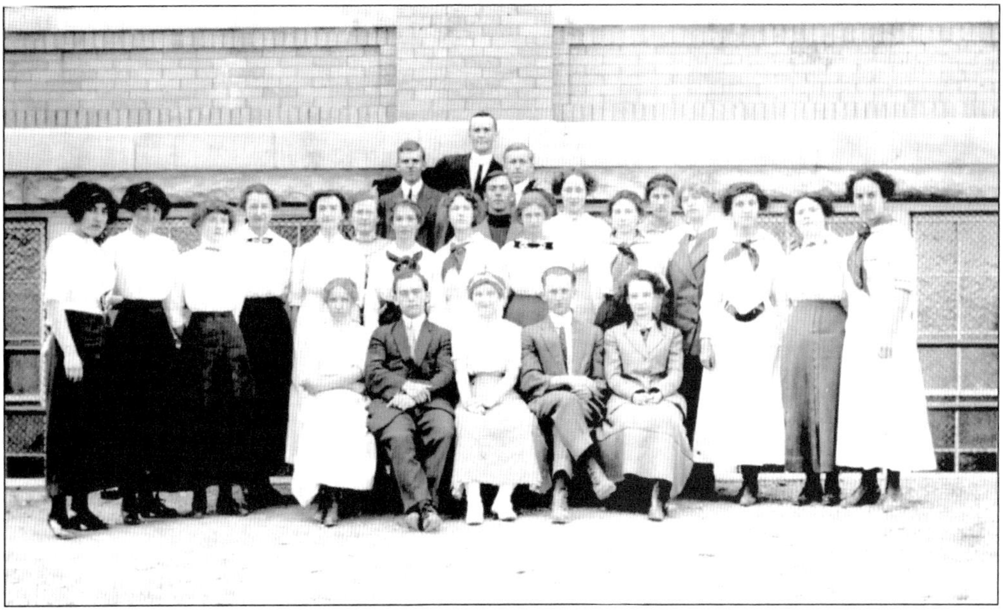

The Brookville High School class of 1913 was the first to graduate from the new high school building. At the time, it was the only four-year high school in the county. Note the students are well dressed for the occasion. This postcard was addressed to Arthur Sylvester, a member of the graduating class who at the time was serving in the U.S. Army in France in World War I.

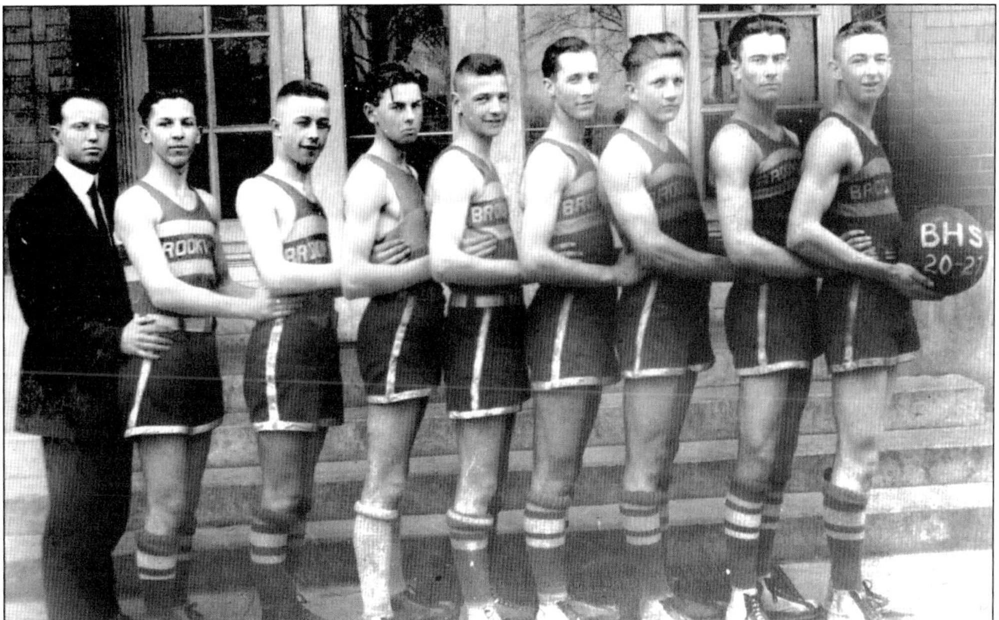

The public school built in 1912 had a gymnasium in the basement. This basketball team of 1920–1921 played in that subterranean pit. When a new aboveground gymnasium was constructed, the old gymnasium was partially filled in and converted to a school cafeteria. A stairway leading to the old athletic facility was rediscovered when the old school was converted to the Franklin County Government Center. (Courtesy Landreth.)

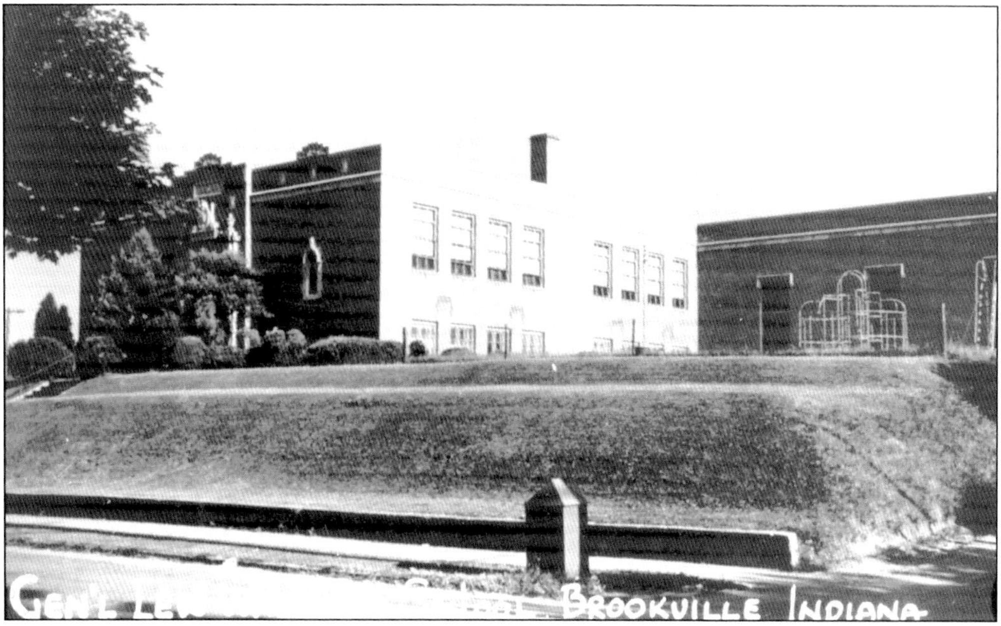

In 1931, school officials built a new elementary school and gymnasium on the hill near the existing 1912 public school. They named it after Lewis (Lew) Wallace, a Civil War general, diplomat, and author born in Brookville in 1827. In 1961, a new elementary school was opened across the East Fork, and school officials converted the building in this postcard into a junior high school. When the new high school opened in 1989, the old public school became the middle school and this building was razed. The old public school, shown below in this photo chrome postcard, stood empty until the county bought it in 2005 and completely remodeled the interior. This Brookville landmark lives on as the Franklin County Government Center. (Below, courtesy Fritz.)

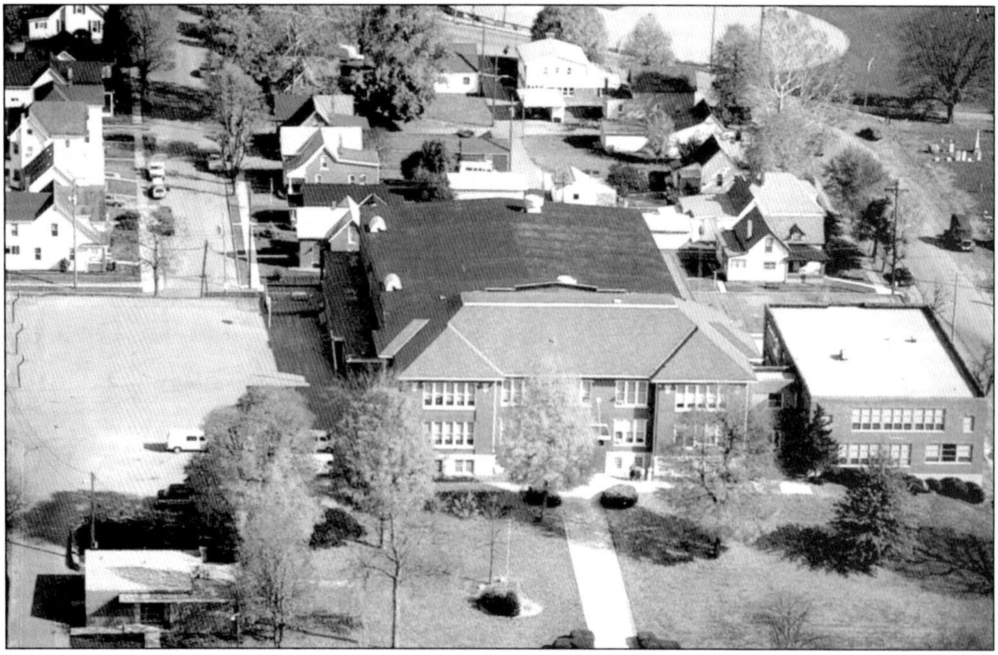

Eight

THE WHITEWATER RIVER

From its beginning, Brookville's defining natural feature has been the river. The first settlers, Amos Butler and John Allen, both built mills on the East Fork. It was the Whitewater River and the hills that drew landscape artists J. Ottis Adams and Theodore C. Steele to live here and Otto Stark and other artists to stay here for extended periods. The river allowed the early development of industry in Brookville, including a paper mill and gristmill on the East Fork. Later, on the West Fork, businessmen constructed a paper mill and a furniture factory.

As the many postcards in this chapter attest, the Whitewater River provided a great source of recreation for local people and visitors. There was fishing, swimming, boating, picnicking, bird and wildlife watching, and enjoying the relaxing sound of flowing water. Fishing, in particular, was a popular form of recreation in the early days of the 20th century, and there were many fishing camps along the Whitewater River, both above and below Brookville. Many families from Brookville and the surrounding areas kept a camp somewhere along the river. There are still a few around. The camps were equipped so that the campers had a place to sleep and a stove to cook their catch of the day. The larger camps were used for other forms of recreation such as eating, drinking, card-playing, and loafing. Residents continue to enjoy the Whitewater at Brookville's town park by the East Fork.

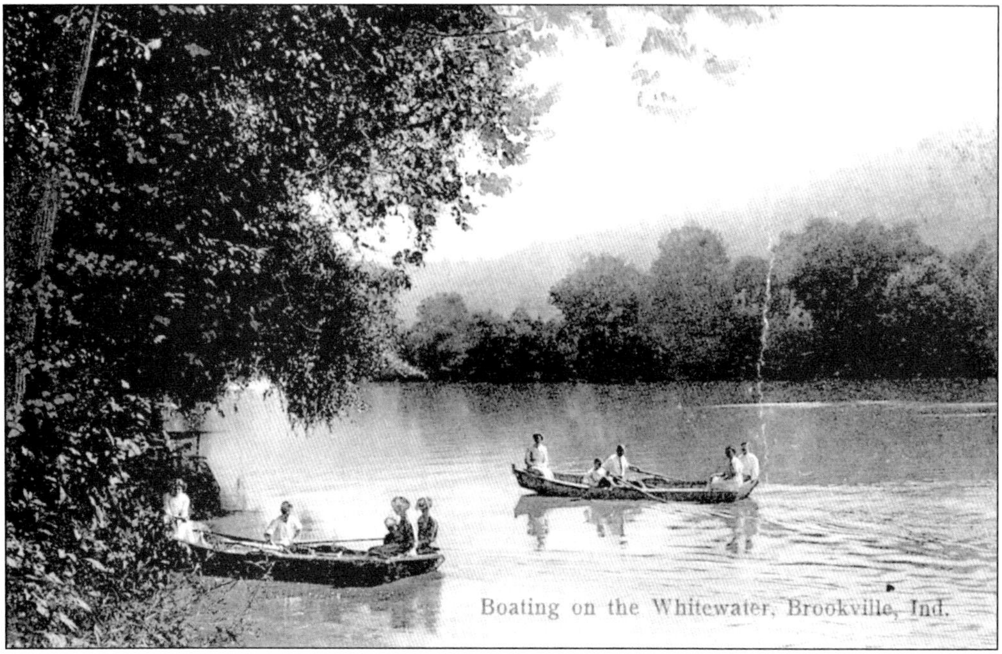

Canoeing and boating have been popular recreations at Brookville over the years. Despite its name, there is technically no true white water on the river, although there are many rapids due to the steep gradient present. In fact, the Whitewater River is said to be the swiftest river in the state of Indiana as it drops an average of six feet per mile. (Courtesy Houchin.)

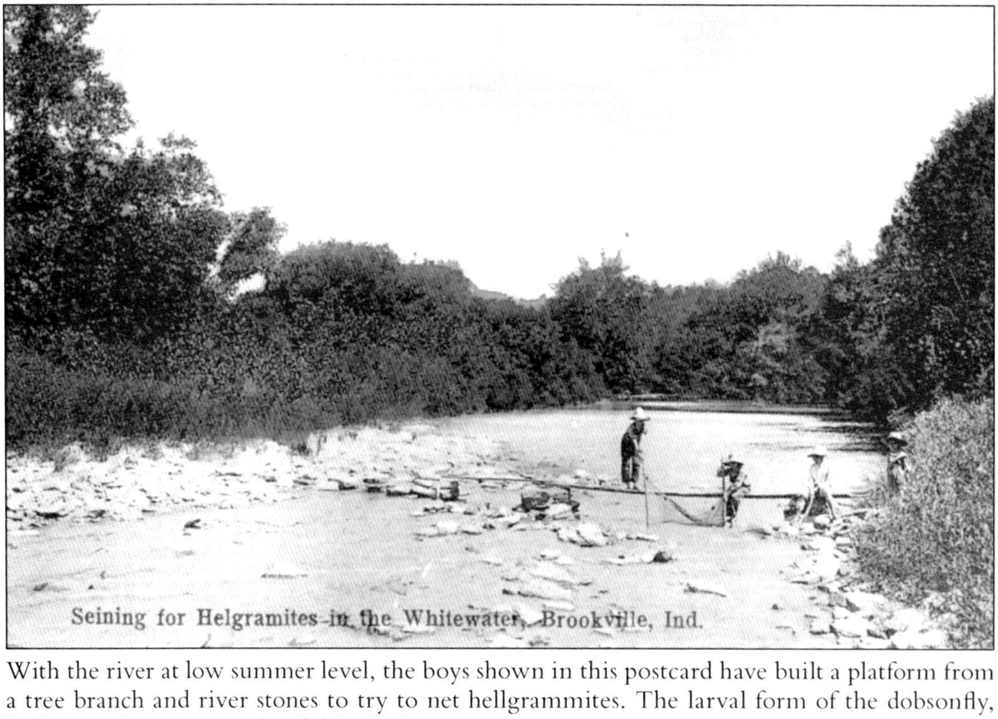

With the river at low summer level, the boys shown in this postcard have built a platform from a tree branch and river stones to try to net hellgrammites. The larval form of the dobsonfly, hellgrammites were used as fishing bait.

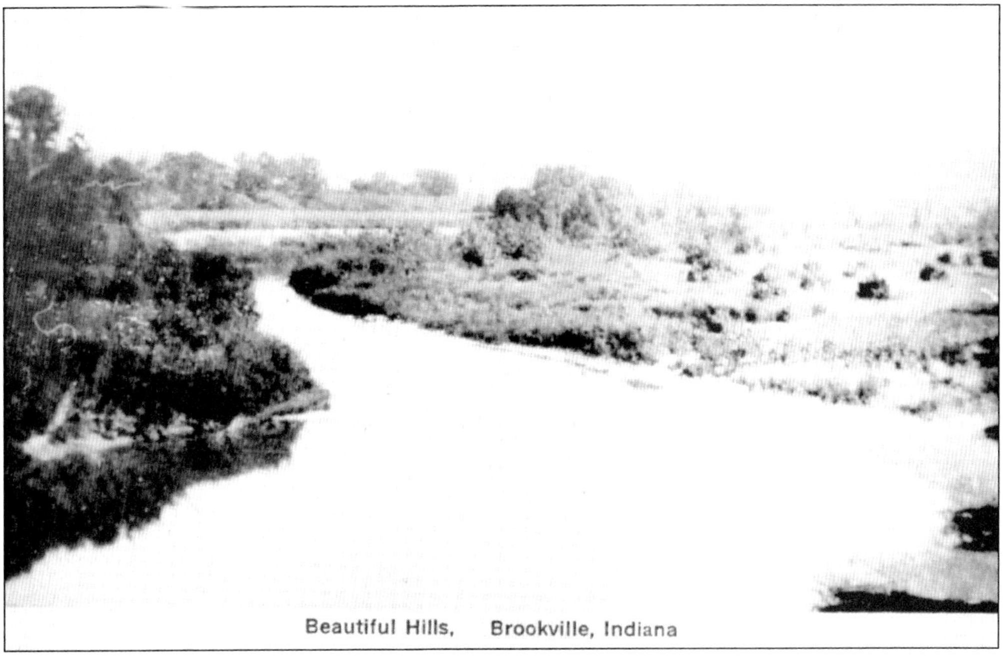

While it is true that the hills around Brookville are beautiful, none are shown in this card, despite the label. This river takes many twists and turns as it flows through Franklin County. This view showing an S-shaped bend cannot be identified due to a lack of landmarks. It is just one of the many river views that define Brookville. (Courtesy Shea.)

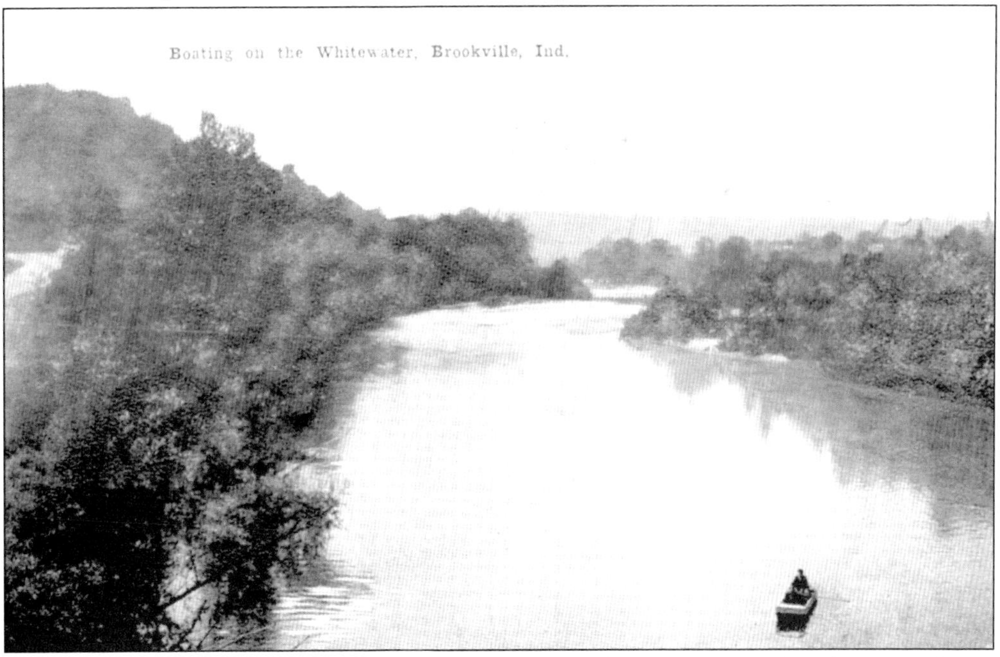

This scene appears to be south of Brookville and below where the East Fork and West Fork join to form the Whitewater River, probably just north of the Poor Farm Bridge. A faint view of a church steeple can be seen at the right, which is probably the St. Michael Church. The dirt road to the left led to the poor farm and is still a dirt road. (Courtesy Schlesselman.)

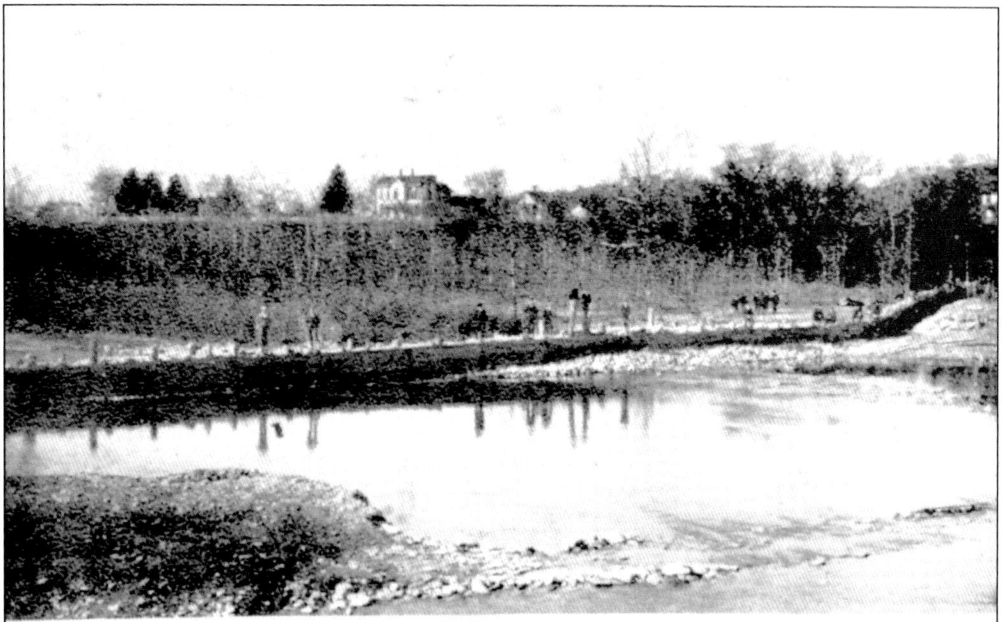
East Fork Dam, Brookville, Ind.

In 1908, a primitive dam was built on the East Fork about a half mile north of the Hermitage. The house, upper center in the card above, was on Fairfield Avenue, near the location of the French Brothers Creamery. The dam was called the Panama Dam and was supposed to control the floodwaters of the East Fork. It was destroyed only a few years later by the March 1913 flood. The bottom card shows the dam that was upriver near the Whitcomb bridge. There was a dam at this location in earlier times, which provided a water flow for the millrace downstream for the gristmill and paper mill. This place would be behind the present American Legion building at the north end of the town park. (Above, courtesy BPL.)

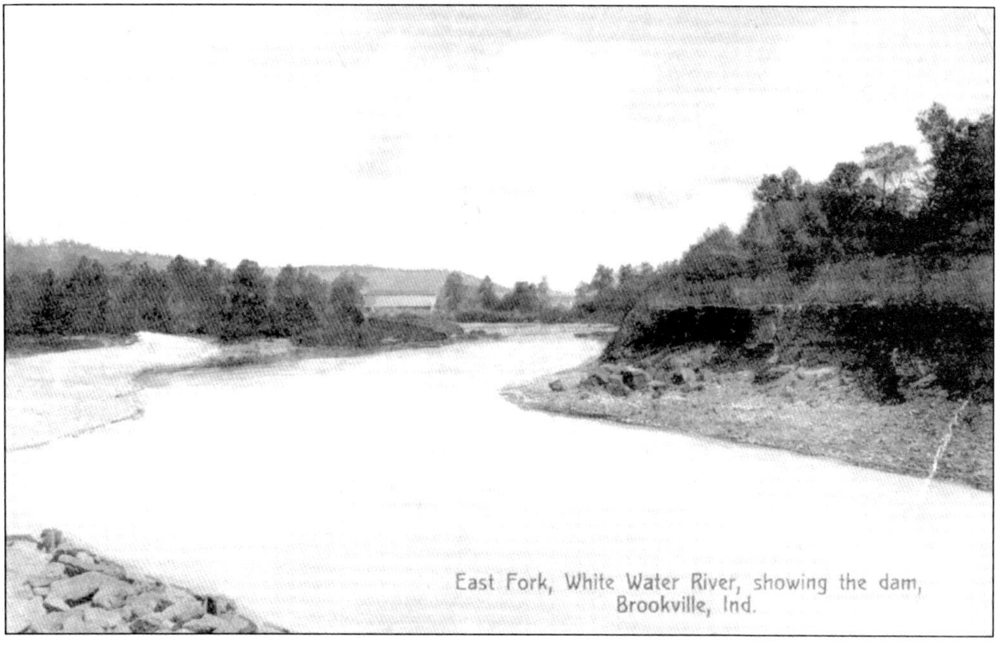
East Fork, White Water River, showing the dam, Brookville, Ind.

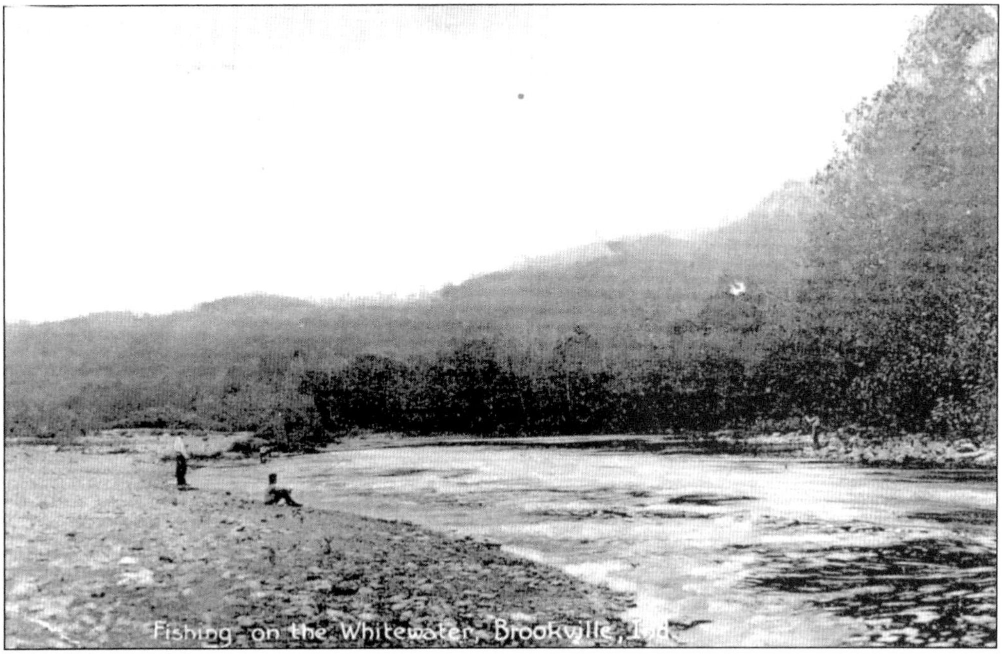

The Whitewater River was formed as the retreating glacial ice sheets melted and water drained toward the Ohio River forming the Whitewater Valley in the process. Thick deposits of sand and gravel were left by the glaciers and characterize the river's bottom today, as evident in the top postcard. The river forms in southern Randolph and Wayne Counties and flows in two main branches, which are scarcely 10 miles apart, before joining at Brookville. From here, the Whitewater flows southeasterly into Ohio, where it eventually joins the Miami River, a tributary of the Ohio River.

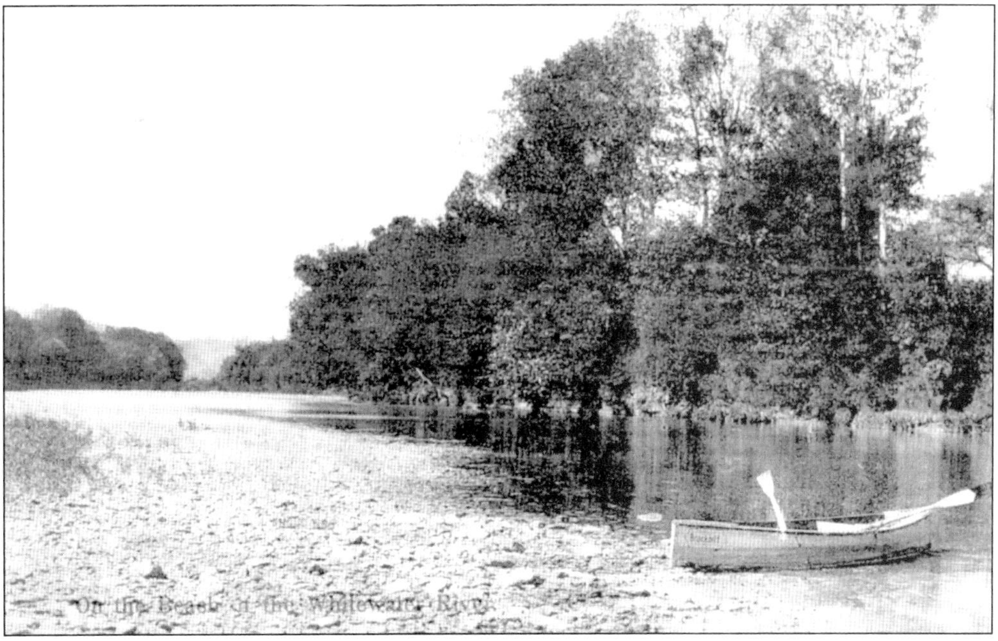

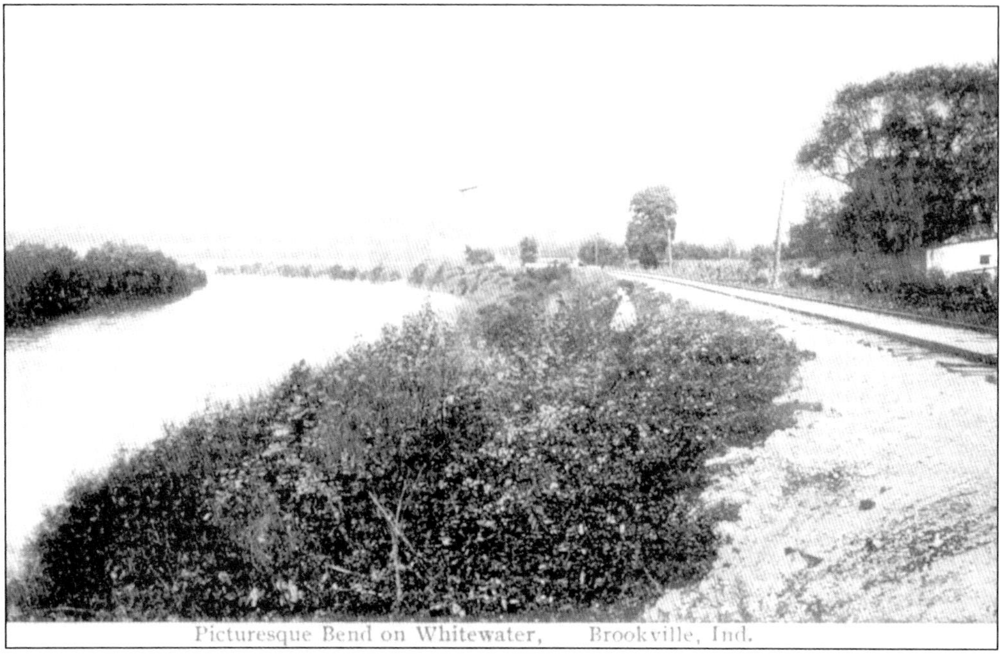

Traveling along U.S. 52 offers some great glimpses of the Whitewater River, particularly south of Brookville. When the railroad was built in the 1860s, it was placed on the towpath of the old canal. This artificial waterway had been situated close to the river out of necessity to maintain the water level in the canal. It was not a great location for the railway because of flooding.

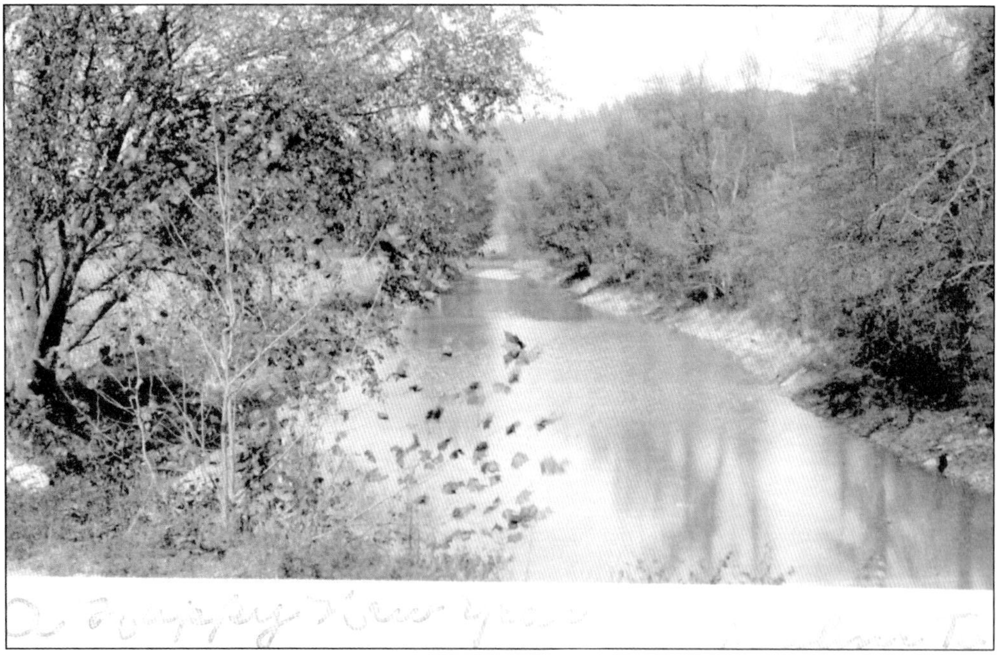

This postcard was postmarked in 1906. During that era, post office regulations determined that the entire back of the card was to be reserved only for the name and address of the recipient. Any greeting was limited to the white space on the front, thus the very brief New Year greeting from Pauline B.

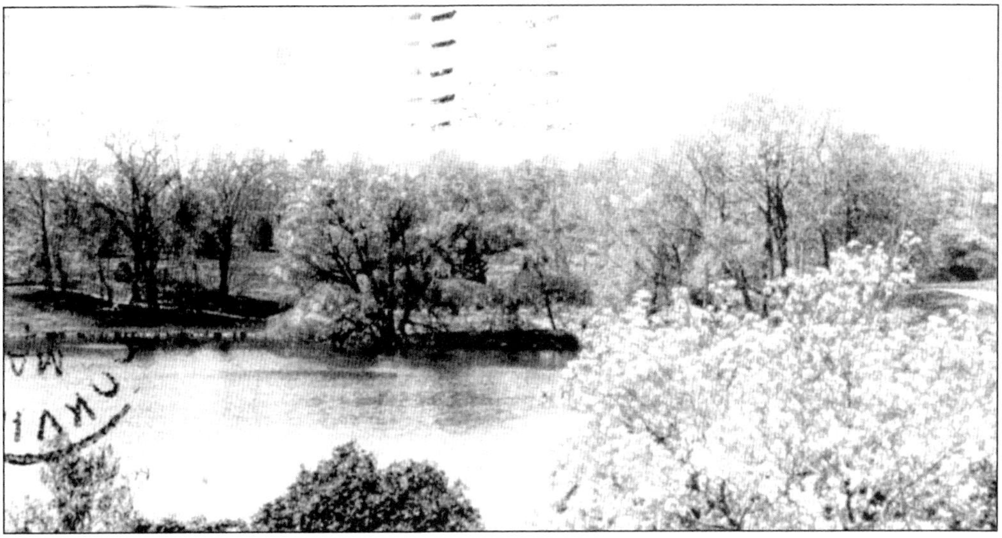

These postcards are both from Gus Baither's variety store. The Willows was a popular spot by the East Fork a short distance north of Brookville. It was a favorite place for fishing, camping, picnics, and, later in the evening, parking. Ben Winans took the photograph for the bottom postcard in 1903; it is likely that he took the photograph for the other postcard also. (Courtesy Glascock.)

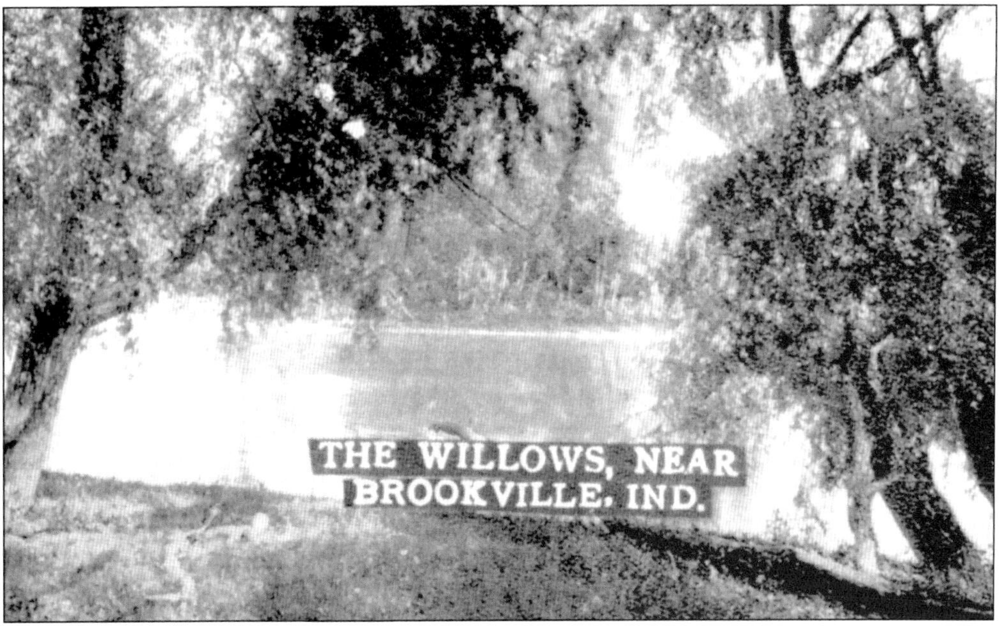

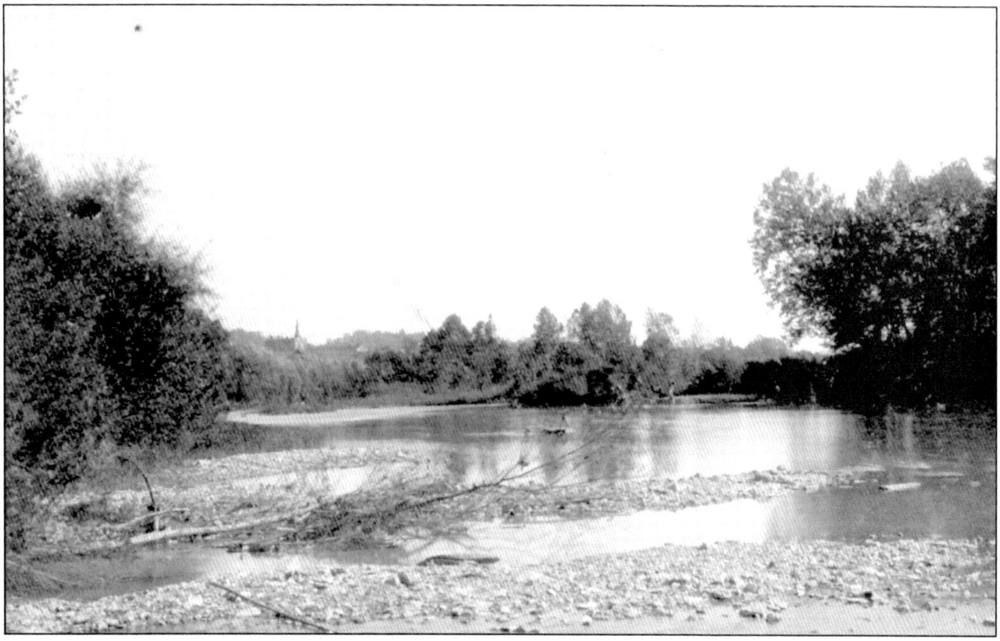

This image shows a typical view of what the East Fork looks like during times of low water, with many gravel bars and brush piles impeding any kind of navigation. The only landmark in this postcard is a church steeple in the distant left center. This appears to be the St. Michael Church.

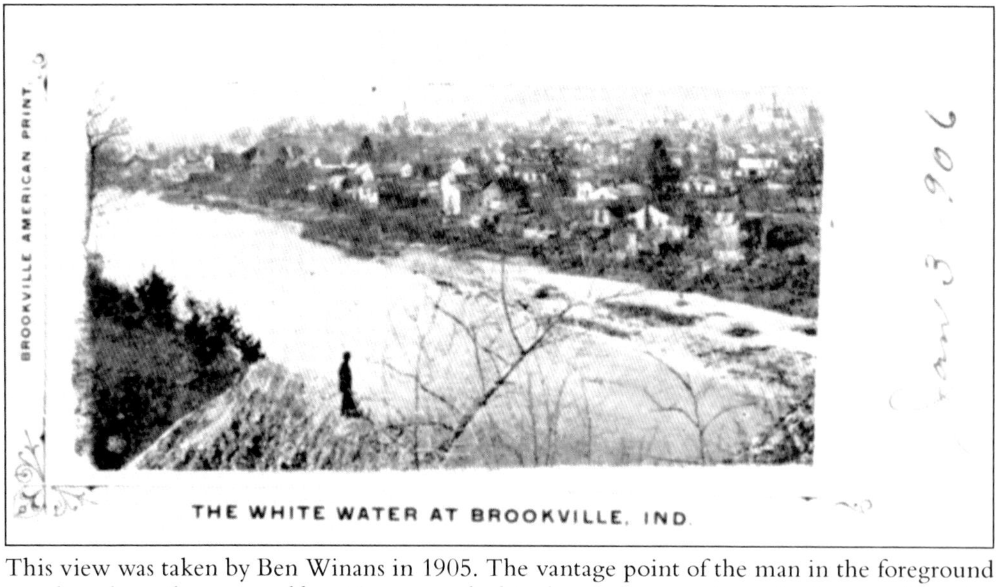

This view was taken by Ben Winans in 1905. The vantage point of the man in the foreground may have been the one used by Winans to take his classic photographs of the Speer mills in the Hermitage chapter. The St. Michael Church is in the upper center, and the courthouse and town building are in the upper right. Across the river, the south valley residential area dominates the scene. (Courtesy Hauberg/Quinton.)

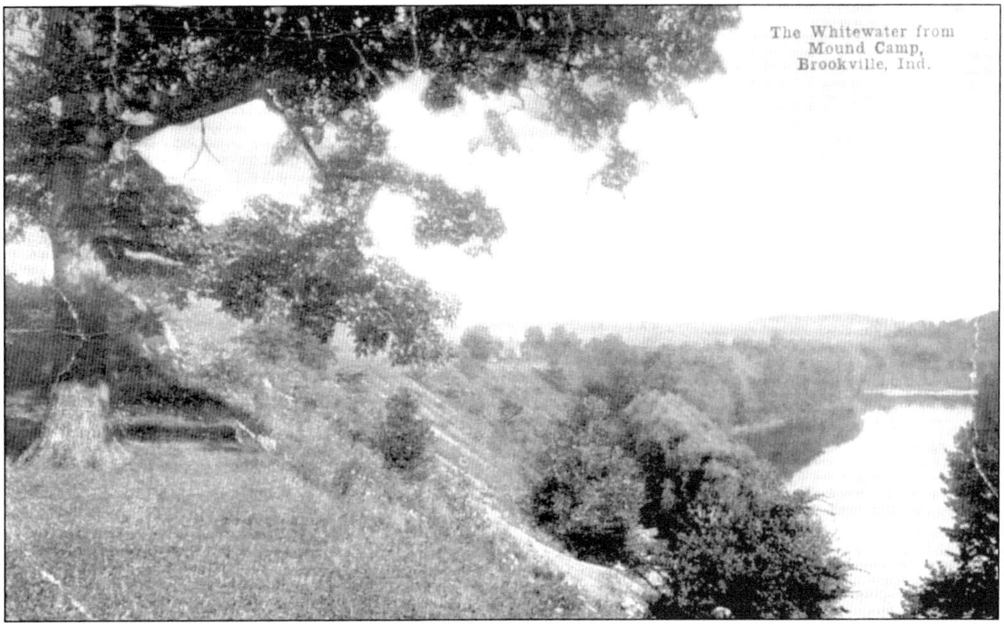

Native American burial mounds on the highest hills near Brookville testify to the historical significance of the area. Evidence collected from these mounds indicates that they were used for burial and ceremonial purposes. It is also believed that since these mounds were built on the highest points of ground along the river, one within sight of the next, that they were also used as a communication network.

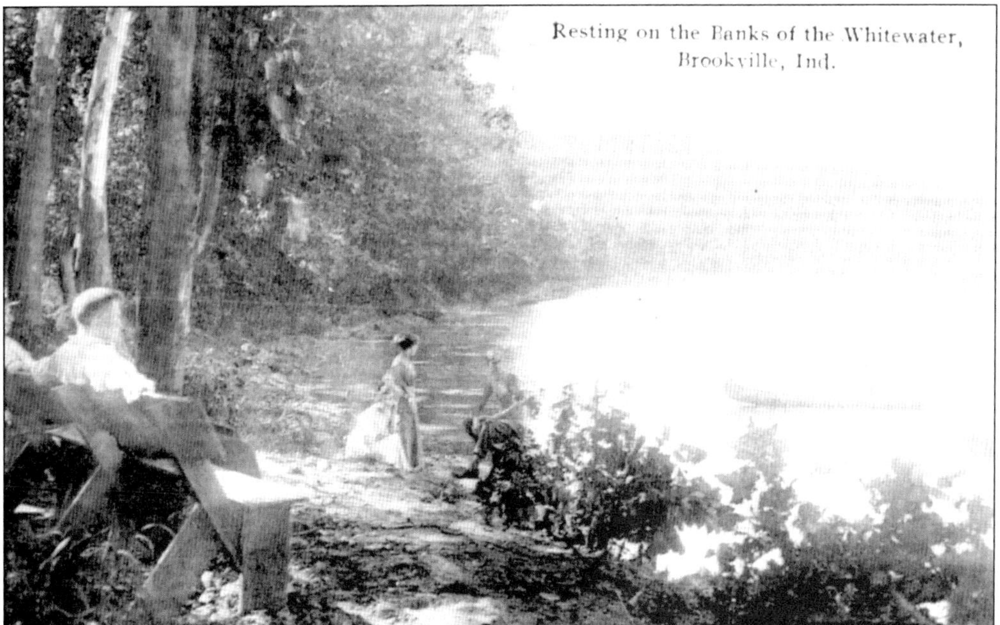

A group of people relax along the river's edge in this postcard, perhaps on a Sunday afternoon. Brookville's unique location between the East and West Forks of the Whitewater River provided people with great opportunities for canoeing and just resting.

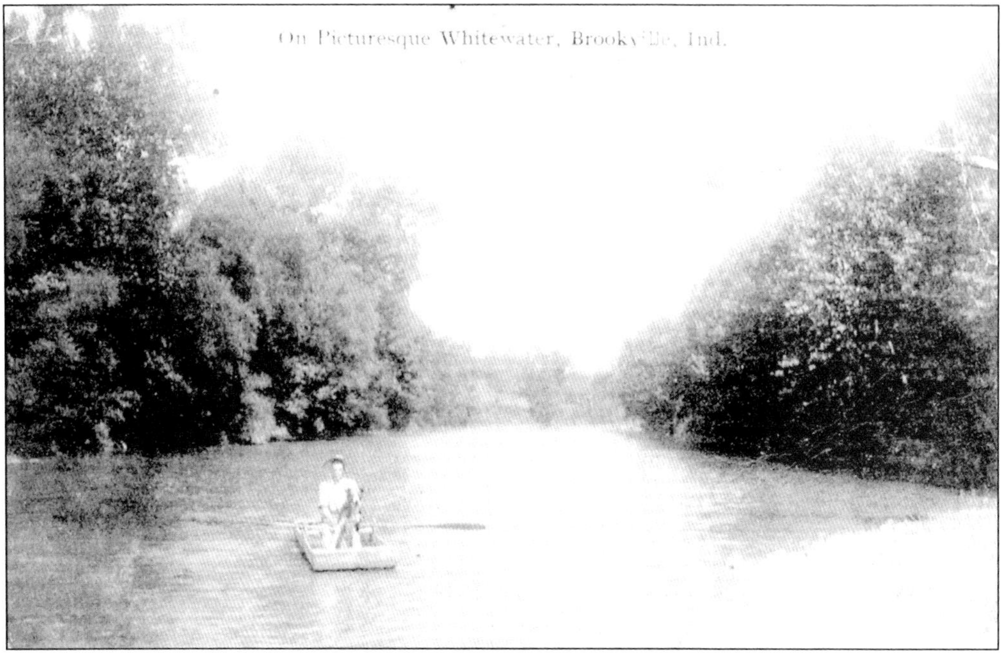

A boy rows his dog out into a quiet pool on the Whitewater River in what appears to be a homemade wooden rowboat. Postmarked in 1915, this postcard shows the river in summertime with the cottonwood and sycamore trees towering along the banks. As this lone paddler shows in the undated postcard below, the Whitewater River has always been popular with canoeists.

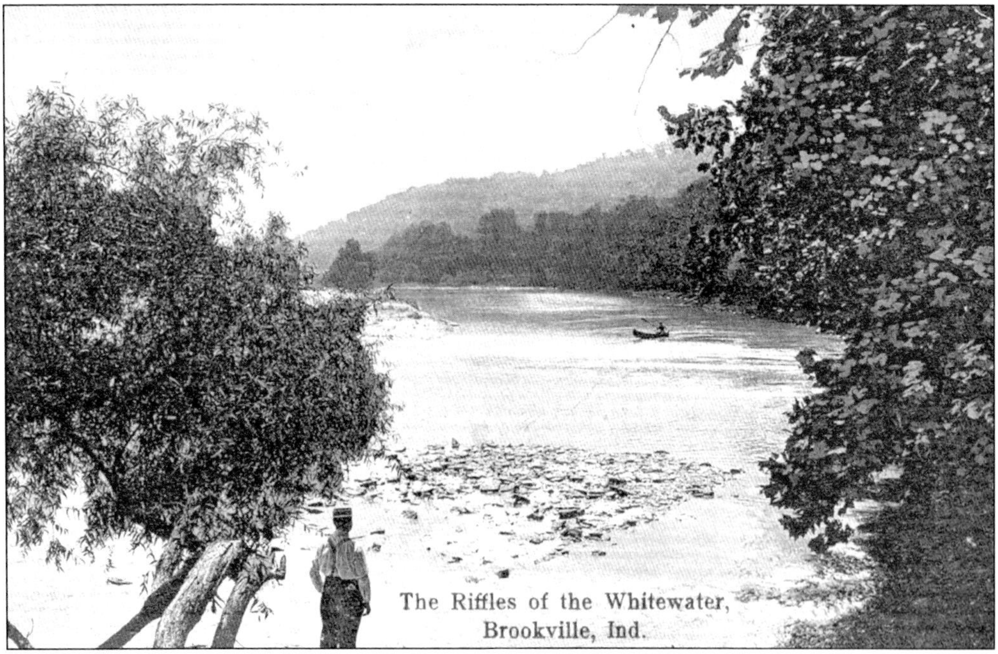

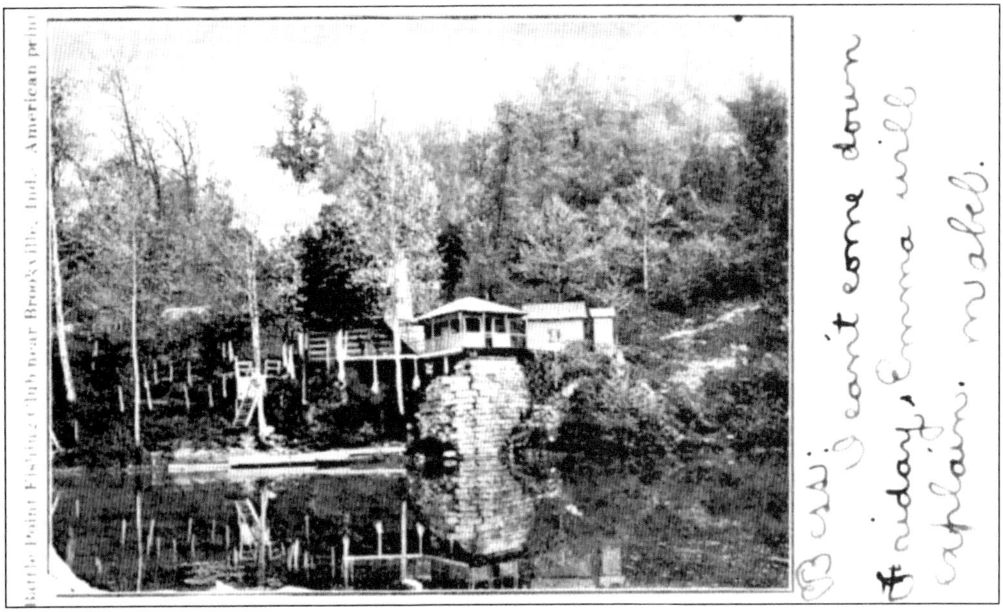

Not much is known about the Battle Point Fishing Club. Battle Point refers to a location along the East Fork of the Whitewater where Native Americans built a crescent-shaped earthwork on top of the hill. It was on the west side of the East Fork between Brookville and Fairfield. When the Brookville Reservoir filled, all traces of the club site were covered by water. The prominent stonework in front of the club buildings was said to be the remains of a covered bridge that was destroyed by a flood in 1898. The larger building probably was used for sleeping quarters and was apparently a log structure, as seen in the top postcard. The two center buildings were likely used for cooking and eating. The small building at the right was an outhouse.

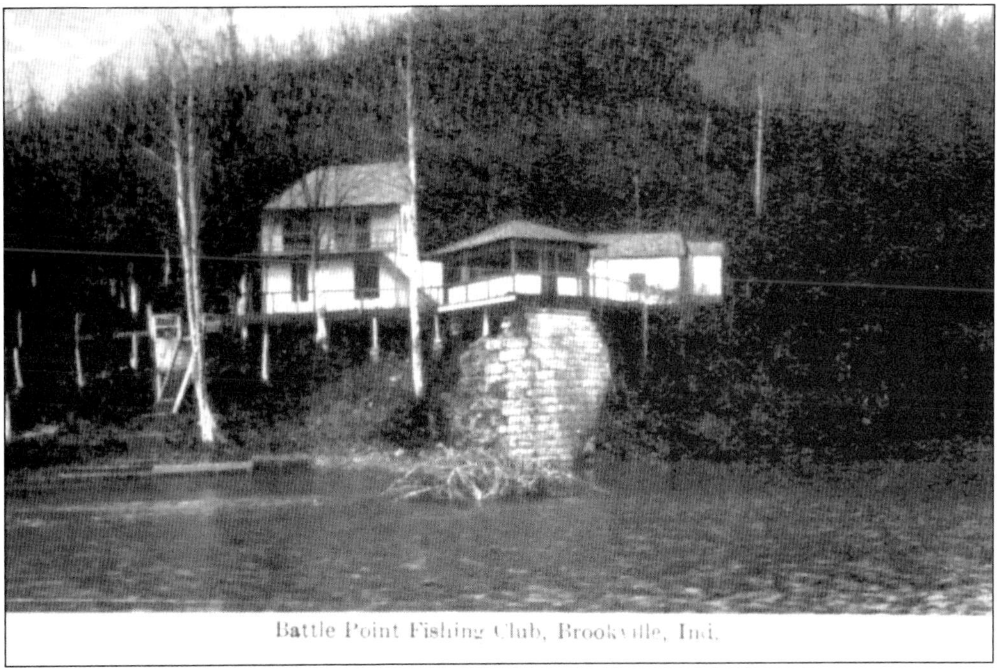

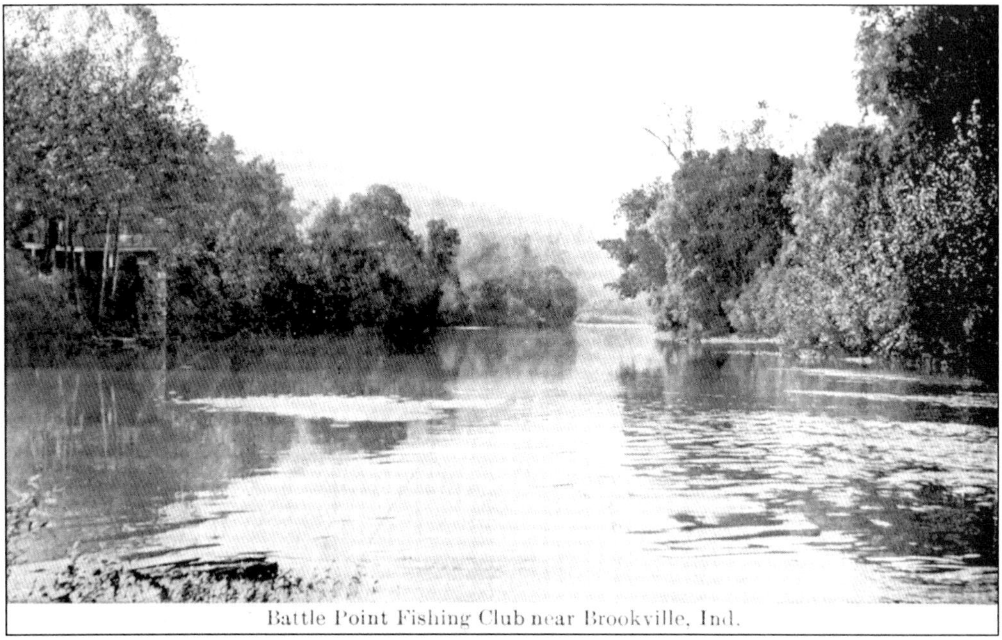

This postcard shows an upstream view of the river and the fishing club. The site for the club was probably chosen as a favorable place for fishing because of the depth of the river channel here. Ben Winans took this image in November 1905.

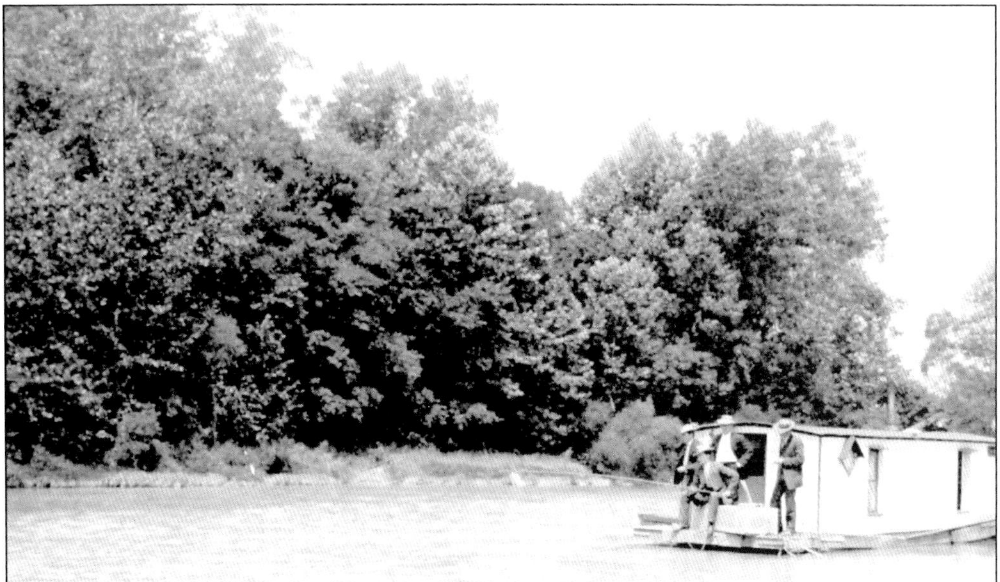

These four well-dressed gentlemen are enjoying a cruise on the river in this card postmarked 1908. The one sitting has a long cane fishing pole. The other three seem to be along for the ride. There was a houseboat resembling this one in a separate photograph by Ben Winans taken in 1903. It was the living quarters of a man named McAdams who docked under the Fourth Street bridge.

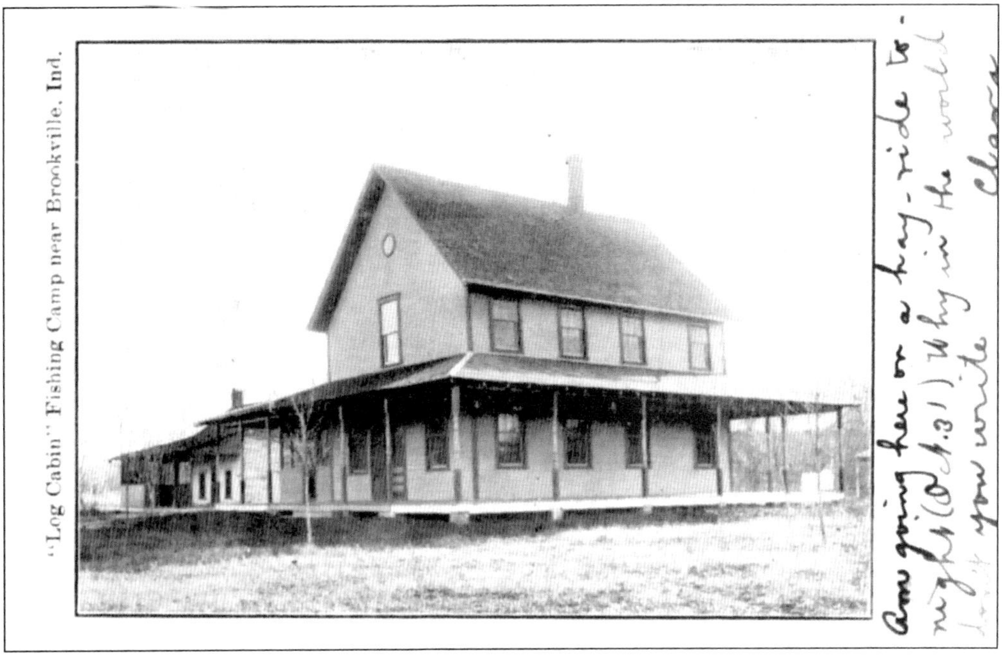

The specific location of the Log Cabin Fishing Camp is uncertain, and it was completely washed away in 1913. The image above was taken by John W. Baker, an associate of Ben Winans, in 1905. It shows an older building at the left; undoubtedly that is where the camp got its name. Evidently the club prospered and was able to build a much larger clubhouse. The bottom postcard suggests that the camps were primarily for men. The smaller camps may have been for families. The message on the back of the card suggests this may have been a rental property as it says, "If you haven't got your supplies yet, write to the Co., giving them a jacking up." A close examination of the postcard at bottom reveals the leaves in the foreground are painted in by hand. (Above, courtesy Rowe.)

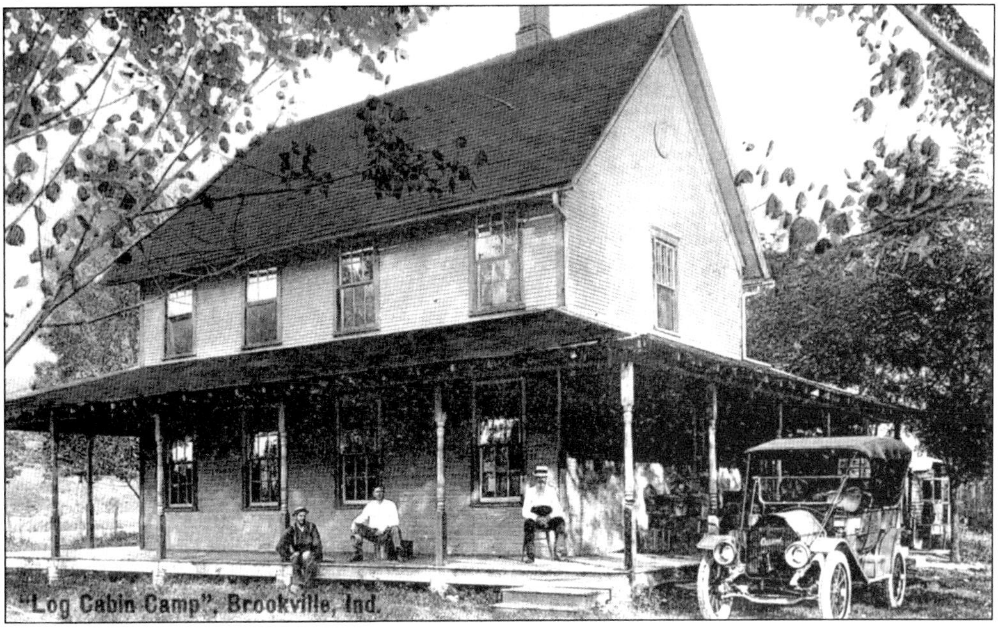

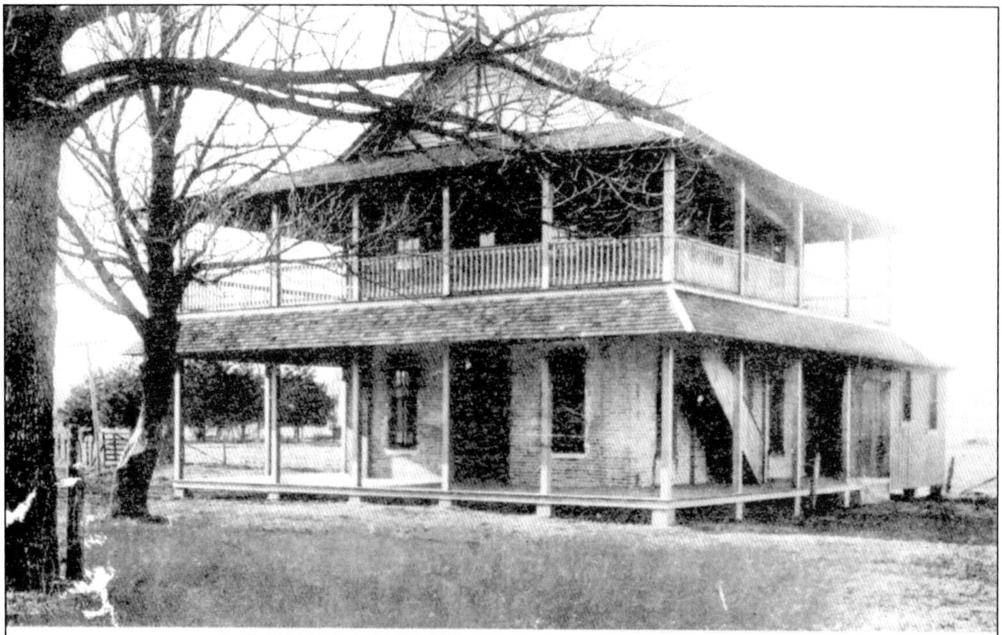

THE "MOUND" SUMMER CAMP NEAR BROOKVILLE, IND.

The Mound Camp was near the Whitewater River about four miles south of Brookville. At one time, there were two Native American mounds near the building, but they were destroyed when the highway was built. The open porches around the upper and lower levels of the building were later additions. The structure inside the porches was a brick building erected in 1883 as the Mound Presbyterian Church. It was a mission church of the Brookville Presbyterian Church. In 1904, the church closed and sat empty until 1910, when Charles Samoniel, a Brookville merchant, bought it and used it for a fishing camp. The Mounds Restaurant opened in the building in 1921; it was famous for its fried chicken. Since 1955, a remodeled dance hall next door has been used for the restaurant. (Above, courtesy FCHS; below, courtesy Schlesselman.)

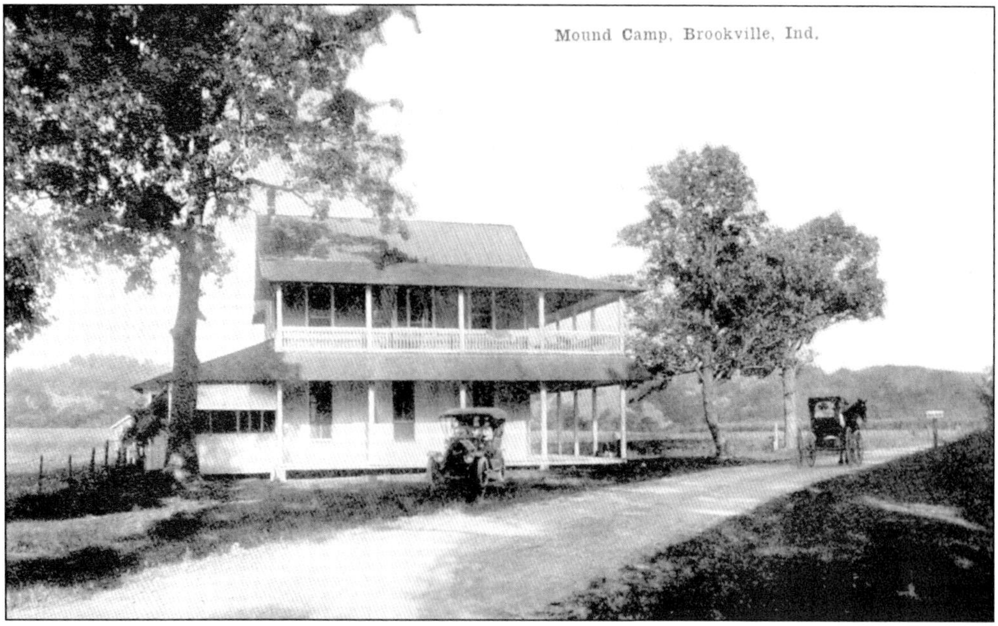

Mound Camp, Brookville, Ind.

Nine

Bridges and Floods

With the East and West Forks of the Whitewater River bordering Brookville, bridges have been vital to the town's transportation and commerce needs. There were five bridges built before 1900. Four were covered bridges, one was an "iron bridge," and none were safe when the Whitewater flooded. According to a 1959 report based on local newspapers, there were at least 18 floods during the years 1836–1959. The earlier floods caused major damage to the canal and the early mills. The 1898 flood had the highest waters within the memory of man up to that time and caused two deaths. But the flood that occurred in March 1913 was much worse. It affected a large area of the Midwest and hit Indiana with devastating force. It was the most tragic flood in the state's history and was responsible for 200 deaths and left about 200,000 homeless. Brookville was hit particularly hard. The National Weather Service archives show that the Whitewater River flood stage was 20 feet, and during the flood, the river crested at 39 feet. The flood caused untold damage to homes and businesses and caused the death of 12 people. Four of Brookville's five bridges were destroyed, and as some of the postcards in this chapter show, many houses in the valley were almost completely submerged.

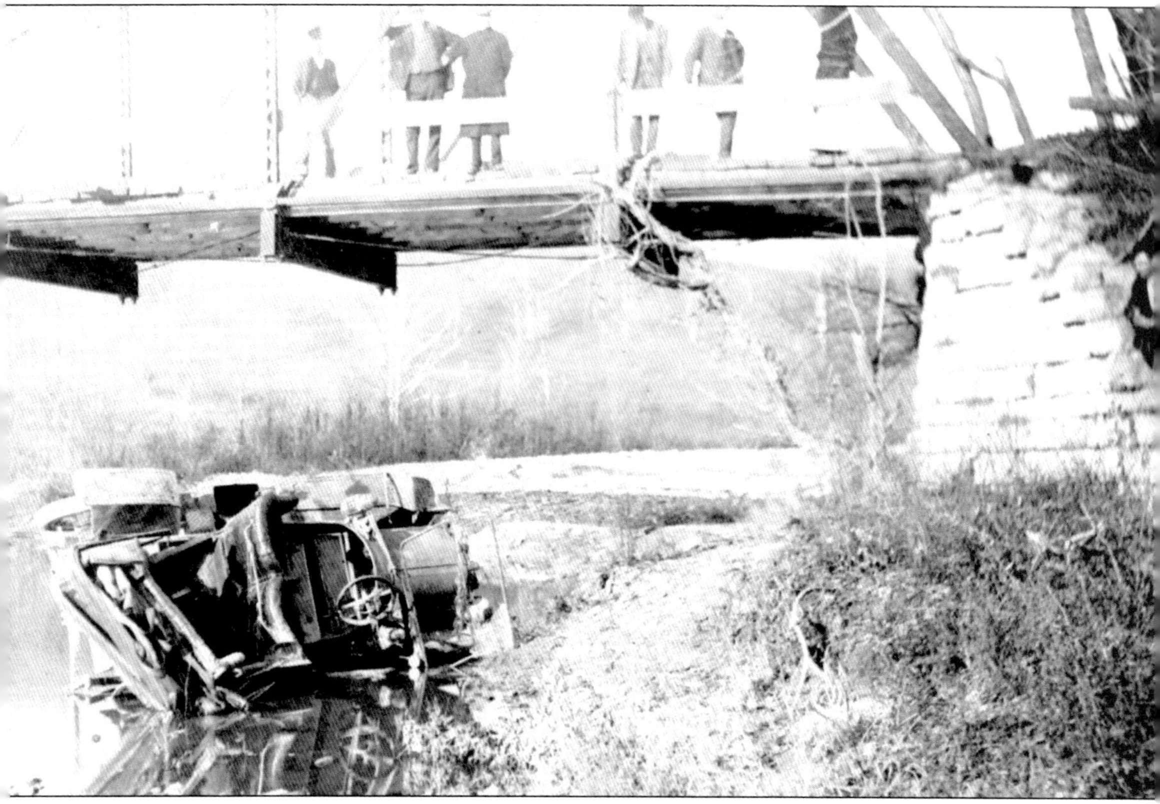

Some unfortunate person lost control of their machine and missed the bridge in this undated postcard. The brakes probably failed or maybe the driver was going too fast. From this perspective it is unclear what bridge this is. This postcard is a great example of the popularity of early photography in recording disasters, large and small, and making a postcard of the event. (Courtesy Jonas/Banks.)

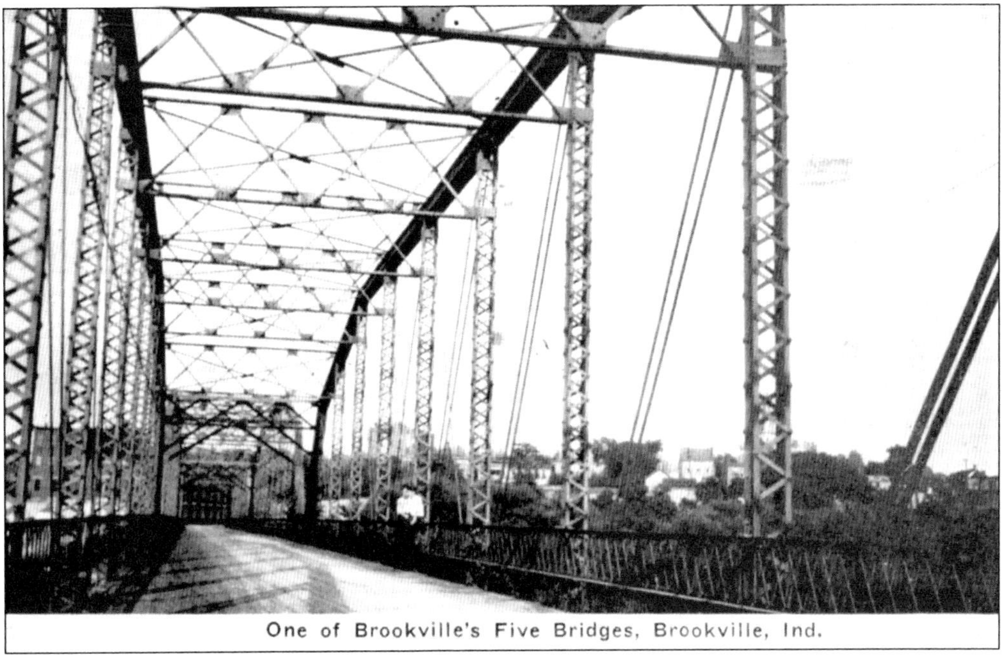

This postcard shows the Seventh Street bridge, which is discussed in more detail below. As this card attests, Brookville had five bridges—three over the East Fork, one over the West Fork, and one south of the place where the two join to form the Whitewater River. The fifth bridge was south of town and outside the town limits. (Courtesy Houchin.)

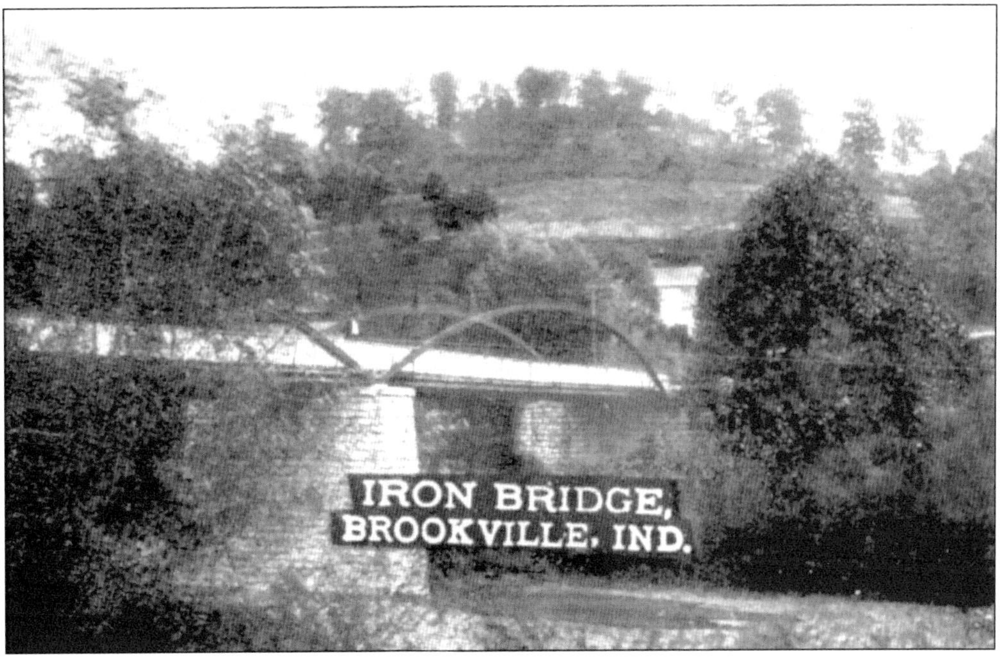

The Fourth Street "iron bridge" was different from all of the other bridges in this area at the time. The other structures were wooden covered bridges, but this one was an open bridge with wood floor supported by two bow-shaped metal trusses on each side. In 1912, a herd of cattle being moved across bridge caused the entire structure to collapse.

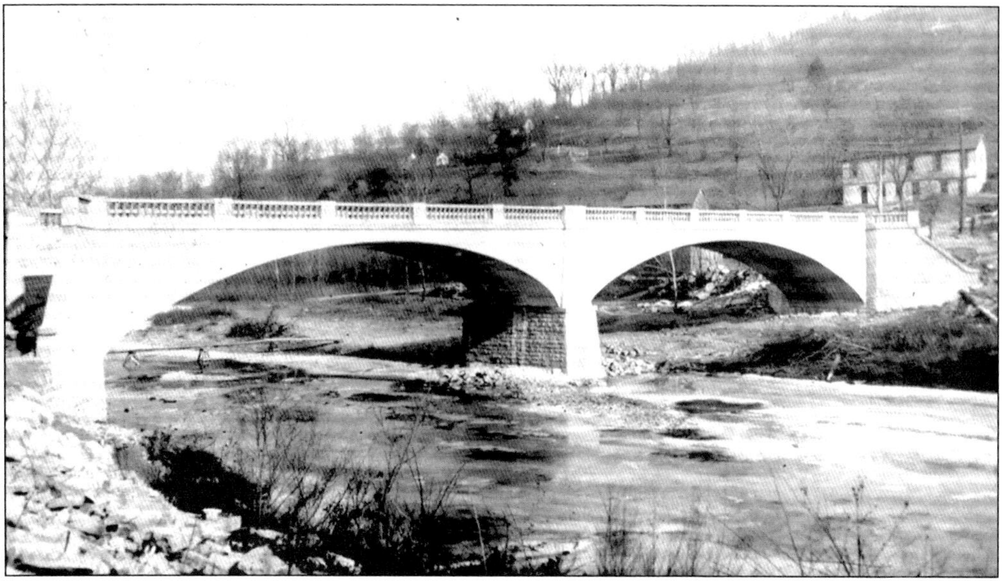

The sender writes on the back of this card, postmarked January 1913, "This is the bridge over the river we forded when we went to Brookville." This concrete bridge replaced the iron bridge but had a very short life. It had just been accepted by the county commissioners when the great flood of March 25, 1913, struck and destroyed it—two months after this postcard was sent. The remains of the ill-fated bridge can be seen in the bottom card. After the flood, a temporary wooden structure was built on the site; it served its purpose until a more permanent structure was built. Most of the debris was removed, but remnants of it could still be seen until a new bridge was built in 1982. (Below, courtesy Houchin.)

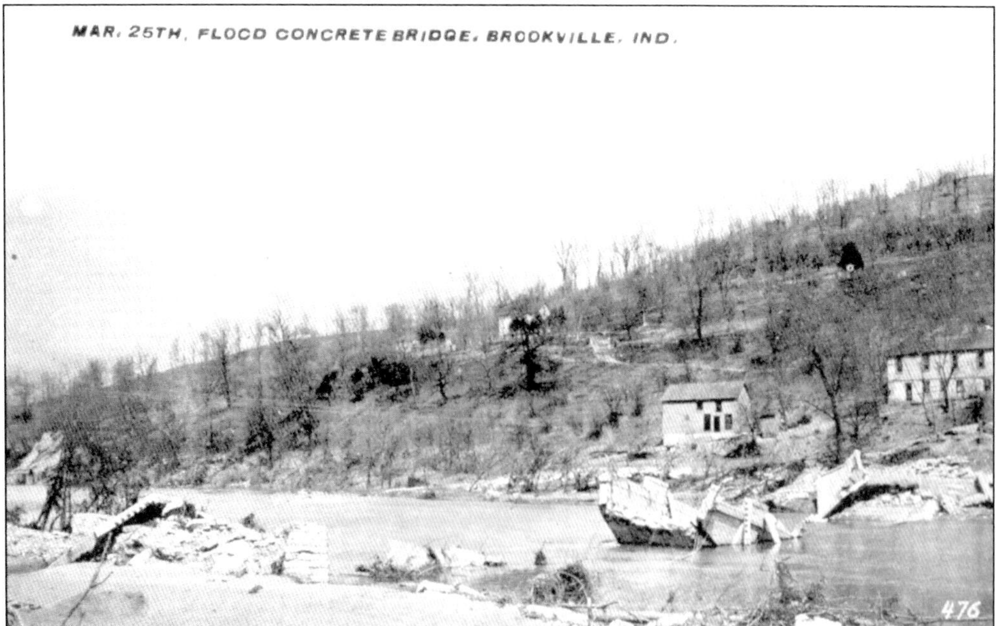

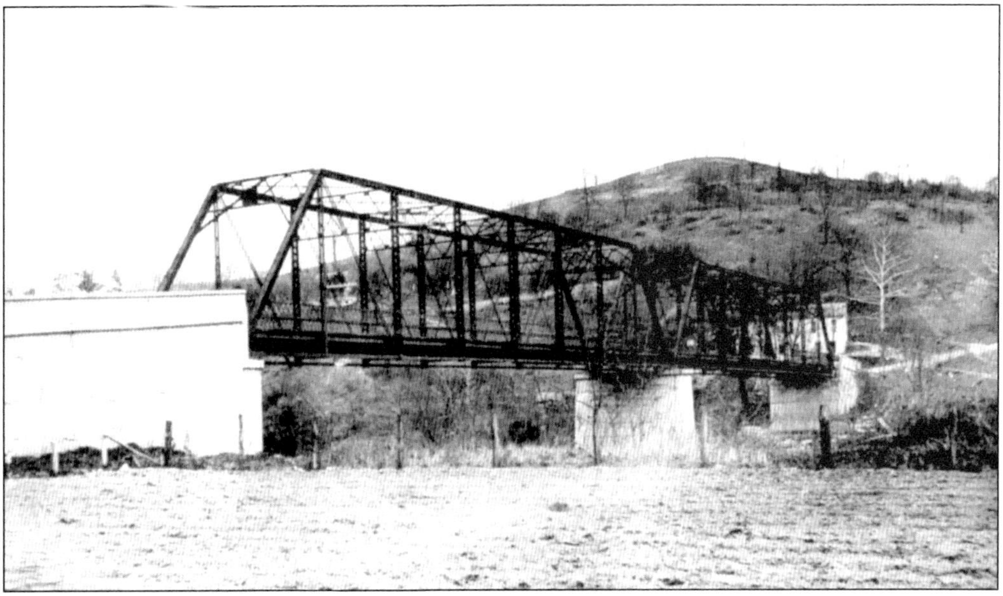

The fourth bridge at East Fourth Street was a steel truss type, built around 1917. This structure served its purpose well until 1973, when an overloaded truck caused a section of the floor to collapse. Repairs were made to allow the bridge to be reopened. In December 1982, the state replaced it with a modern concrete bridge. Unlike earlier designs, the current bridge is not level but was built on a slight incline allowing a more gradual approach to the Mount Carmel hill. (Courtesy FCHS.)

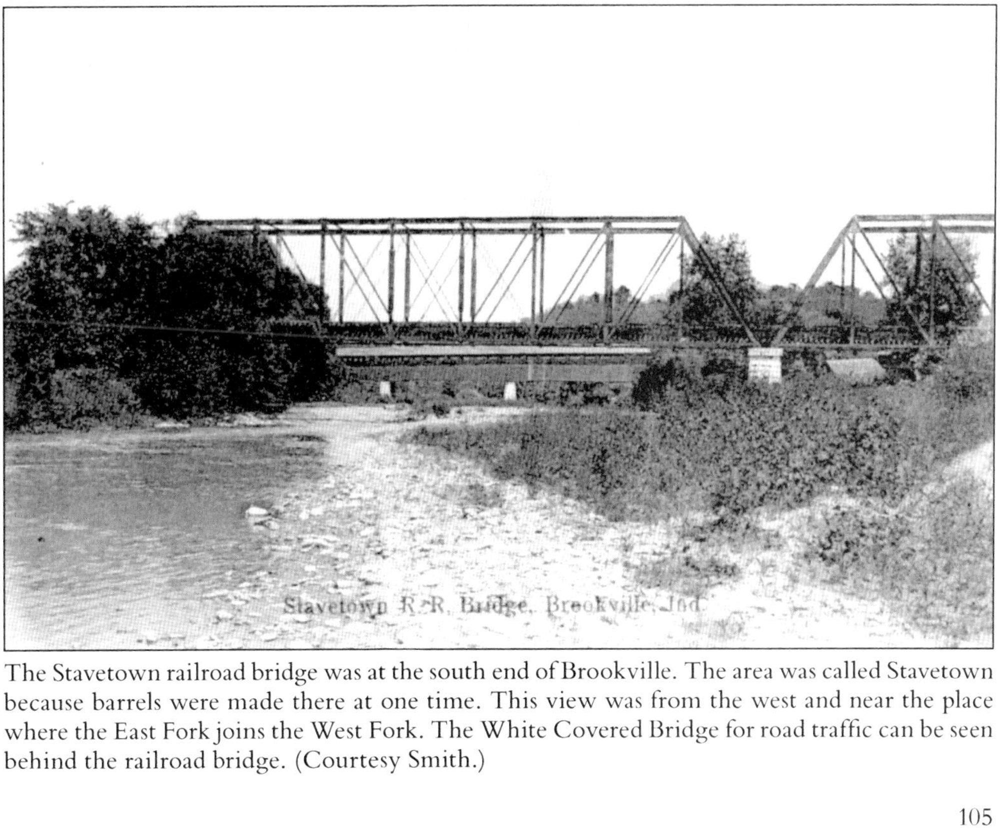

The Stavetown railroad bridge was at the south end of Brookville. The area was called Stavetown because barrels were made there at one time. This view was from the west and near the place where the East Fork joins the West Fork. The White Covered Bridge for road traffic can be seen behind the railroad bridge. (Courtesy Smith.)

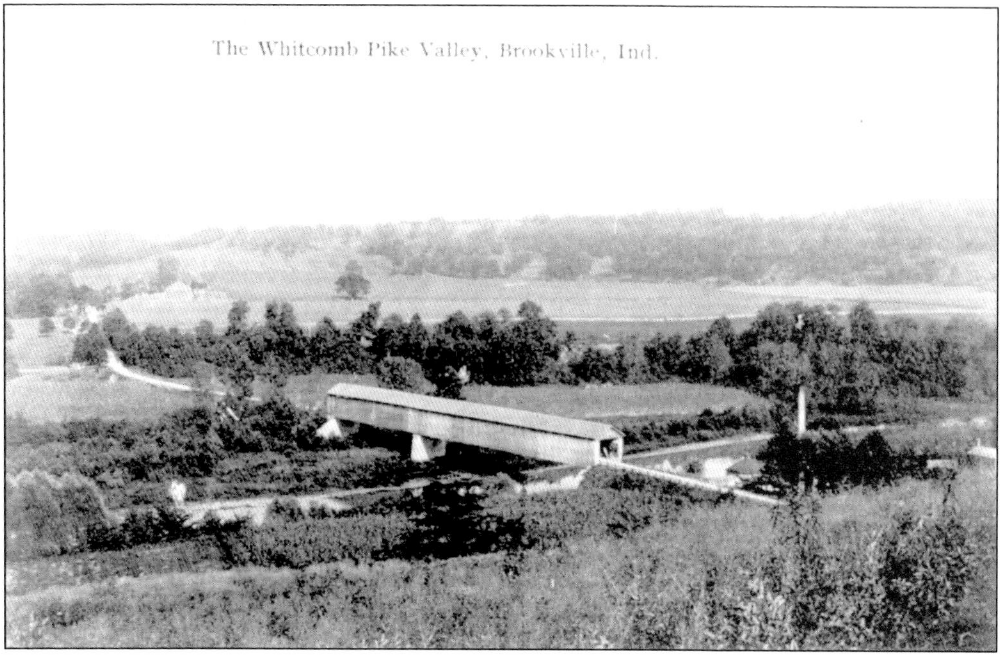

There were three bridges on the East Fork of the Whitewater River at Brookville. This is the upper bridge known as the Waterworks Bridge. The smokestack for the waterworks building is visible in the center right of this photograph. This bridge was the only one of five that survived the 1913 flood. The bottom card shows the west end of the bridge after the approaches were washed out in March 1913 and an extension was constructed to allow the bridge to be put back into use for horse-and-buggy traffic. The waterworks' stone well tank at the left partly blocks the view. This covered bridge was replaced by a steel truss bridge in 1934; that bridge has since been replaced by a reinforced concrete bridge and is now on State Route 101. (Below, courtesy Lamont.)

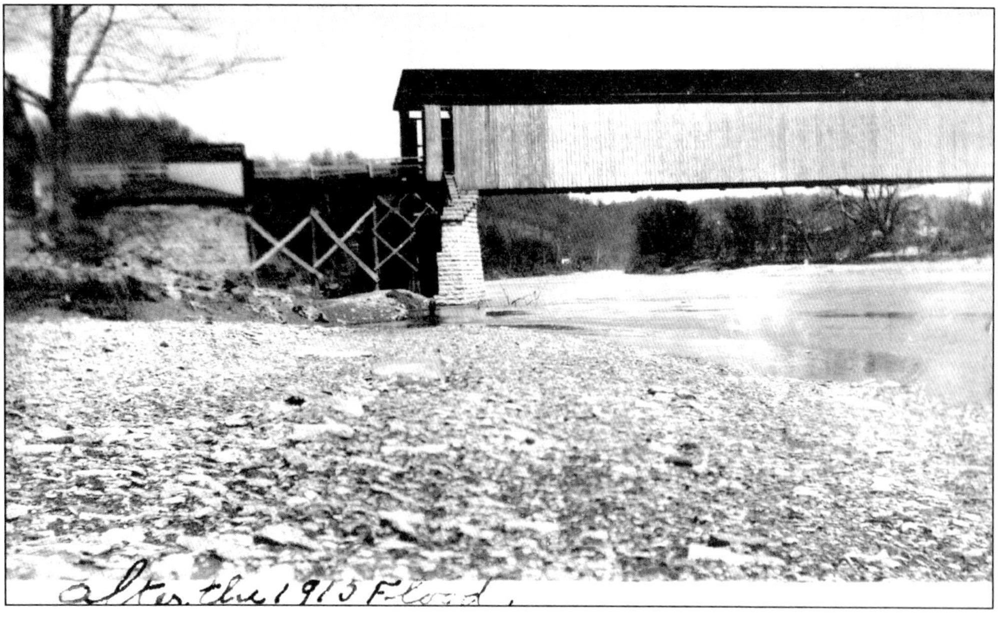

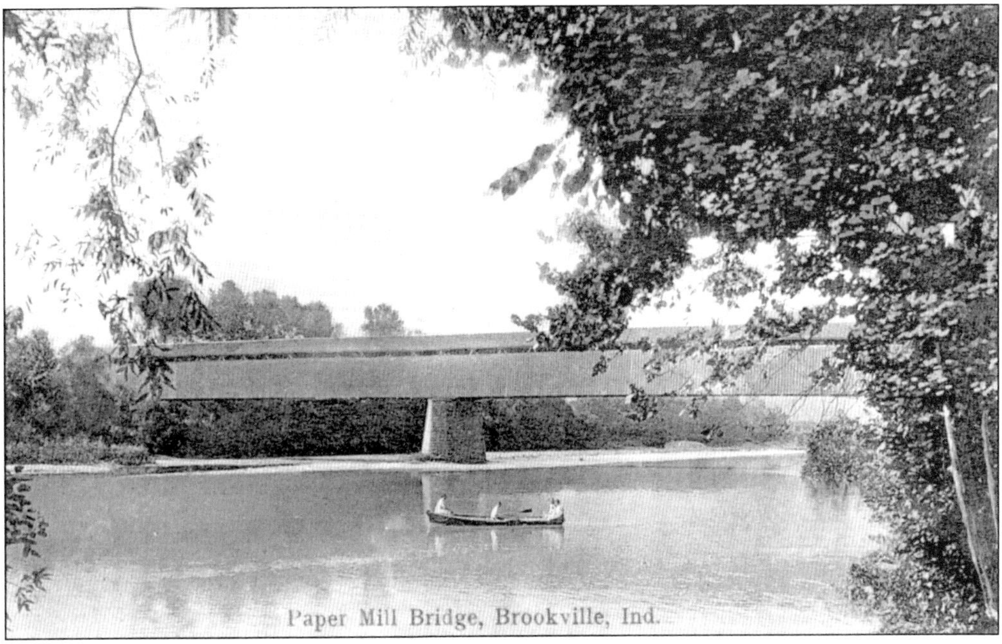

This bridge was just south of the paper mill and was known by that name. Like most covered bridges in the area, it was swept away by the 1913 flood. It crossed the West Fork and connected Seventh Street with St. Mary's Road. None of the bridges were rebuilt as covered bridges, and the structure that replaced this bridge was a triple-span steel truss bridge. This steel bridge was replaced in 1979 by a reinforced concrete bridge, but the remains of the steel bridge stood in place unused until it was taken down in 1996. The postcard below is looking from the west and toward the town. (Above, courtesy Rowe.)

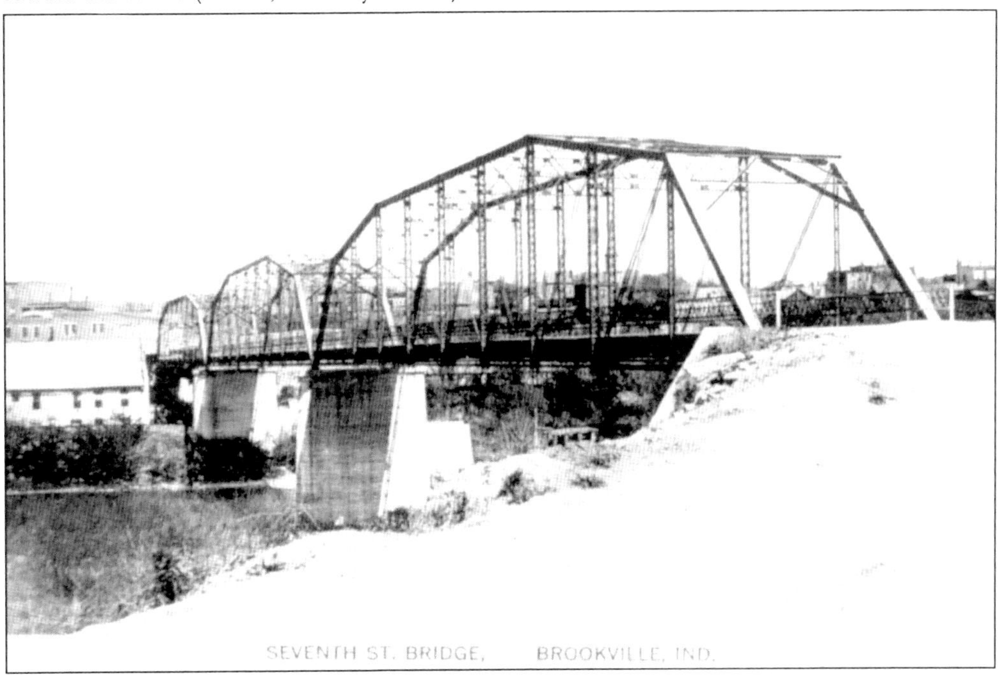

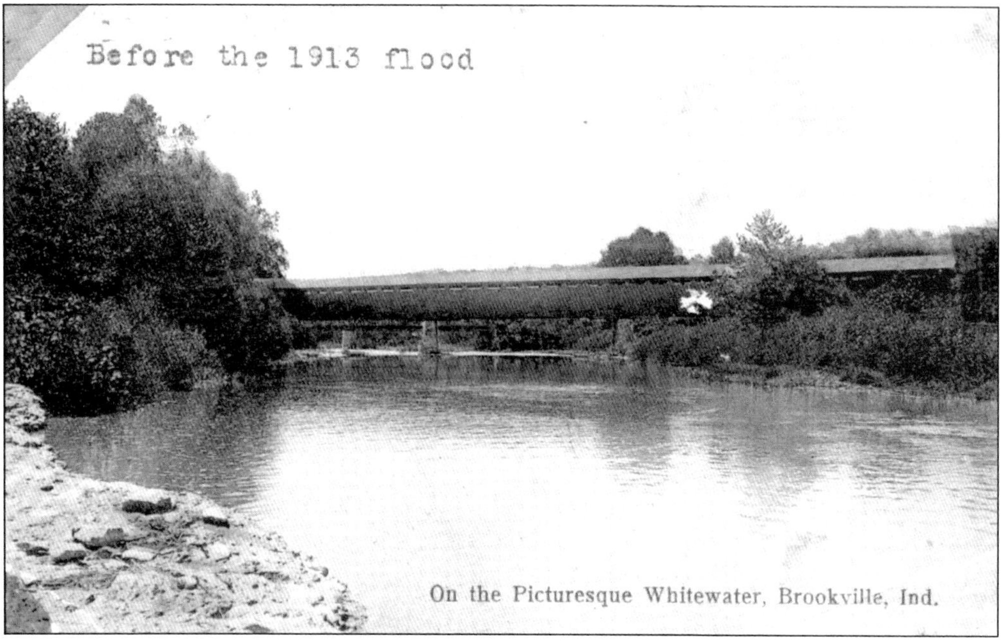

This card shows the White Covered Bridge from upstream. The stonework at the bottom left in this card was called the "cement" by the locals and was the jumping-in spot at this favorite swimming hole. The photograph below is a winter scene and a bit less inviting for swimming. Both the covered bridge and the railroad bridge were destroyed by the 1913 flood. While the railroad bridge did not float away, it was so badly damaged that it had to be replaced. It was replaced the same year as the flood; a plaque on the newer bridge says, "American Bridge Company of New York, U.S.A., 1913." This steel bridge had been fabricated in large sections and shipped here by railcar. (Above, courtesy Houchin; below, courtesy Lamont.)

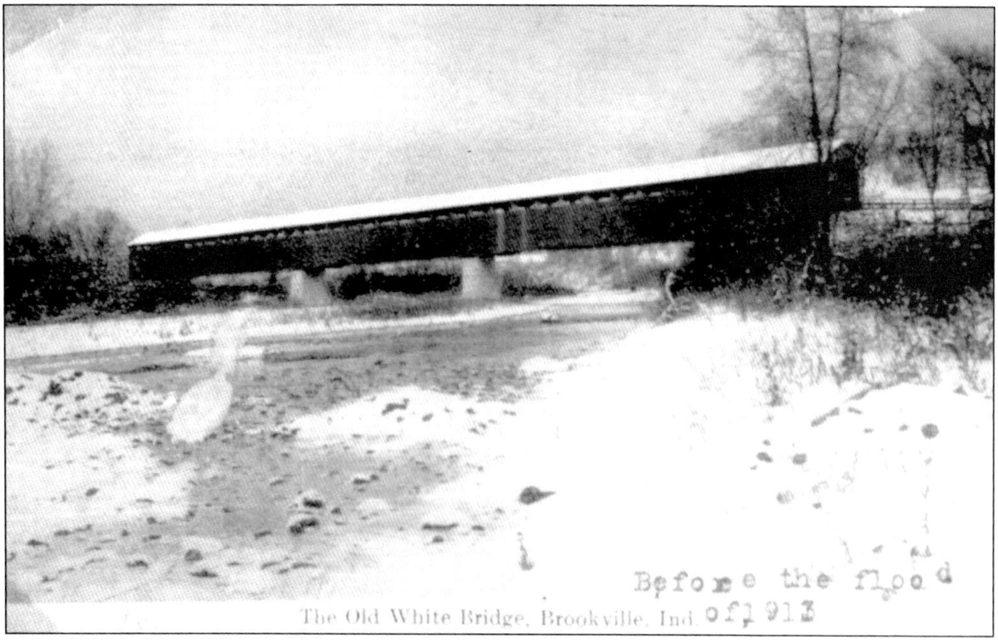

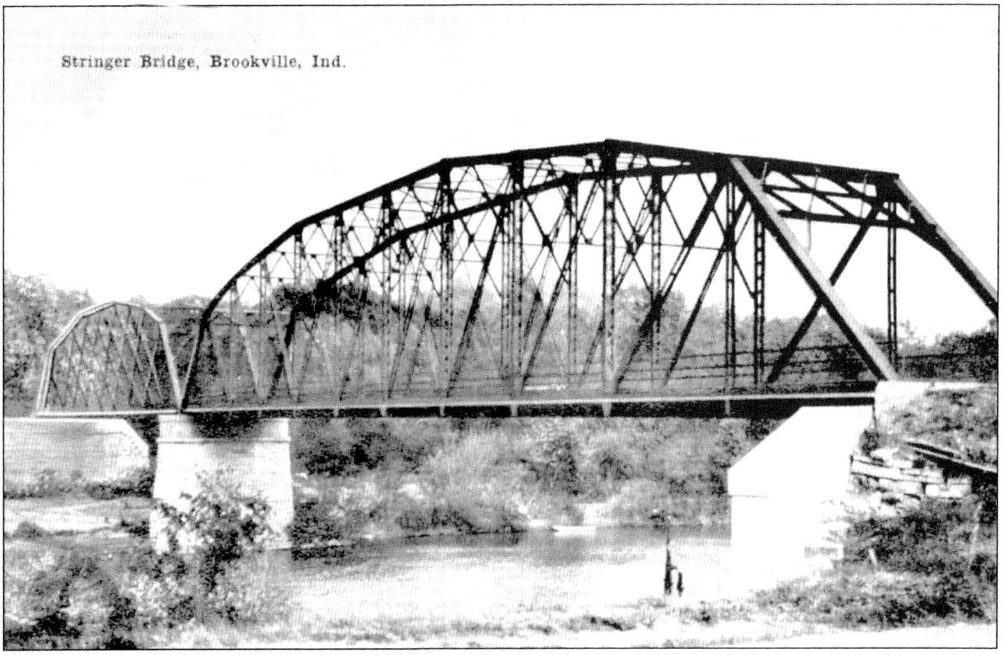

The Stringer Ford Bridge and the Poor Farm Bridge were one and the same. Stringer was the owner of the property that became the poor farm in later years. Before the bridge, there was a river ford on this spot, which was just south of the place where the two forks join to form the Whitewater River. The earlier bridge was a covered bridge, but it was destroyed in 1913. After the flood, the steel truss bridge was the engineering marvel of its time, but these were eventually replaced by reinforced concrete bridges with no visible supporting trusses like the covered bridges and the steel bridges. Today there is only one steel truss bridge remaining in the county; it is over Pipe Creek in Metamora Township.

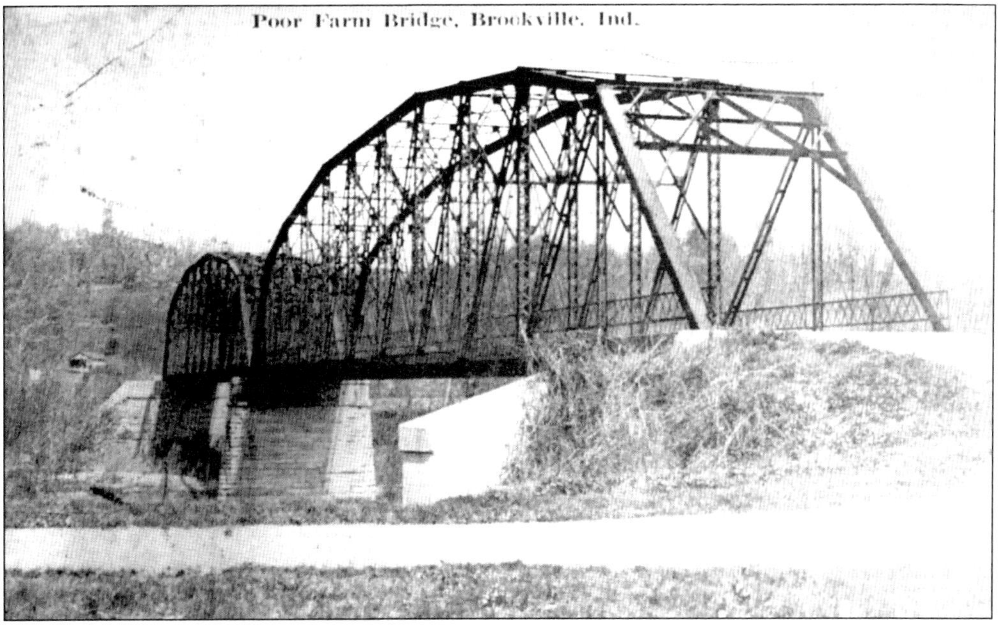

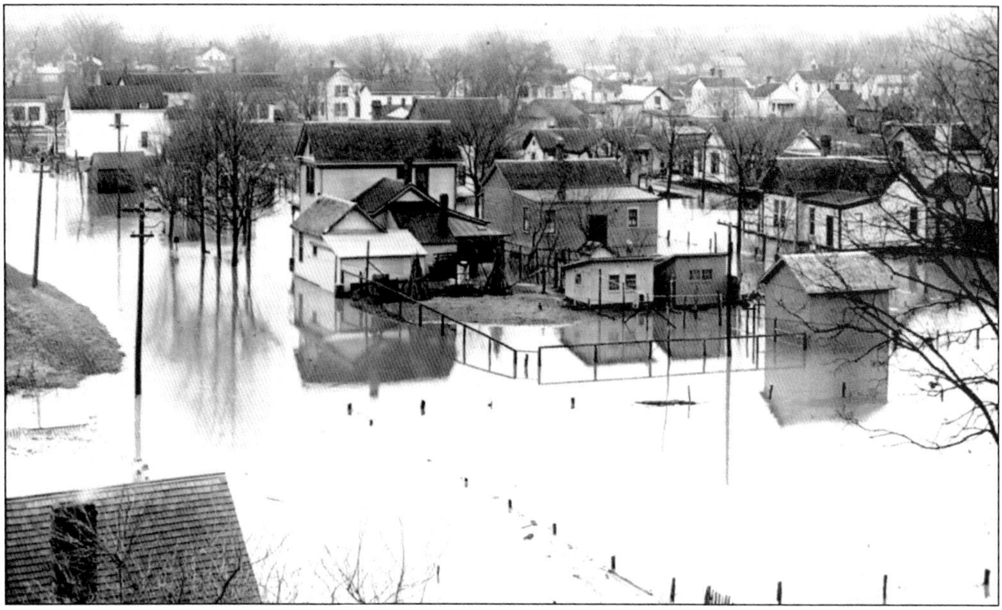

This postcard shows the view, taken from Bracken Hill, of some of the houses in the valley after the water had begun to recede. The postcard below shows the houses along Fourth Street after the water was gone. The two-story house at the right is the John Cleaver house at Fourth Street and Weber's Lane. The street was covered with mud and so were the lower floors of the houses. At the far left, the new Fourth Street concrete bridge is gone. Up and down the street groups of people are discussing their sad situation and the work they face to return their homes to habitable dwellings again, but no one appears to be working. Most of them were successful in cleaning and repairing the damage, but some homes floated off their foundations and were ruined. (Courtesy FCHS.)

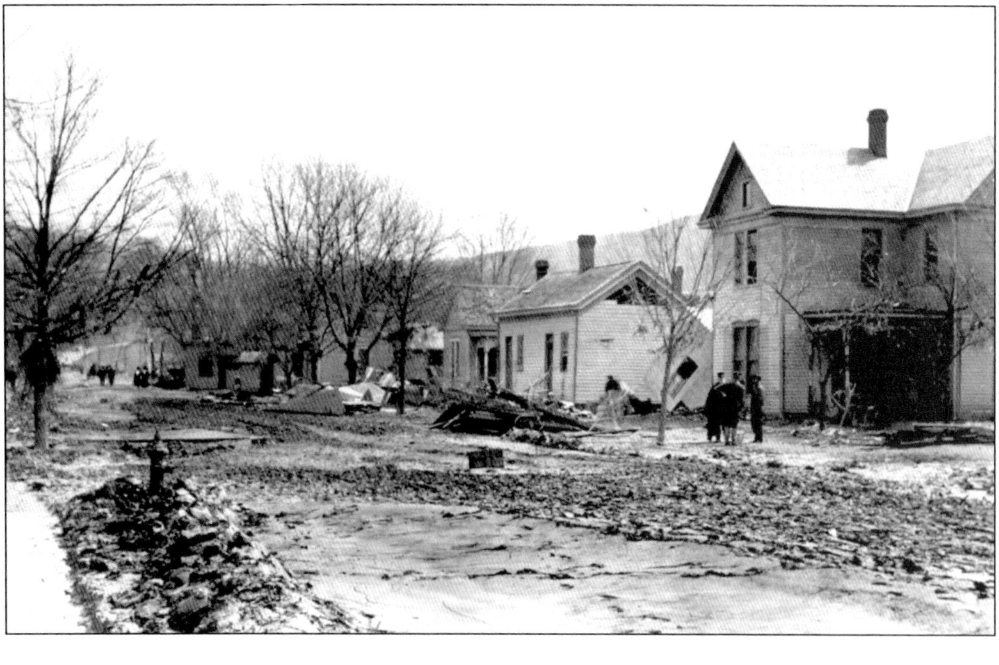

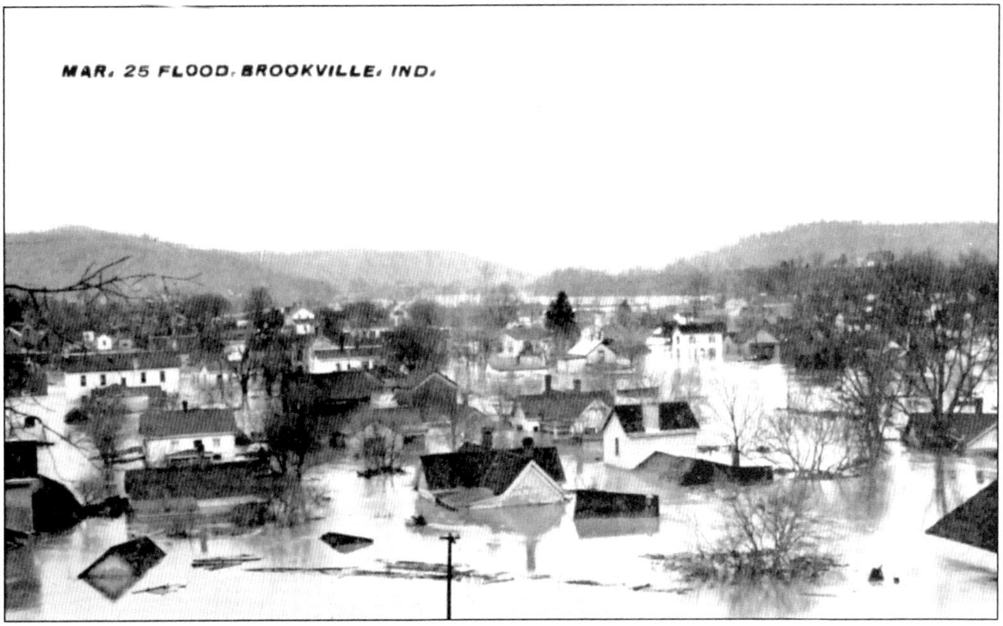

This postcard shows high water in the valley across Fourth, Fifth, and Sixth Streets where the water was the deepest. Seventh, Eighth, and Ninth Streets are on slightly higher ground. The photograph on this card was taken by Jacob Harry Swayne, but it was a Ben Winans photograph that told the photograph was taken "from Adam Peters'," which was by the hillside steps leading to Bracken Hill and the St. Michael Church.

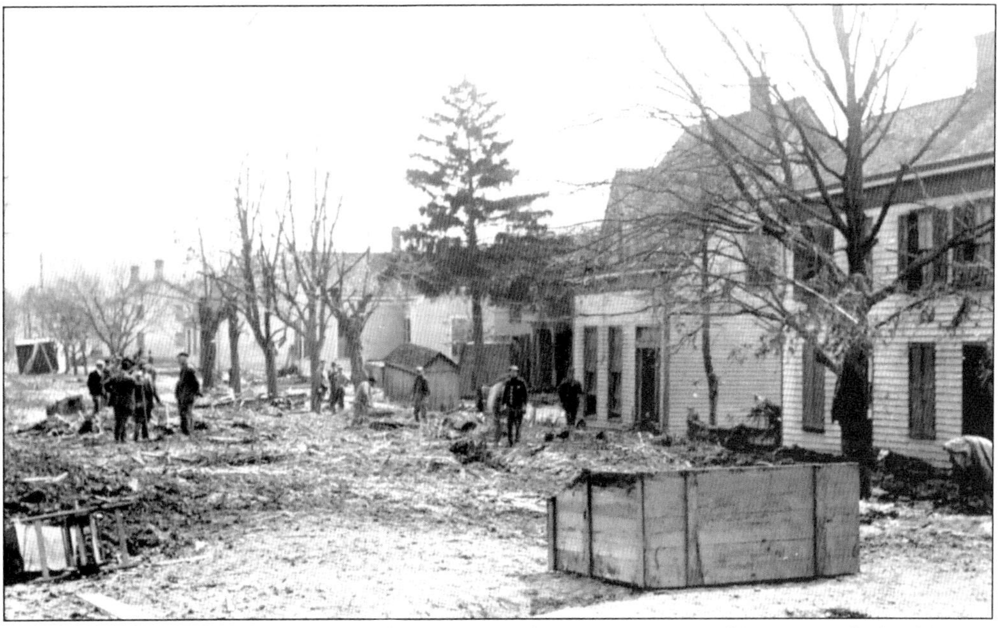

This postcard shows the aftermath of the flood on homes on lower Fifth Street. The building at the far left is the Franklin County Seminary, then a private home. Men and boys are gathered around but do not appear to have dug in yet to get the work done. Even today, mud can still be found in the inner walls and crawl spaces of buildings in the valley. (Courtesy FCHS.)

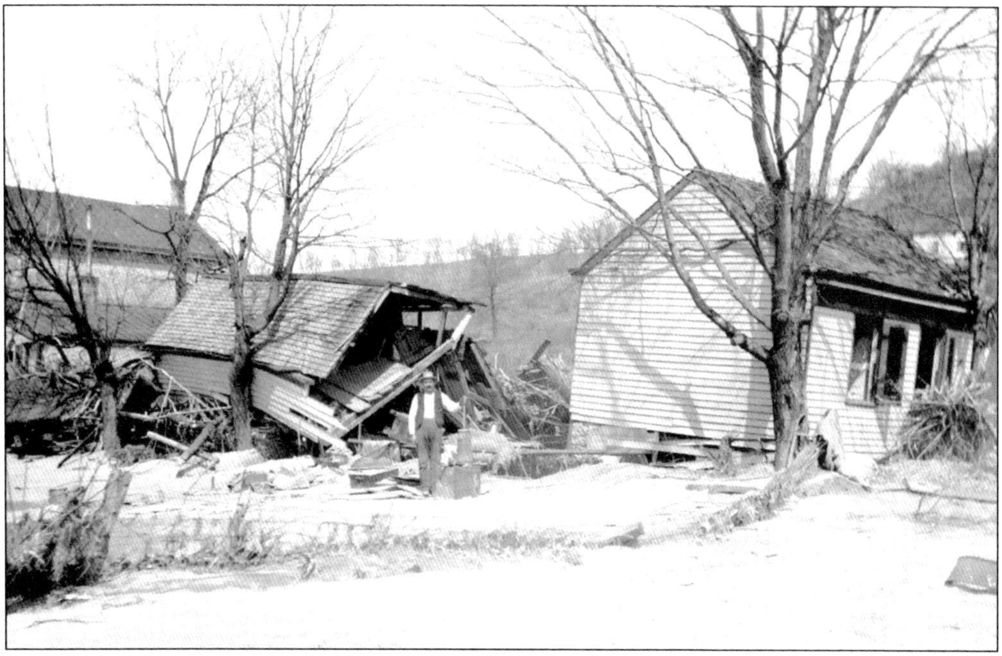

Small buildings, like the one at the left of center, were no match for the high waters, and many of them floated away and were broken in the process. Somehow the small house on the right seems to have remained on its foundation despite its close proximity to the East Fork. (Courtesy FCHS.)

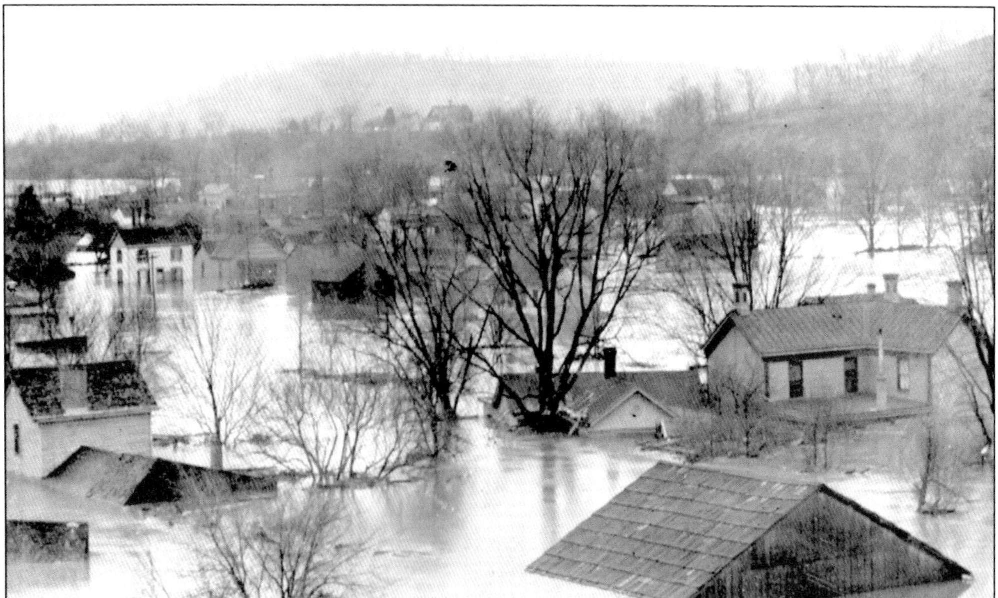

According to the 1913 flood report, this view was taken from the county jail at Fourth and Main Streets. It is looking toward the northeast and shows a general view of high water in the valley. It shows that the one-story houses and buildings were nearly covered. Some people who lived in two-story houses went to the second floor when the water rose and were rescued by boat later. (Courtesy Hauberg/Quinton.)

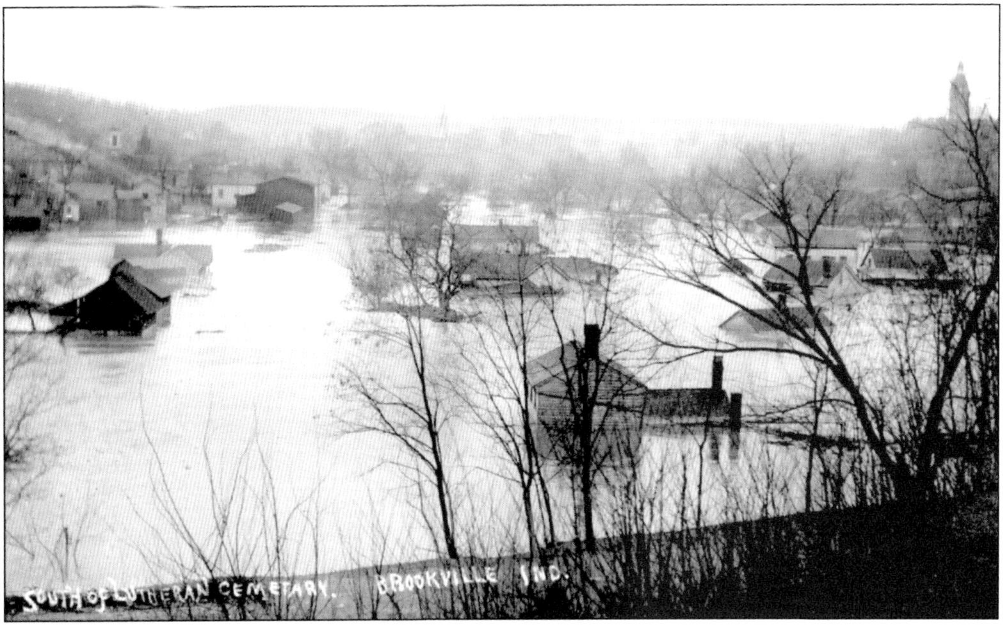

This view was taken from the Lutheran cemetery (town cemetery) on Tenth Street looking south directly at the St. Michael Church. The Lutherans were still using the old brick church in the cemetery in 1913. The Franklin County Courthouse, like the Lutheran church and the Catholic church, was on high ground and untouched by the floodwaters. (Courtesy FCHS.)

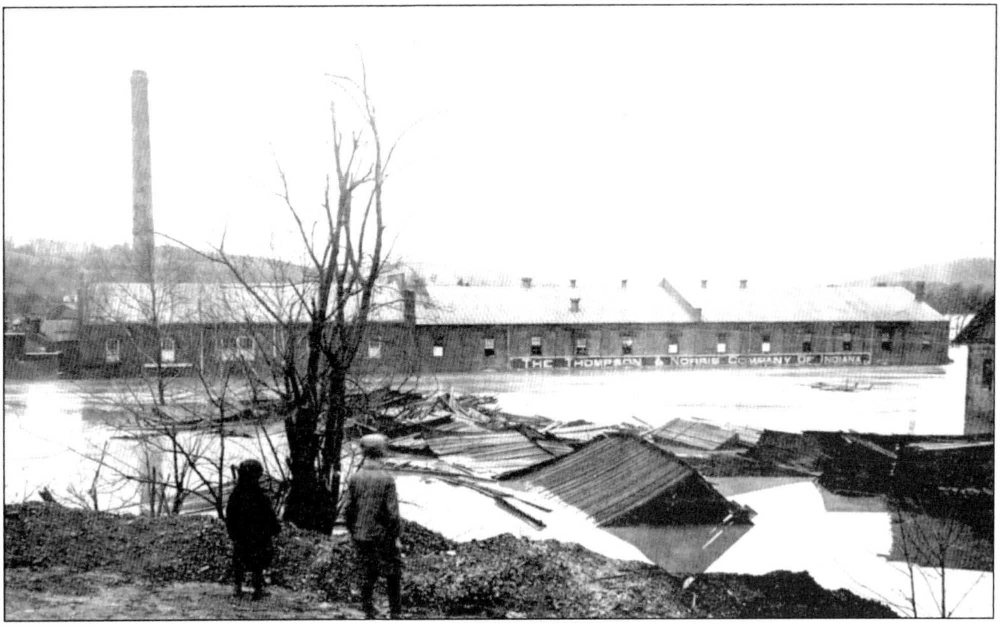

These children peer across the floodwaters at the Thompson and Norris Company of Indiana paper mill by the West Fork, which ordinarily was behind the factory. They are standing on the high ground near Seventh Street looking west. All traces of the river bridge and the train depot are underwater. (Courtesy Houchin.)

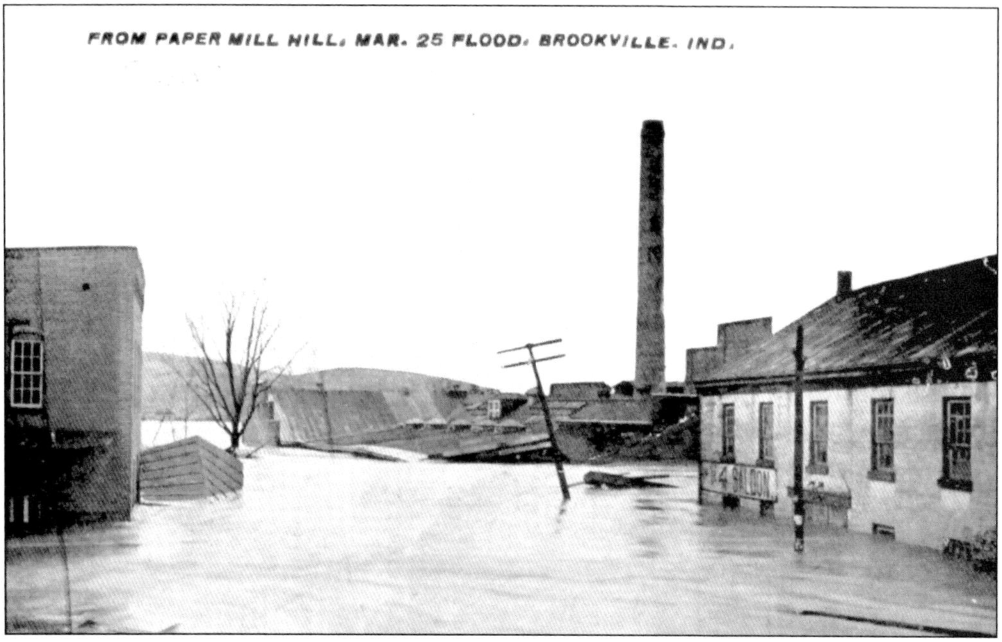

This postcard shows the office section of the Thompson and Norris building, to the left of the telegraph pole, almost completely underwater. The postcard below is from the same viewpoint after the water has receded and the roof has collapsed. The Big 4 Saloon is at the right. Since it was constructed of brick, it was not heavily damaged like the frame houses and outbuildings. (Below, courtesy FCHS.)

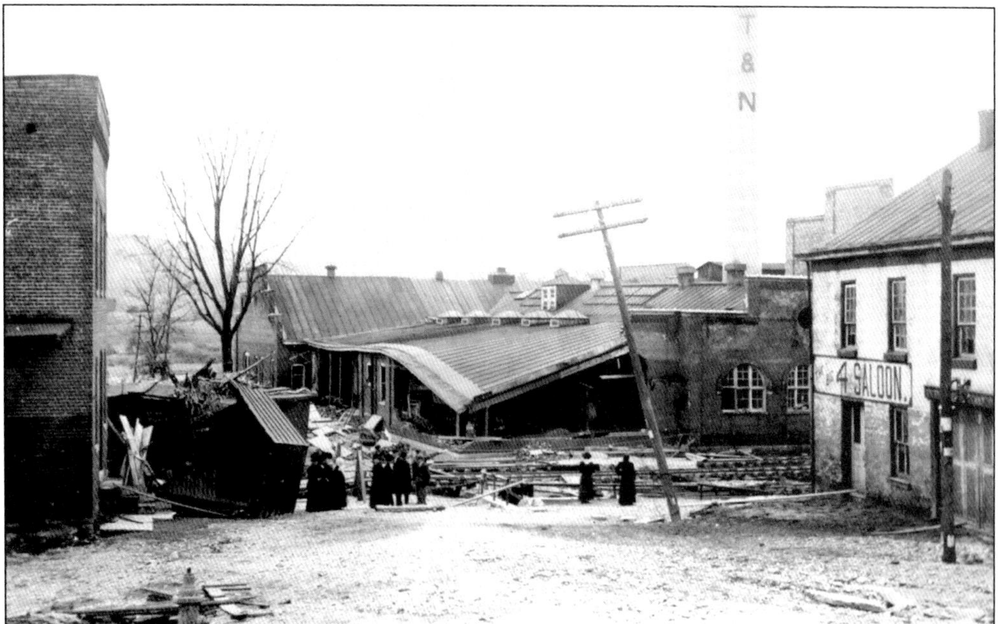

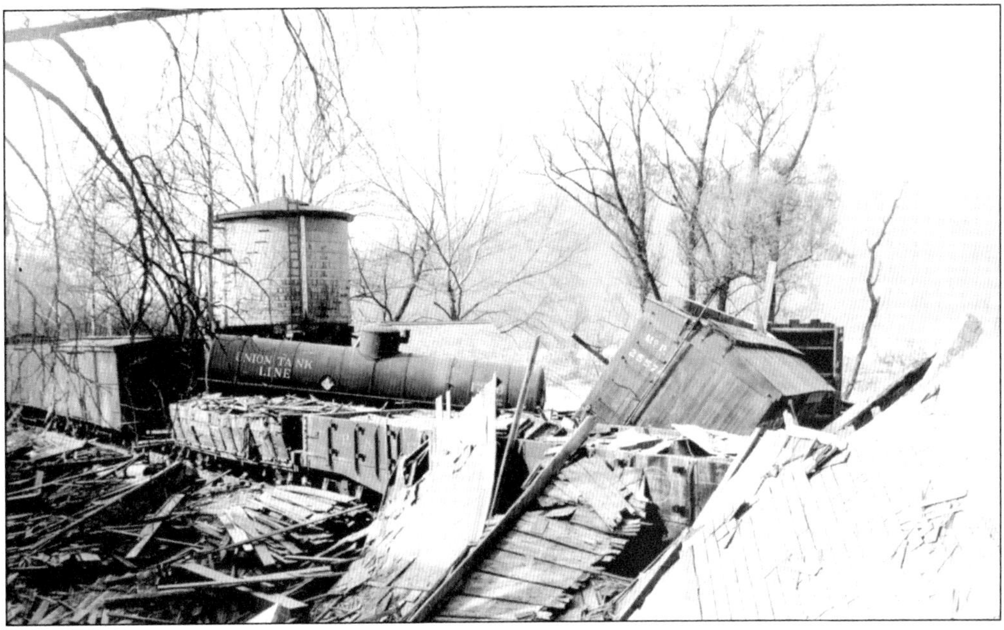

This scene was just a short distance south from the Thompson and Norris paper mill. The railroad's water supply tank has survived, but it is surrounded by the wreckage of the railroad cars both on and off the tracks as well as the rooftop and debris of a stray building. The depot nearby was washed away, and a great deal of labor was required before the tracks could be cleared and repaired. (Courtesy FCHS.)

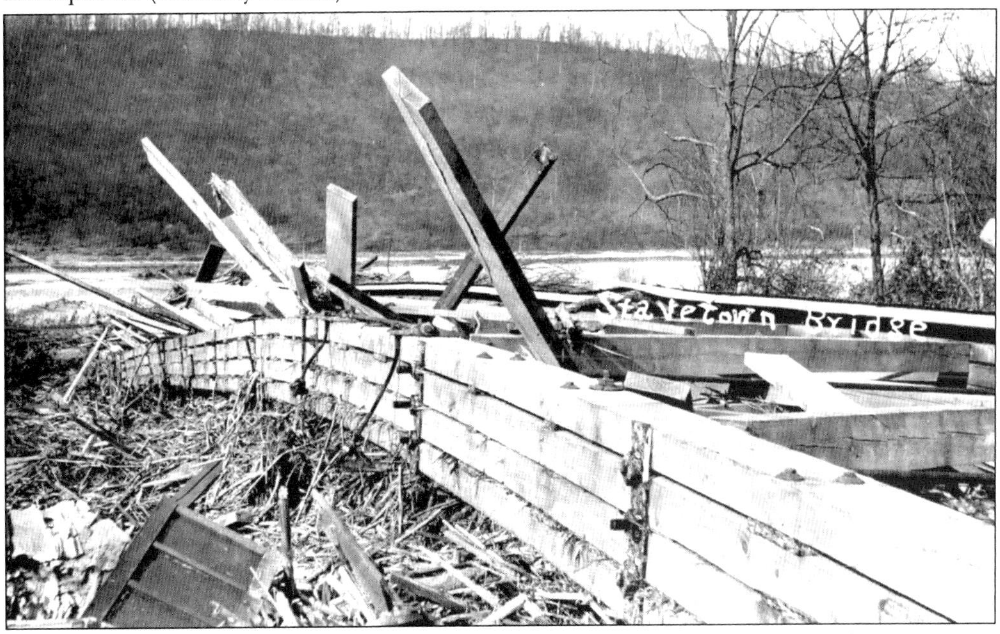

This card shows the splintered remains of the Stavetown bridge at the south end of town. It gives an idea of the force that destroyed the bridge. Trees and other debris lodged under the bridge, blocking the river and causing a buildup of water against the bridge itself. Visible in this shot are the floor supporting members and truss assembly. When the high water subsided, the bridge was left high and dry on the riverbank. (Courtesy Schlesselman.)

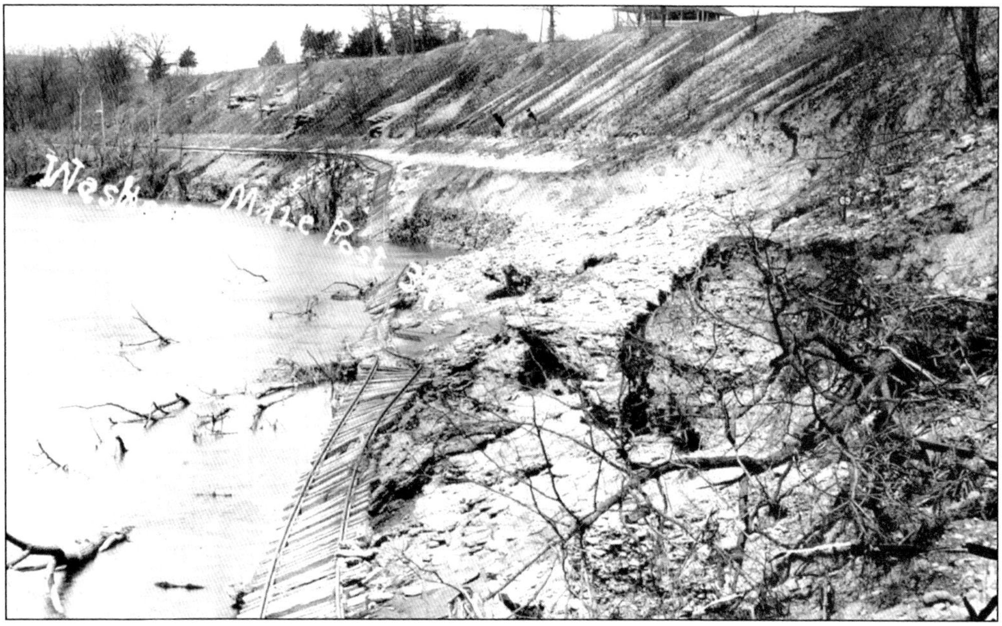

This card, "Washout Mile Post 39," shows the severe damage to the rail line south of Brookville. This is near the Mound Camp, which can be seen slightly right of center at the top. The damage to the line was repaired, but it required many men to return the rails to their original location. They used mules and slip scoops to fill in the damaged railroad bed. (Courtesy Houchin.)

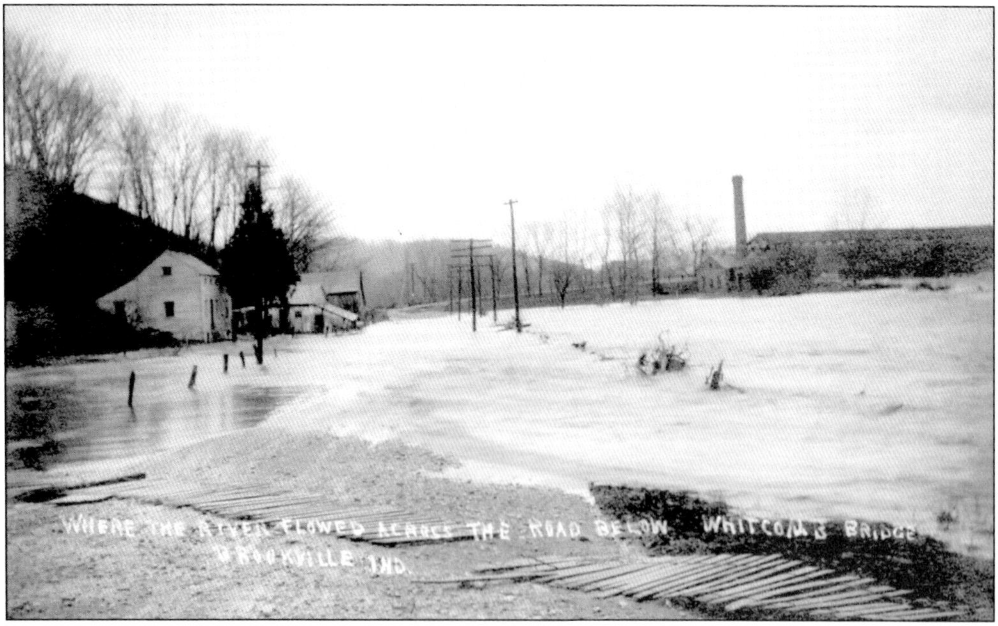

The photograph in this postcard was taken from present-day Fairfield Avenue. It is marked with the notation, "Where the river flowed across the road below Whitcomb Bridge." The waterworks stack is at the right of the bridge. This bridge was not washed away by the high waters of the flood because its earthen approaches washed out first. (Courtesy Houchin.)

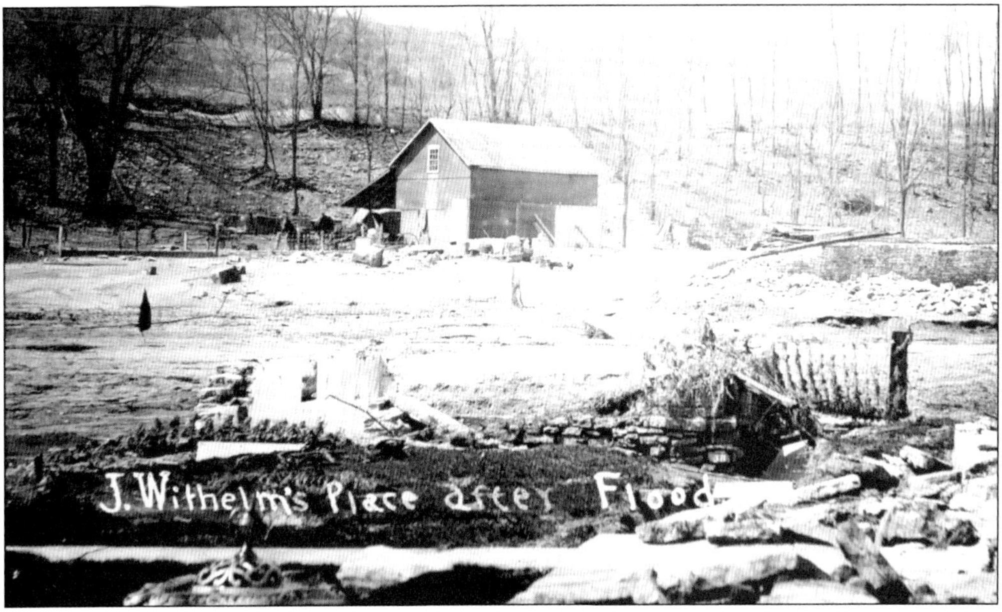

Jacob J. Wilhelm lived near Cedar Grove. A biographical sketch written about him in 1915 said, "On March 25, 1913 . . . occurred the great disaster of Mr. Wilhelm's life. . . . His house, barns, fences, grain and everything which he owned, except himself and family, were swept away by the disastrous flood." It concluded, "He has since erected five new buildings." (Courtesy FCHS.)

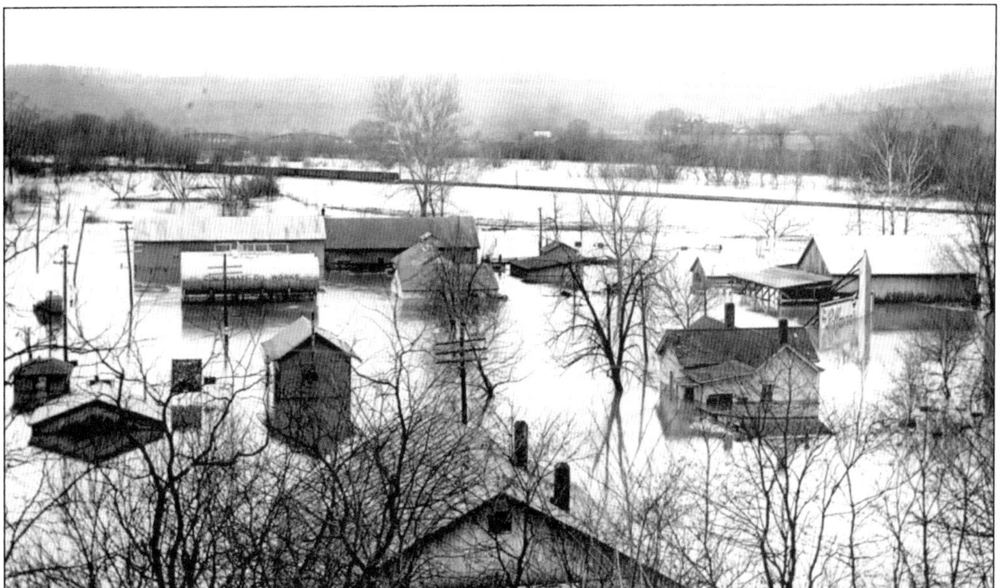

This postcard is marked 1913 flood on the back, but it is of a later time of high water, probably 1929. The bridge across the Whitewater River to the county infirmary in this photograph is a steel truss bridge, which was constructed after the covered bridge washed away in 1913. The steel railroad bridge, which was replaced in 1913, is just below the infirmary bridge in the photograph. The tank at the left center is marked the Cincinnati Oil Works. (Courtesy FCHS.)

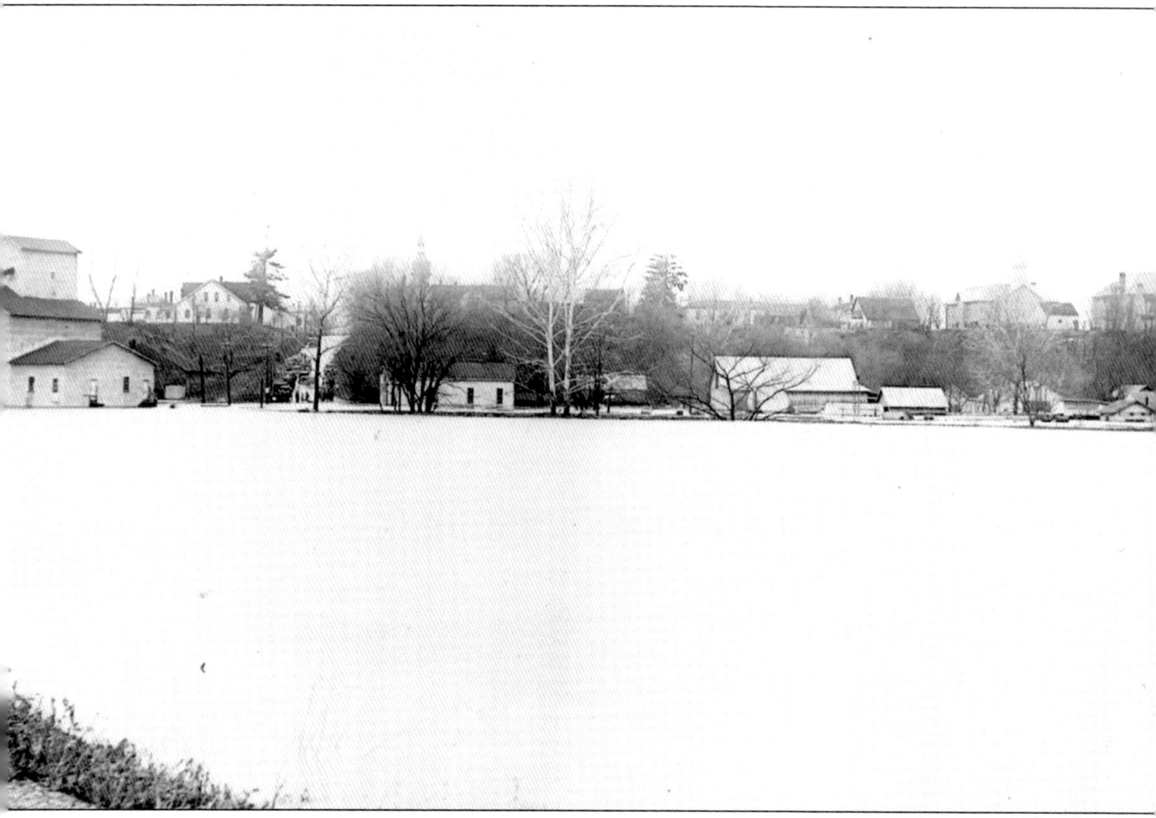

This postcard is somewhat of a mystery, but the best guess is that it was also taken during the flood in 1929. The area in the foreground is a basin and was used by the local baseball team as a playing field in the early 1900s. The Frank Wright grain mill is at the left. The canal basin was behind the mill. (Courtesy FCHS.)

Ten

The Whitewater Canal and the Railroad

In 1836, the Indiana legislature passed the Mammoth Internal Improvements Act. It provided for three major canal projects. One of these was the Whitewater Canal to allow southeastern Indiana a means of transportation to the big cities and access to their markets for the region's farm products. At that time, there were few roads that would allow anything but traveling on horseback. In September 1836, state officials, canal commissioners, and congressmen held a groundbreaking ceremony in Brookville for initiation of construction of the Whitewater Canal. Gov. Noah Noble, former governor James Brown Ray, and Lt. Gov. David Wallace, all former Brookville residents, were present. The canal, when finished, extended from the National Road at Hagerstown, Indiana, to the Ohio River. At Harrison, Ohio, one branch of the canal went to Lawrenceburg, Indiana, and another to North Bend, Ohio, where it passed through a tunnel and then on to Cincinnati. The canal had a short life due to low water at times and frequent floods at other times that caused heavy damage resulting in high financial costs for maintenance and extended periods when it was shutdown. With the advent of the railroad, the canal could not compete for freight traffic and transportation. In 1863, the canal property was sold to the railroad interests, and the rail lines were laid on the canal towpath. Rail traffic began in 1868. The canal and other projects of the state's Mammoth Internal Improvements Act caused Indiana severe financial problems in the late 1830s and 1840s. A 14-mile section of the canal from the Laurel Feeder Dam and through Metamora was restored in 1944–1946 through the efforts of a statewide group formed locally. The state accepted responsibility for the project in 1946, and it is now maintained by the Indiana Department of Natural Resources as a state historic site.

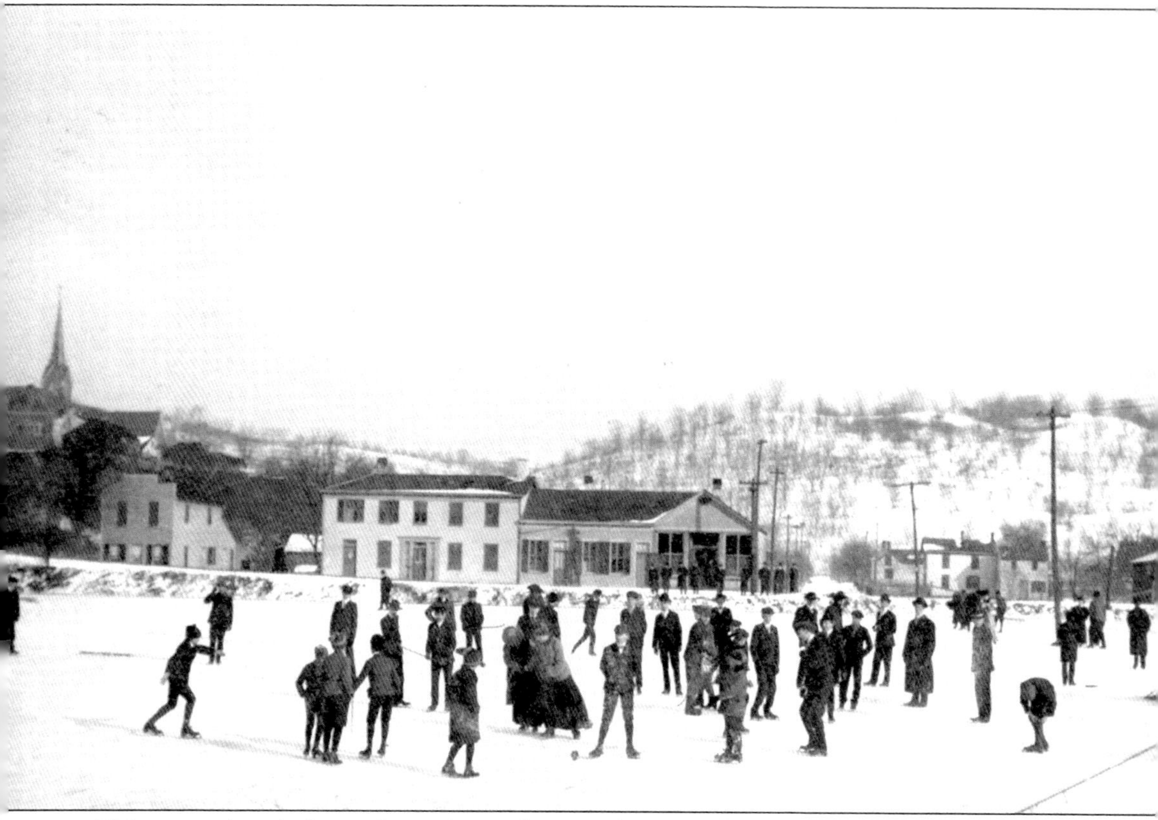

This postcard made from a Ben Winans photograph is one of his most popular. It shows that the young people of Brookville have found a use for the old basin long after it ceased being used by the canal company. The photograph is not dated but is estimated to have been taken sometime between 1902 and 1905. The canal basin was not filled in but was drained and has been used for business operations.

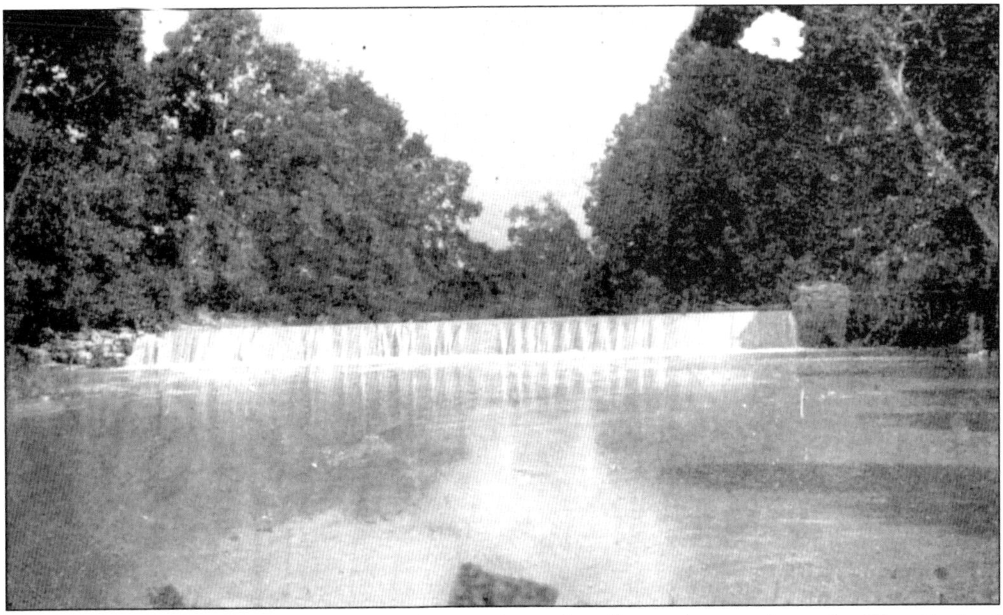

The feeder dam near Laurel was one of seven dams that diverted water from the West Fork of the Whitewater River to the canal. The earlier dams were constructed of logs and brush with stone abutments. These washed out frequently in times of high water. The last wooden dam failed in 1937 and was replaced by this concrete dam in 1944. (Courtesy Houchin.)

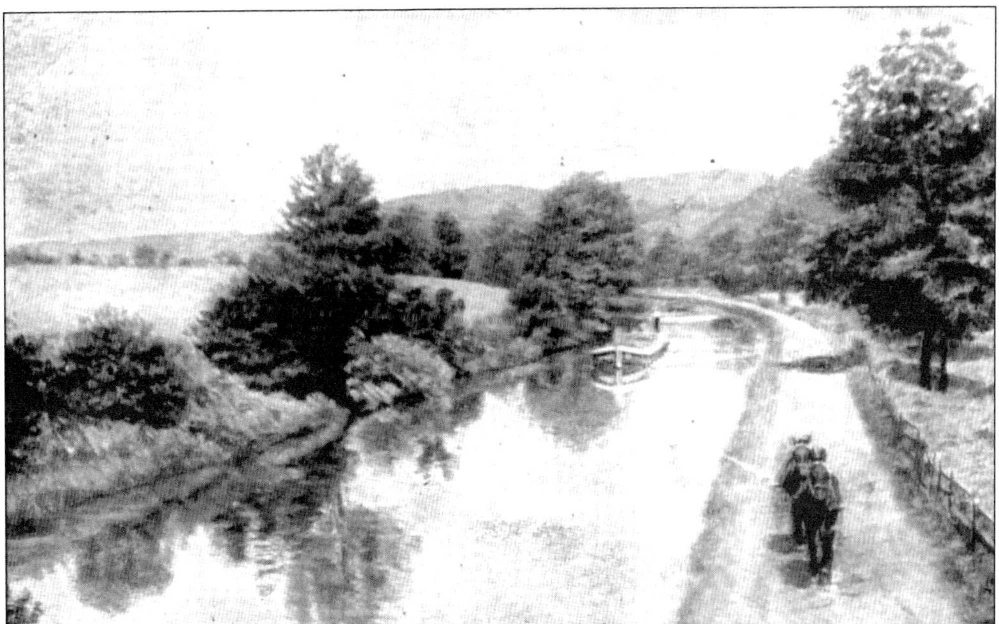

This early card shows two mules on the towpath pulling a canal boat through the Whitewater Canal. The boat could have been carrying lumber, produce, grain, or even passengers to some destination. (Courtesy Houchin.)

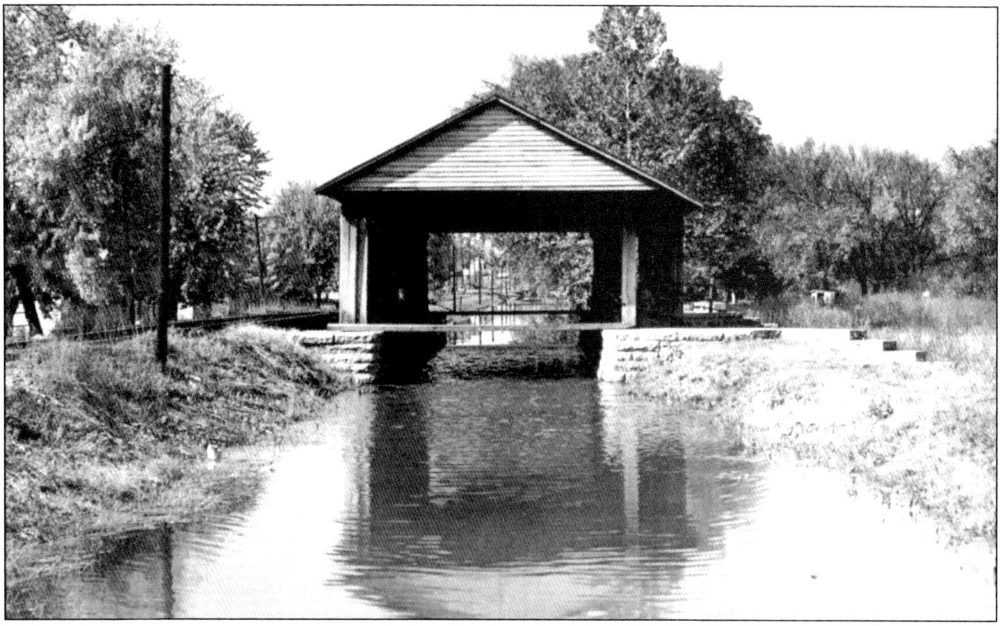

The Duck Creek Aqueduct at Metamora is the only one of its kind remaining in the United States. It resembles a wooden covered bridge with timber trusses to support the load on the floor, and it carries the water in the canal over Duck Creek. There are two restored canal locks nearby, as well as a restored gristmill at the upstream lock—all part of the state historic site. (Courtesy Cowan.)

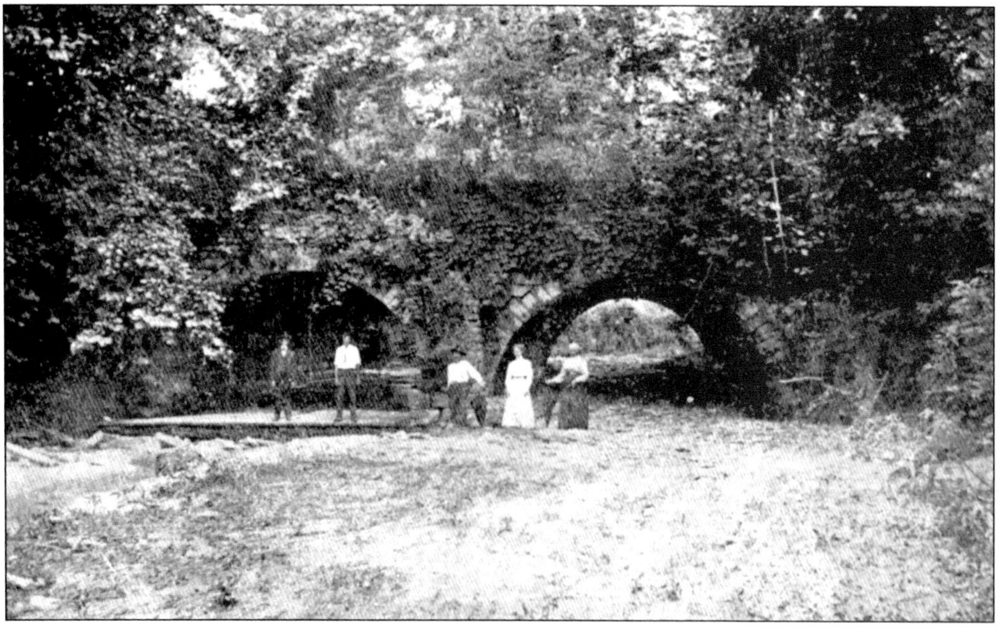

Beneath the vines and other vegetation, there was an abandoned massive stone "twin-arch aqueduct." Like the wooden aqueduct at Metamora, it carried the canal over a small stream, Yellow Bank Creek in this case. Sadly it was razed during the Depression as a "make work" project. This postcard was made from a photograph made by Ben Winans in the early 1900s. (Courtesy Houchin.)

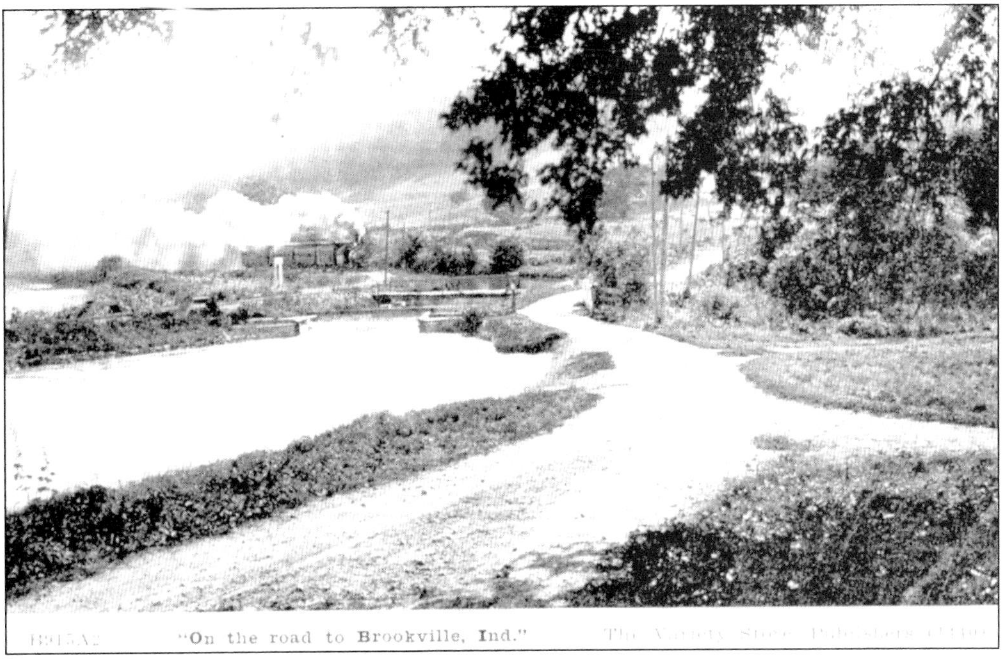

"On the road to Brookville" shows three modes of transportation—the canal, the railroad, and a dirt road. This card was made from a photograph by Ben Winans taken in 1902 near present-day Yellow Bank Road. The road that connected Brookville with Indianapolis became U.S. 52. The railroad rails have been removed here, and the restored canal ends near here.

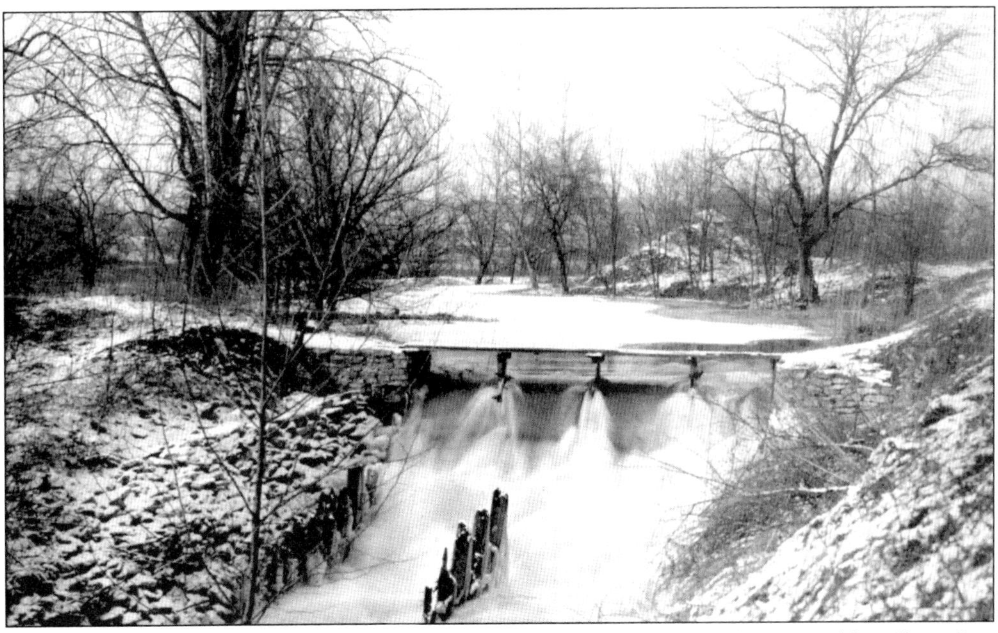

A Ben Winans photograph, taken in 1902, identifies this as a "tailrace at old mill site" at Brookville. He did not say which mill, but it probably was near Wright's Mill south of the canal basin. This was an image taken for its picturesque quality as a winter scene. The railroad is not shown, but a bit of the roadbed is shown at the center right.

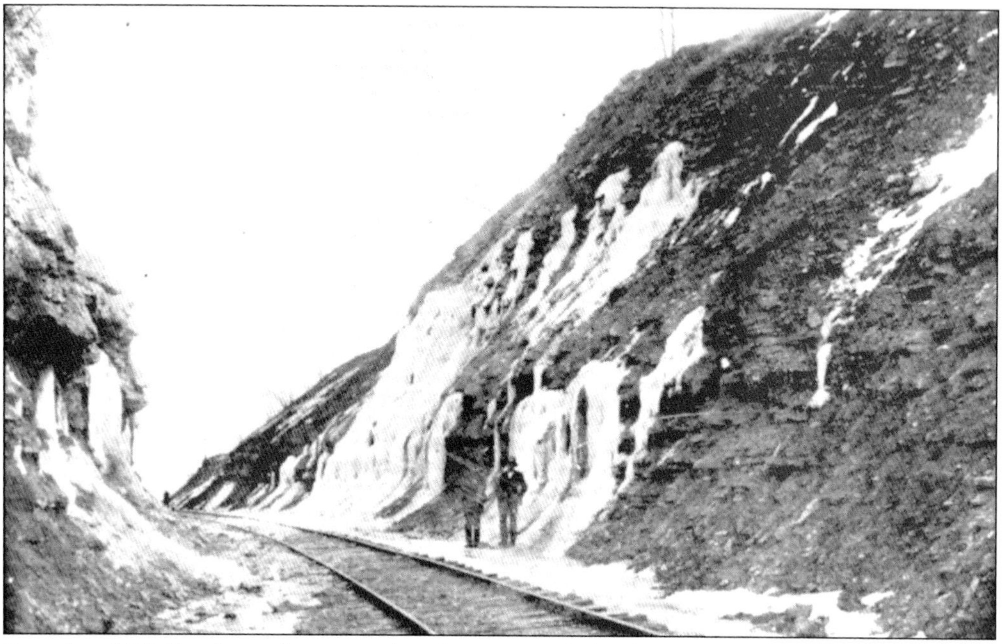

Boundary Hill Cut shows the excavation that was made for the railroad tracks at Boundary Hill between Brookville and Metamora. This had to be a major project requiring many men and mules to move so much dirt to make a gradual slope that the steam locomotives could climb and descend. This was near the boundary formed by the Greenville Treaty of 1795 with the Native American tribes of the Northwest Territory. When the Greenville Treaty was negotiated, the United States gained ownership of all the land east of the treaty line, which eventually became the state of Ohio and a triangular section of land running to the Ohio River called the "Gore" that became part of the state of Indiana. The land west of the Greenville Treaty line still belonged to the Native Americans at that time. (Below, courtesy Jonas/Banks.)

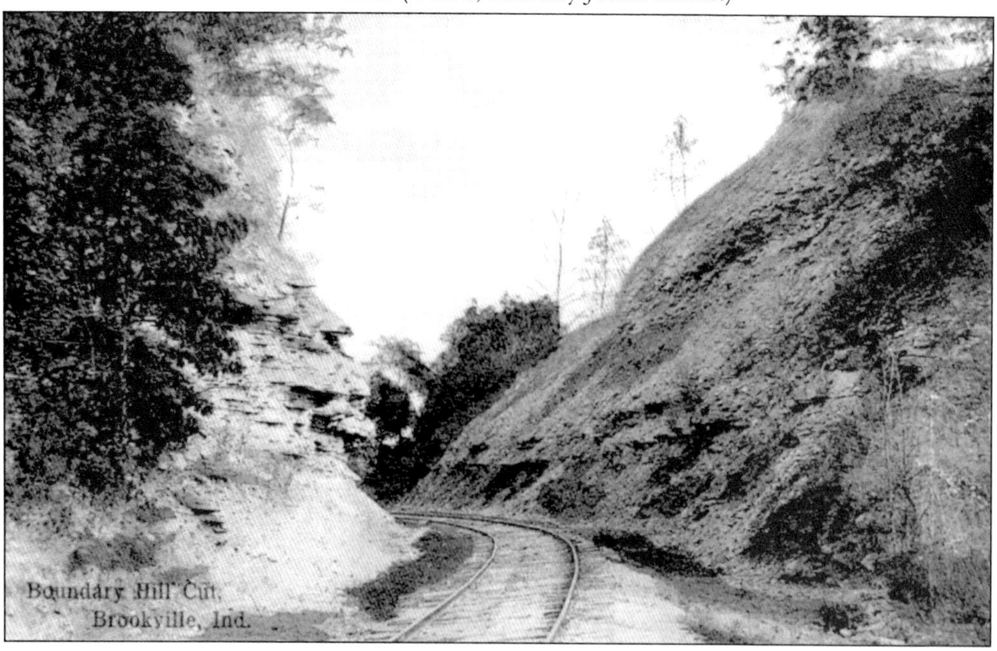

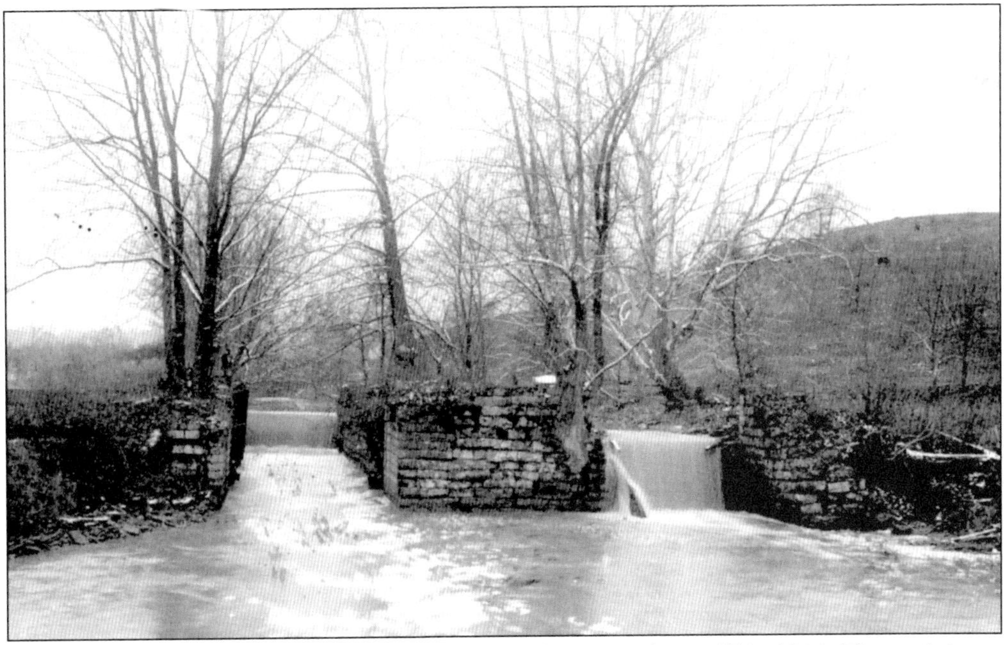

The postcard above shows the abandoned canal lock at Boundary Hill in 1906. The card shows the abandoned canal lock at Yellow Bank, which was near the twin-arch aqueduct. Canal locks were necessary because of the uneven terrain through which the waterway passed. In general, the canal route descended from north to south following the river route nearby. Locks were designed to allow the canal barges to be raised or lowered from one level to another. In these views, the lock gates are open so there is a waterfall as the water flows from the higher section of the canal to a lower section. Today these locks are in a much-deteriorated condition. The remains of the Boundary Hill lock can be seen by turning at the road to the Franklin County Landfill and Recycle Center.

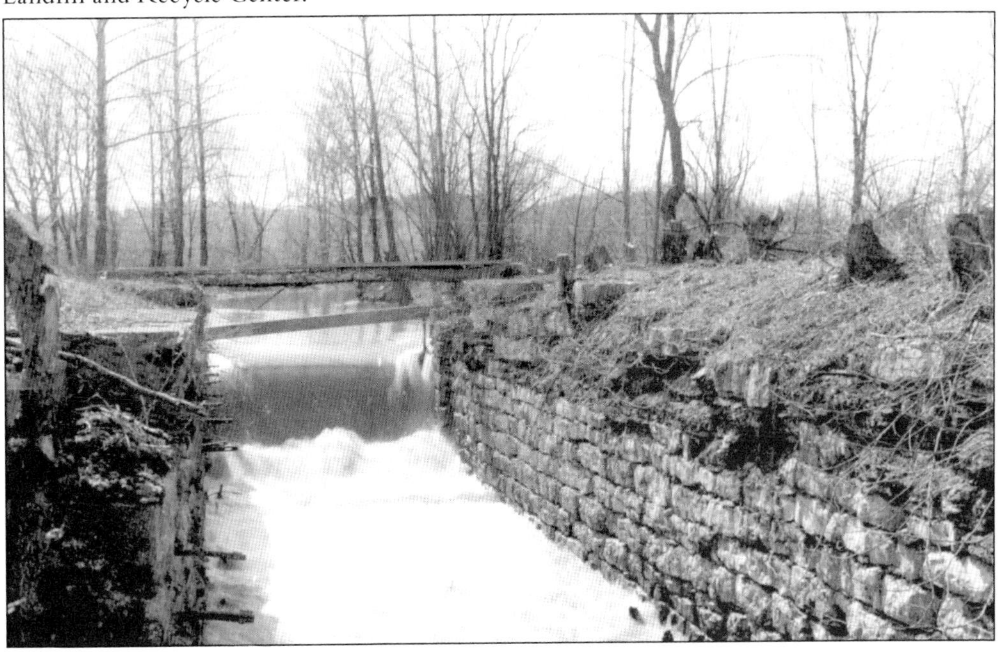

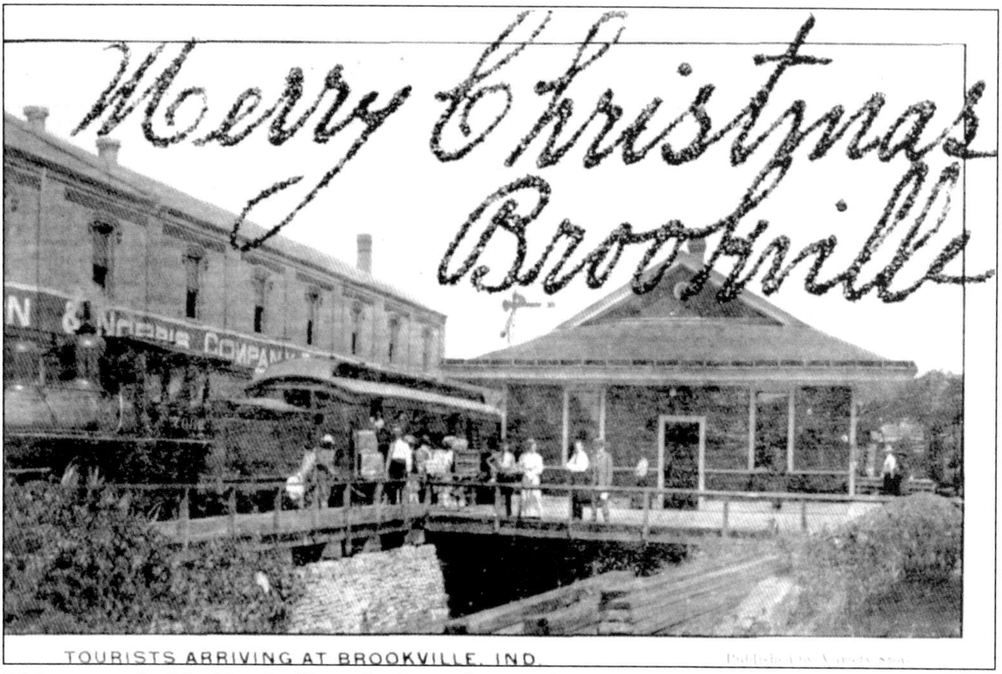

This postcard of the Brookville train depot shows a do-it-yourself decorating step. Stores sold a small kit of glue and metal shavings that people could use to personalize their greeting, a process called tinseling. In 1913, these cards were banned from the mail unless they were sealed in an envelope after an incident in which a New York postal employee required surgery to attend to an infection he received from handling these cards.

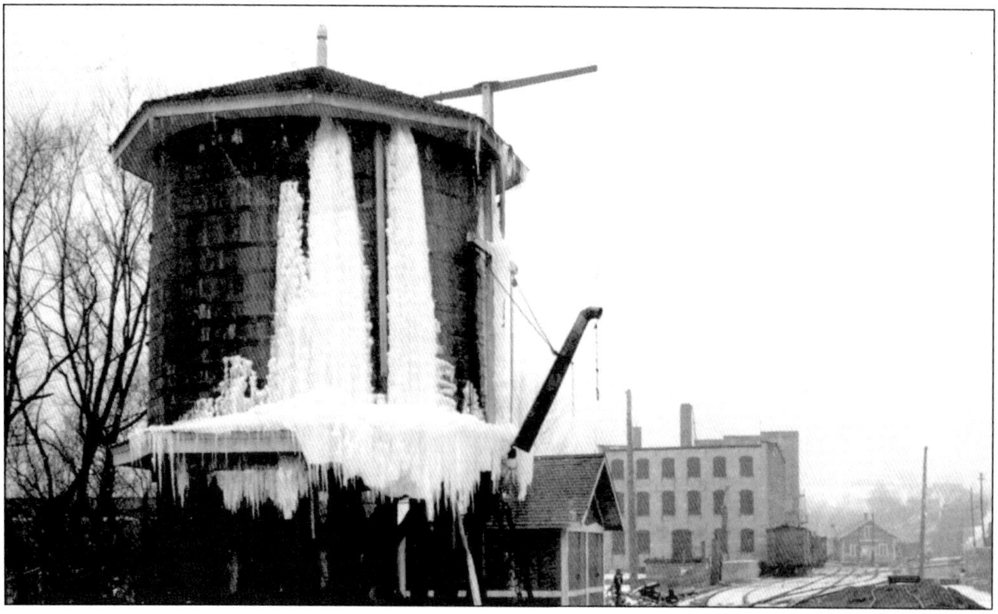

The frozen water tank in the foreground was there to provide water for the boilers of the steam locomotives. The three-story building in the background was a whiskey warehouse. The train depot can be faintly seen between the tracks in the far background. This image was taken by Ben Winans in 1905.

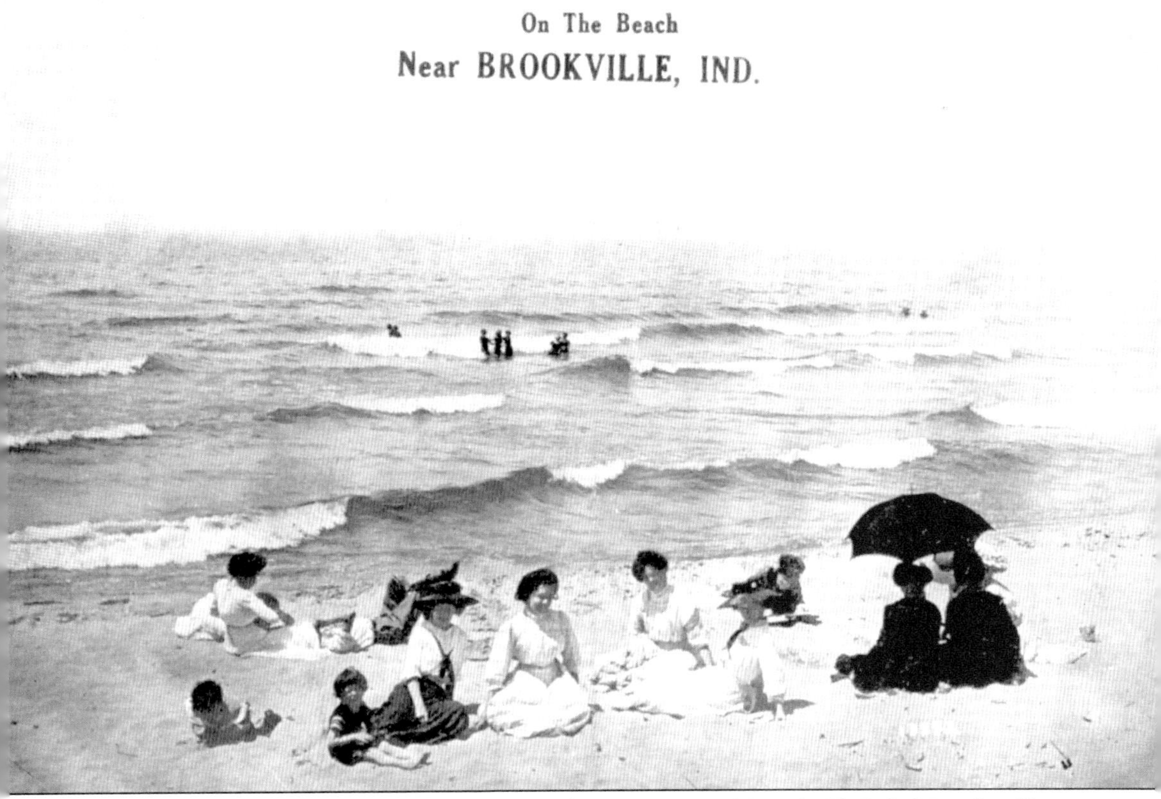

Was this photograph taken on the canal? The Whitewater River? Brookville Lake? Local residents should not spend too much effort trying to determine the exact location of this waterfront scene. Generic postcards were very popular as a general greeting, and sometimes the subject matter was a bit of a stretch. Although Brookville is landlocked away in southeastern Indiana some 800 miles from the nearest ocean, that did not keep this postcard publisher from creating this dreamy beach scene, complete with whitecaps. Nor did the sender make note of the unusual location in the message when she sent the card in 1913.